D0015635

WALKING PREY

How America's Youth Are Vulnerable to Sex Slavery

Holly Austin Smith

Foreword by Mira Sorvino

palgrave
macmillan

To my school teachers. And to all the teachers who strive to lift their students to the greatest heights possible.

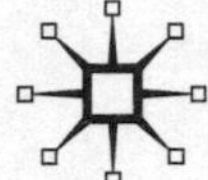

WALKING PREY

First published in 2014 by PALGRAVE MACMILLAN® in the U.S.—
a division of St. Martin's Press LLC, 175 Fifth Avenue, New York, NY 10010.

Where this book is distributed in the UK, Europe and the rest of the world, this is by Palgrave Macmillan, a division of Macmillan Publishers Limited, registered in England, company number 785998, of Houndmills, Basingstoke, Hampshire RG21 6XS.

Palgrave Macmillan is the global academic imprint of the above companies and has companies and representatives throughout the world.

ISBN: 978-1-137-27873-9

Library of Congress Cataloging-in-Publication Data
Smith, Holly Austin.
Walking prey: how America's youth are vulnerable to sex slavery / Holly Austin Smith.
pages cm
ISBN 978-1-137-27873-9 (hardback)
1. Child prostitution—United States. 2. Child trafficking—United States. 3. Sexually abused children—United States. 4. Sex crimes—United States—Prevention. I. Title.
HQ144.S657 2014
362.760973—dc23

2013033088

A catalogue record of the book is available from the British Library.

Design by Letra Libre

First edition: March 2014

10 9 8 7 6 5 4 3 2 1

Printed in the United States of America.

CONTENTS

FOREWORD

I FIRST MET HOLLY SMITH AT THE NATIONAL CONFERence of State Legislatures' Fall Forum in Washington, D.C., December 2012. I was keynoting for the second time at one of their conferences, pushing for more and stronger anti-trafficking legislation on the state level, and I had asked the National Survivor Network, created by the Coalition to Abolish Slavery & Trafficking, if they had a member that lived near the conference. I felt very strongly that a survivor of human trafficking would be her or his own best advocate, and boy did she prove me right.

Holly walked on stage, a lovely, professional-looking blonde woman, looking every bit the part of a conservative politician's daughter. She then further disarmed the audience by projecting a picture of her fourteen-year-old self hanging out with her young friends. Any preconception that underage sex trafficking could only happen to *other people's children* flew right out the window.

The story Holly briefly outlined that day, and has further detailed in this book, is painful, ugly, yet *familiar.* She systematically builds her case that just by being a child in America—in this culture obsessed with consumerism, sex, and the objectification of women—anyone is potentially vulnerable to being trafficked for sex or falling prey to CSEC (commercial sexual exploitation of children). Add to that the terrible insecurity that often accompanies adolescence, a need for love and escape from painful home environments, and Holly's young self reads an awful lot like how I remember feeling at thirteen and fourteen. She then factors in various elements such as prior sexual abuse, parental substance abuse, and an economic need that make her falling into the hands of a pimp trafficker almost unsurprising, if terrible.

She details all the steps that led her to that fateful situation, and is very clear that though she was not held at gunpoint, this was the only option she felt at the time was a viable means of surviving, of having some modicum of power, love, and attention, though she soon found out these were illusory. We are brought into the thought processes of a very young person, and are shown how pimp traffickers and gang traffickers have systematized how to take advantage of young people.

Holly has a unique way of making the extremely personal resonate on a universal level. Then she takes the research and science on predisposing factors and environments and folds them seamlessly with vetted best practices into sound recommendations. One, for preventing vulnerable children from being trafficked, and two, for successfully treating survivors so they are able to fully move forward and away from the cycle of sex trafficking. In all of this we are continually reminded that she knows whereof she speaks, because she knows exactly what did and did not work for her, and what could have been done better. She shines a light on survivor and non-survivor led methods of outreach prevention and aftercare that should be emulated, and replicated, on a national scale.

She focuses the light on the buyers of underage sex, and how any attempt to eradicate this system must focus on reaching these very average men, in every community, who pay for sex everyday with young people and who not only think nothing of it, but suffer very few consequences. Programs to target these current consumers have to be implemented, but it can't stop there. A culture of empathy must be engendered here, and the advertising culture that sexualizes young kids, and especially girls as objects (sometimes even as objects of abuse), must be changed. Boys have to be raised to respect and honor girls and women, not to exploit them.

One of the kinds of legislation that I continually advocate the robust passage of is Safe Harbor. What this involves is a new lens for law and order to view underage victims of sex trafficking and kids in commercial sexual exploitation. Essentially, it replaces the old criminal designation of "child prostitute" with minor victim of sex trafficking or sexual exploitation. It recognizes that children and teens in these situations are being used and abused by adults who exploit and profit from them, and that they are not criminals but victims, due a full gamut of services that help them reclaim their lives and move forward. It raises the criminal penalties of the traffickers to the highest levels, requiring sentencing commensurate with the other most serious crimes such as arson, rape, and murder. It expunges criminal records, so that child victims will not be haunted by their past throughout their lives, as they pursue higher education and gainful employment. In its best form it allows the minor victims to seek civil redress.

These laws are in harmony with the United States Federal Government and the United Nations Palermo Protocol's official recognition that anyone under the age of eighteen does not need to provide evidence of force, fraud, or coercion to be deemed a victim of human trafficking. It is based upon the understanding that a child or teen does not have the legal, psychological, neurological, or emotional capacity to make an informed choice to be sexually exploited—so any assertion by law enforcement, the court system, or the youth themselves that their presence in prostitution or commercial sexual exploitation is by their own will is invalidated. Sadly, only 11 of 50 states had some version of the Safe Harbor legislation in 2012; and some of those were weak, meaning that in many states youth in commercial sexual exploitation are still deemed "child prostitutes" and considered criminals. It is overwhelmingly the child victims who are arrested, not the pimp and not the john, i.e., the adult buying their young bodies for sex. Policemen without crucial training for child sex trafficking still see these kids as bad seeds; and sometimes they end up not only in the juvenile system, but in adult jail, though they are minors and have not committed serious crimes.

In other cases child victims are diverted to mandatory treatment programs, where they are locked up and forced to complete the programs in order to avoid criminal charges. Although these programs are well-meaning, there is a serious flaw in their philosophy of treating victims like criminals given a second chance. In no other crime are its victims locked up. It is a serious dilemma because authorities fear for the minors' wellbeing and fear they will fall back into the hands of traffickers. Holly debates the pros and cons of this approach. I think we all feel there is an ideal approach out there, just not perfected and put into place in a widespread enough way to do good at present.

I believe this book will go a very long way toward enlightening policy makers, law enforcement, social services, legislators, and the public at large on what the real, brutal experience of child sex trafficking here in the United States is. Just as she debunks the myth that all underage sex trafficking victims are kidnapped at gunpoint out of their sandboxes at the local park, she just as clearly shows us the error of seeing the child or teen in this situation as the one perpetrating a crime. She makes the unfamiliar familiar, and the reprehensible tactics of the traffickers comprehensible. I think *Walking Prey* will help the efforts to decriminalize and help restore the lives of these kids enormously, making this country a safer place to be a child, and a more compassionate one.

I am in awe of Holly's courage to reveal so much of her painful personal experience for the better good, her fierce intellectual engagement on this issue, and her brilliant ideas for change. She inspires me, and I am grateful for her leadership in this global fight to end human trafficking.

Mira Sorvino
United Nations Office on Drugs and Crime
Goodwill Ambassador to Combat Human Trafficking
January 10, 2014

PROLOGUE

JUNE 1992, SOUTH JERSEY

I was looking for something.

It was the summer after my eighth grade middle school graduation, and I had been looking ever since that school year had begun. The song "When It's Love" by Van Halen was still popular, and I would turn up the radio dial to listen to the lyrics. Sammy Hagar sang about waiting and wanting to connect with someone—I was the same way. I stared into the faces of strangers as they passed by me in large crowds, a habit I had picked up that year. I was looking for someone to acknowledge me in some way. I thought that if someone noticed me, if somebody, *anybody,* didn't look away when I bumped into his view, then I would *know* that I was *really there*—that I was alive and solid and visible.

And then one day, somebody did.

I was walking through the mall with friends, searching each face, when I noticed a man watching me. I held his stare, waiting for him to turn away, and then he raised his finger and curled it back, motioning for me to come over to him. I blinked and looked behind me, thinking for sure he must be talking to someone else; but nobody was there. I looked back at him and he curled his finger again, motioning for me to come over.

I shook my head *no.*

He dropped his fist and continued to watch me. I looked around to see if anyone noticed the exchange. My best friend and her boyfriend had stopped at the Piercing Pagoda, my other friends loitering around them, and everyone else in the world continued to look over me, past me, or through me. Only *this guy* noticed my existence. It was a moment for which I had been waiting—a stranger who lived *out there* in the *real world* spotted me and invited me in. I was unsure of what to do, hesitant; yet I was equally afraid I might miss this opportunity—but for what? I didn't know, but I wanted to find out.

"I'll be right back," I said to Crystal, my best friend, who shrugged as she held a pair of silver hoop earrings against her ear.

Didn't this scare you? I've been asked. No, it didn't. What scared me in middle school was the idea of losing my friendship with Crystal, the threat of never finding a *real* boyfriend, and the fear of social humiliation especially from losing in a public fistfight. Although I pretended to be tough, I was secretly afraid of getting beat up in high school. I felt like a coward, and I feared exposure. Strangers, however, were low on my radar for danger. I wasn't afraid of them; I was intrigued by them. I saw them as portals into another world outside of Tuckerton, New Jersey, a world I so badly wanted to join.

Even the few times I hitchhiked to school, I felt an electric sense of freedom being so close to a stranger. Yes, I had heard about assaults and kidnappings on television, but at ages thirteen and fourteen, I didn't think anything like that could *actually* happen to me. Only one guy ever really made me nervous: a trucker who pulled over to give me a ride. I climbed into the cab of his truck and gave directions to my school. I can't remember much about him except that he was a white man wearing a ball cap. He inched closer and closer to me over the long, leather seat, steadily, like he was getting ready to grab a fat frog. I jumped out of the cab, landing hard on my feet.

The guy in the mall didn't appear creepy or threatening, though—he looked *cool:* early twenties, wearing a B.U.M. sweatshirt with gold chains around his neck. Most important, I felt special that he pointed *me* out of the crowd instead of Crystal, or one of her more outgoing *new* friends, all of whom I believed to be prettier or cooler or just more fun than me. More than once, I had been voted last when the neighborhood boys rated our *hotness.*

I was more nervous than fearful about approaching the guy in the mall. I worried he would turn me away, realizing he had made a mistake, and leave me feeling stupid. I quickly concocted a plan to ask him for pot if the introduction was awkward. I had tried pot only once, and I did it out of spite more than curiosity. I had heard that Crystal started smoking pot with her boyfriend, and I was jealous not only because we had pinky-sworn that we would never do drugs but because she had made such a serious decision without me. I thought that if I could gain a connection for pot from this guy, then maybe I could gain a solid spot in Crystal's new crowd. Yes, this was my great big concern in middle school—the fear of being left out and left behind. It turned out that my nervousness was for naught; the man with the gold chains leaned out of the pay phone booth and said very directly to me, "Remember this number." And then he said a phone number.

"Got it," I said.

He then turned away from me and pulled himself back into the booth as though the conversation was over.

"What do you want me to do?" I asked.

He hung up the phone and wrote the number on the palm of my hand.

"Call anytime," he smiled broadly.

And that was it. That was how I met my trafficker. There was no violence, no threats, no screeching car on the street, and no screaming or kicking abduction. There was only mystery and an offer of friendship. I walked back to my friends and shrugged at Crystal's puzzlement.

"Oh, that guy," I said. "That's one of my dad's friends."

Looking back, I realize this quick exchange between us was purposeful. The man with the gold chains probably didn't want to call attention to the fact that he had just engaged with a random young girl. Just as passersby took little notice, so did my friends. And I was equally relieved by the brief exchange between us. I talked to him on my private phone line as I had done many nights with my friends, and my friends' friends, and my friends' older brothers and even their friends. Unfortunately, I didn't know that my new friend, Greg, was actually a pimp.

"WHAT'S UP, GIRL?" GREG SAID THAT FIRST NIGHT OVER the phone, as if we were just picking up an ongoing conversation. My worries over an awkward silence with this stranger melted away. I stretched the phone cord across my bed and relaxed. Greg asked me about myself—about school, about my friends, about my parents, about my life. It was an instant friendship without any pressure or pause. I realize now that this was a tactic. Teens can be socially awkward; if a person or conversation feels uncomfortable, then a teen may shy away. Child traffickers are charismatic; they make it their business to be sympathetic and relatable to a teen's troubles.

I can't say exactly why I kept talking to Greg only because I don't remember many specifics about our conversations. He didn't call too often or come on too strong; and he didn't push any sketchy topics like sex or running away because *that* would have raised red flags. He was casual and cool. What I liked most about Greg was that he talked to me like I was an adult; he seemed to really consider my thoughts and opinions. Crystal's friends scoffed at any kind of genuine discussion; if anyone made a smart or sincere comment, it was typically met with sarcasm. I learned to keep quiet around them.

"You're too mature for high school," Greg said. "You're pretty enough to be a model."

I don't know if I believed him or not, but I know I *wanted* to believe him. I wanted to know what it was like to be loved by an older guy. Greg said he was from Tennessee, and I imagined going there with him. I imagined going anywhere, really. Rock bands like Warrant, Poison, and Skid Row all had MTV videos that showed snippets of live concerts, complete with smashing guitars, stripping girls, and screaming fans. MTV served as my only keyhole into the world outside of Tuckerton, and I felt like I was missing out on a huge party.

"We can go wherever you want," Greg said. "You can drive my red corvette across the country."

This surprised me. "But I don't have a license," I said.

"That's OK," Greg said, "I'll get you a fake one."

I twirled the phone cord and imagined myself driving down a highway with wind in my hair, high school behind me, and California dreams ahead. I wanted to go to Los Angeles, I told him. The Doors got started in Los Angeles; as did L.A. Guns, Mötley Crüe, Guns N' Roses, and other bands I liked. I wanted to write songs for a rock band. I carried with me a spiral-bound notebook with lines of angst-ridden song lyrics throughout eighth grade. I had been studying song lyrics ever since intermediate school when I discovered the Guns N' Roses album, *Appetite for Destruction.* I would sit in front of my stereo with album inserts spread across my bedroom floor. With headphones on, I pored over the song lyrics, credits, and album artwork.

By middle school, I discovered a local aspiring band called Absent Child. They practiced at Miller's, a seedy bar on Main Street known for fistfights and go-go dancers. Just days before I met Greg, I dressed in my tightest jeans, curled my bangs, and hitchhiked to Miller's. I wanted to show my song lyrics to the members of Absent Child. I was convinced that, if they saw my poetry, they would invite me to join their band. I fantasized about going on tour with them and becoming the most popular girl in high school. I sat outside the bar for a long time, but I couldn't work up the courage to knock on the door. I kicked at the dirt in the parking lot, until I finally picked up my notebook and walked back home.

Days later, after I had met him at the mall, Greg casually mentioned that he knew musicians.

"You know singers?" I asked.

"Yeah, girl," he said, "I know singers, actors, models; I hang out in the same clubs as Boyz II Men."

Dance songs like "Rhythm is a Dancer" by Snap! and "3 A.M. Eternal" by The KLF conjured images of young adults drinking, flirting, jumping, and dancing inside nightclubs. I considered clubs to be the epitome of adulthood and independence. Not only did I want to be an adult; I wanted to be as happy as I imagined the adults inside those clubs were. I would have followed Greg down a dark alley if he had said a club waited at the end of it, especially a famous club with famous people inside. Through the mirage of genuine conversation and compliments, Greg tapped into my interests, and he constructed glamorous opportunities for a better life. This alone, however, did not cause me to run away. I hesitated.

Greg was patient, though. He laid the groundwork, and then he waited.

He waited for a phone call from a teenage girl who was ready not only to run *toward* a new life, but also ready to run *away* from her old life. I made that desperate call approximately two weeks after meeting Greg. When the pressures of my teenage world boiled over; I packed a bag with my favorite pair of jeans, pictures of Crystal, and my notebook of scribbled song lyrics. And I ran away.

GREG AND I HAD AGREED TO MEET AT A DIFFERENT shopping mall, the Shore Mall, which was farther away. I got a ride from an older guy who worked at a restaurant in the mall. I sat on a bench between Boscov's and Clover for so long that the cashiers started to look at me suspiciously. I knew that sitting in the same spot would draw attention, but I didn't know what else to do. Greg was late, and I began to worry that I had made a mistake. I looked at the pay phone and wondered if I should call Greg again, or my mom. But I couldn't bring myself to call home. I knew that if I called my parents I would be caught in a lie about my afternoon plans and I'd get into trouble. I felt like I was always in trouble; I was always doing something wrong.

"How long have you been sitting there," Greg asked when he finally showed up.

"This is where you said to meet," I said, too tired to complain and also a little intimidated by him.

Greg seemed annoyed. I immediately sensed a difference between the Greg on the phone and the Greg in person. Although he was the same man I had met at the original mall, he was now distant and unfriendly, not like he had been on the phone. Twenty years later, I learned that the man I'd been talking to on the phone actually was a completely different person. I drove 300 miles from Richmond, Virginia, to the Atlantic County Prosecutor's Office in New Jersey to collect police records from my case. I held in my hands two different mug shots: one showed Greg (the man I met in person), and the other showed a man whom I had never before seen. This other man, apparently Greg's cousin, pretended to be the man I had met at the mall. Clearly, Greg's cousin was skilled at gaining a girl's trust; while Greg was skilled at spotting vulnerable girls. I wondered how many others were swindled by this same scheme. Unfortunately, as Greg stood before me on July 1, 1992, I knew none of this. I assumed he was annoyed because I looked so conspicuous in the mall.

Greg bought a bottle of hair dye from Clover, and then he led me to a clothing store. My feelings of uncertainty waned with the prospect of shopping. I ran my fingers through a rack of jeans, but Greg led me to the back of the store. His eyes skimmed over some dresses of a variety that I would have called "slutty." He asked the sales girl to pull a few dresses off the wall, and then Greg told me to try them on. I hurried in and out of the dressing rooms. I didn't like dresses—they made me feel naked, awkward, and ugly. I usually wore tight jeans with half shirts. But I assumed dresses were necessary for dance clubs, so I kept quiet. When we left without buying anything I was relieved.

Greg then took me across the street to Kinney Shoes. He picked up a red high heel shoe and asked, "What size are you?"

"Five," I said.

Greg held the shoe up to a sales girl. "You got these in size five?" he asked.

"The smallest size we have is seven," she said, eyeballing me.

"OK," he said, "I'll take 'em."

I said nothing. I was feeling disappointed about the shopping trip, and Greg must have noticed.

"You want some sneakers?" he asked.

Of *course* I wanted sneakers; the only shoes we could afford at home were "bobos" from Kmart. I picked out a pair of Nikes, and then followed Greg toward the door. As we walked out of the store, I ran into Danielle Hughes, or Dani, a classmate from elementary school.

"Hi Holly," Dani said with a big smile.

I hesitated, "Hi Dani."

She was with her mom whom I recognized from field days, school plays, and class trips. Even if I had been with my mother, Dani probably wouldn't have known her. I think Dani may have seen my mother only once at a Thanksgiving play. Dani and I were close friends in fourth grade; she laughed at all my jokes and stories. But I had parted ways with many of my friends from elementary school. I was jealous of them and their clarinet lessons, softball and field hockey games, and wholesome family vacations. I had wanted my mom to be like their moms. I wanted her to bounce me out of bed for orange juice and egg sandwiches; and I wanted her to tote me around town for gymnastics, dance, or karate classes. With both of my parents working full time, home life for me seemed different than that of my friends at school.

Once, I had called my friend Nick's house and he answered the phone with a chipper "Banchik residence!" I imagined him leaning over a bright yellow kitchen counter with a bowl of fruit in the background; I hung up on him. My jealousy turned to spite; and I kept a distance from my friends. Or maybe they had distanced themselves from me. I was, after all, barred from playing at Melissa's house, another elementary school friend, because her mother had overheard me cursing. Her mother also frowned on the fact that I had turned their television set to MTV.

This was about the time I befriended Crystal, who was a year older than me. Crystal didn't seem to give a damn about anybody, or anything, except having a good time. I didn't need other friends or family vacations, I thought; all I needed was Crystal. Greg stood over me and didn't say anything. Mrs. Hughes looked at Greg, and then at me, and then pulled Danielle inside the store.

"We need to get you more hair dye," Greg said.

He bought another bottle of blond hair dye from the Thrift Drug next door, and then he called for a taxi.

"We're goin' to Atlantic City tonight," he said.

I assumed the high heels were necessary to get into a dance club, and I resolved to be adventurous. Greg asked the taxi driver to stop at Burger King, and I munched on French fries as we passed motels and casino billboard signs with pictures of money stacks and pretty girls in swimsuits. I pushed aside concerns and looked forward to my new life. We pulled into a motel parking lot, and Greg knocked on the door of room 115.

An older girl opened the door, and Greg pushed inside to a small room. The girl yawned and smiled; she was in her early twenties, and she was beautiful. She was tall and thin with an oval face; smooth, dark skin; and a gleaming smile with straight, white teeth, all at perfectly right angles. Not like my teeth. Kasper Borkowski called me "bucktooth beaver" in elementary school—a revelation that hit me like a slap on the face. I stopped smiling with an open mouth after that, and I covered my mouth when I laughed. This girl must be a model, I thought; she looked just like Naomi Campbell.

"This is Nicki," Greg said.

She rubbed her sleepy almond-shaped eyes, and I wondered if her career began with Glamour Shots, a photography chain that promised to boost modeling portfolios. Greg headed toward a back hallway and said to Nicki, "Get 'er ready." I sat on a couch and unwrapped my cheeseburger. I had the burger halfway to my mouth when Greg turned and glared at me. He looked mean and mad, intense, like he was daring me to say something to him.

Then it registered what he had said to Nicki: *Get her ready.*

Greg suddenly looked very big to me; he took up most of the hallway in his jacket and boots. I set the burger in my lap and held Greg's stare. Something didn't feel right. I thought about the mall. *Could I find my way back there?* I doubted it, and I had no money for a taxi. Even if I did have money, though, I had no idea how to hail a taxi. I could hitchhike home, but I didn't know in which direction to go. I rarely paid attention to my surroundings. I began to wonder if we were really going to a club. I thought back to my phone conversations with Greg. One night he mentioned knowing prostitutes who worked at casinos and made a lot of money.

Oh, I could never do that, I said, unsure if he was suggesting it.

The topic changed so quickly that I didn't think of it again until that moment. I knew that by then my parents would have realized I had run away again, and I knew that if I went back home I'd be grounded. I would be trapped in my bedroom knowing that Crystal was continuing to drift further and further away from me. I thought about the stillness and suffocating silence of my bedroom. Somehow I knew this was my one chance to object to whatever was happening, but I said nothing. I *couldn't* go back home. It wasn't even an option.

Greg finally turned and headed into the back room. I looked at Nicki, and she smiled.

She turned on MTV and said, "C'mawn, baby, let's dye your hair."

MONICA MANCINI AND HER MOTHER MOVED FROM NEW York City to Mystic Islands, New Jersey, when I was in seventh grade. At that time, Crystal and I lived about a mile away from Mystic, and we walked there in the summertime. Monica was one of the first of Crystal's *new* friends. She had silver braces, a New York accent, and a New York attitude; she also had a closet full of knock-off purses and designer-brand clothes for Crystal to borrow. I could *not* compete with Monica. The first time I heard that Crystal was sleeping over at Monica's house, I ran down a flight of stairs in school to catch Crystal at her locker.

"You're sleepin' over at Monica's?" I blurted.

"Yeah," she said, "Her mom's takin' us shopping tomorrow in New York City."

She was excited, but I couldn't breathe. What pained me most was Crystal's flip attitude about it. She acted like nothing was out of the ordinary, as if *we* didn't go skating every Friday night and then sleep at *my* house. As if I didn't make her pancakes every Saturday morning because she said French toast was just soggy bread. Seventh grade had been stressful as I tried to fit in with Crystal's new friends. I slept over at Monica's house once for a slumber party, but I got into trouble. We were all outside flirting with a carload of boys, but I was the only one who dared to crawl inside the car. My nerve was the one attribute that set me apart from the others. Mrs. Mancini called my parents to have me removed from the party. My parents showed up after midnight, drunk and angry.

Nicki spoke with a heavy New York accent, and I couldn't help but feel like she was my own personal Monica Mancini. Nicki was *my* new friend, I thought. I bonded with her easily and immediately; and it felt like an instant slumber party. She had all kinds of lotions and shampoos, eyeliner pencils and mascara bottles strewn over the bathroom vanity. I sucked in my cheeks as she applied blush and blue eye shadow, and I puckered my lips for the red lipstick. I felt like I was getting a makeover. I wasn't sure why Nicki and I were getting ready; maybe I still thought we were going to a club. I didn't question her, though; I trusted her completely. She was like a big sister.

"Go rinse your hair out, shooga," Nicki said.

I knelt over the bathtub and held my hair under the faucet as I had done a million times at home. Getting ready to go skating in seventh grade was serious business. If I couldn't get my bangs to flip just right, I would wash the hairspray out and start over again. Such a process could frustrate me to tears. Nicki blow-dried my hair, and I stared into the mirror. My hair looked unnaturally dry and yellow; and my eyebrows looked dark. It was a shocking change from the dirty blond I'd been an hour or so earlier. I looked at Nicki.

"Aww, you'll get used to it," she said. "Try my dress on."

I pulled Nicki's red dress up and looked in the mirror. I felt flat-chested and pale as I usually did in dresses. Nicki gave me the high heels to wear, and my bare feet slipped around inside. I had to half-drag them with me to walk since they were two sizes too big. Greg emerged from the bedroom and sat me down to go over what he called *The Rules.*

"Don't talk to *any* black guys," Greg said. "Don't talk to 'em, don't look at 'em. Most of 'em are pimps."

"OK," I said, while trying to decode what Greg had just said, especially because he was a black guy.

"Don't smoke crack," he pointed his finger at me, "I won't deal with any fuckin' girl on crack."

I thought about the frying pan commercial: *This is your brain on drugs.* I had never tried drugs except for the two hits of pot that year. Even Alice Cooper said drugs were stupid.

"Call me," Greg said, "as soon as you have five hundred dollars. If a cop stops you, tell'm your name is Stacey Combas. Tell'm you were born June 10, 1974, and that yer eighteen. Tell'm you live at 201 White Horse Pike."

Greg told me to repeat these details back to him, and I struggled to remember everything.

"If the cops give you shit," he said, "act up! Tell'm to stop botherin' you when there's plenty other hoes walkin' around."

Nicki chimed in. "Jus' give 'em attitude, girl," she said, "Give 'em lip for fuckin' wich you and they'll back awff."

I worried about breaking one of the rules, of messing up, of letting them both down. I didn't want them to think I was too immature to handle what they both seemed to think I could manage.

"Whatever you do," Greg lowered his voice, "don't tell'm 'bout me. I will *never* go back to jail again." He slammed his fist into his open palm, and then he pointed his finger at my face.

"Never," he said. "Understand?"

I understood.

Nobody said the word *prostitution.* It just hung in the air like a slab of meat. Everything was moving so quickly. Nobody asked me any questions. Nobody asked me if I was OK with this, or if this was what I had signed up for, or if I wanted some time to think about it. Nicki called for a taxi, and the two of us were on our way to Atlantic City.

"Here, baby," Nicki put two condoms in my hand, "I gotta get some mo'."

I was quiet.

"Now when dudes pass you," she said, "say things like '*C'mere, honey, you wanna good time?*' or '*You wan' some company?*'"

I nodded.

"First say two hundred dollars'n hour; go down to a hundred if they get rowdy 'bout it."

I nodded.

"Ask 'em if they got a room, and you meet them at the room. If they don't got a room, you tell 'em go get one and come back."

She must have sensed my anxiety.

"Don' worry, baby," she said, "sometimes they don' even want sex, some tricks just wanna talk to you."

The cab dropped us off on Pacific Avenue. Nicki walked to a corner store to buy more condoms, and then she stopped in front of Caesar's.

"This is *our* corner," she said, "Always meet me here."

I walked behind Nicki as she called to random men passing by. Lights flashed from the casinos and the passing traffic was loud and overwhelming. I hoped she wouldn't leave me out there all alone.

An old, pudgy white man passed by and smiled at me.

"How old are you?" he asked me.

"Um, eighteen," I said.

Nicki smiled her pearly teeth smile: "You wanna date her?"

"How much?" he asked.

"Two hundred," she said.

The man left and returned quickly with his car.

"Go 'head, girl," Nicki said when he pulled up.

I climbed into his car and watched Nicki through the rearview mirror as the man pulled away.

"I don't kiss on the mouth," I said to the man, after we were inside his Trump's Castle casino hotel room.

I tried to sound mysterious like Julia Roberts in *Pretty Woman.*

"Why?" the man asked.

"It's too personal," I quoted.

The man stripped off his clothes and left the socks on his feet. I looked from his wrinkled body up to his face. He kept smiling this friendly old-man smile.

"This is my first night," I said.

"I could tell," he said. "I'm honored."

And then he told me that I reminded him of his granddaughter.

I was fourteen years old. The following night separated life as I knew it into two parts: before Atlantic City and after Atlantic City.

INTRODUCTION

WHEN I FIRST BEGAN SPEAKING, AUDIENCE MEMBERS struggled to see the connection between my story and human trafficking. However, my testimony exemplifies a common form of child sex trafficking in America: pimp-controlled prostitution of children. My story also illustrates a common means by which traffickers, especially pimps, obtain their victims: they lure them in with a façade and false promises. The United States' Trafficking Victims Protection Act of 2000 (TVPA) clearly states that force, fraud, and coercion are not necessary elements to constitute cases of child sex trafficking. Although the traffickers in my case *did* use fraud and coercion, their manipulative tactics did not match with the extreme preconceptions of my audience members. I often heard the same questions after speaking:

Did they drug you?

Did they beat you?

But, how'd you get captured!?

This last question came from a sincere man wearing a pained look of confusion over his face at an event in Virginia. Another woman, a reporter, who also seemed sincere but bewildered, asked me, "Is there any way you were ever dropped on your head as an infant?" She simply couldn't understand my naïveté and compliance to a trafficker's demands. These questions no longer surprise me, considering some of the current messages in America surrounding the topic of child sex trafficking. Many images show bruised and battered children bound by chains or rope. Indeed, these images represent the atrocities of which traffickers are capable; however, they do *not* represent all situations of child sex trafficking.

Many children in the United States are lured into trusting their traffickers, or they are intimidated or exploited by traffickers and/or buyers[1] because of their lack of options. Because their situations do not match those widespread anti-trafficking images depicting violence, these victims are often left feeling as if they are at fault. Or worse, fault may be projected onto them by the public. Awareness campaigns must include images of *all* potential cases of trafficking and other forms of exploitation. Otherwise, society will continue to label certain kids as "child prostitutes" or "teen prostitutes" as opposed to *victims.*

With such labels that imply choice and fault, these victims are often ignored, arrested, or otherwise misidentified. It is on behalf of these children that I share my testimony. As difficult as it may be to expose the details of my story throughout this book, it is necessary to close the gap between sensationalism and reality. Misconceptions cloud public opinion and weaken the methods used to prevent child sex trafficking, making it difficult to identify, protect, and care for child victims. This book will serve as a survivor-informed introduction to the topic of child sex trafficking in America; and it will offer insight into prevention, aftercare, and advocacy efforts to community members, anti-trafficking advocates, and criminal justice and mental health professionals alike.

SO, WHAT IS HUMAN TRAFFICKING? IN 2000, THE PURpose of the Trafficking Victims Protection Act (TVPA) was defined "to combat trafficking in persons, a contemporary manifestation of slavery whose victims are predominantly women and children, to ensure just and effective punishment of traffickers, and to protect their victims."[2] In the United States, the terms "human trafficking" and "trafficking in persons" are often used interchangeably, and both terms typically refer to the U.S. definition for a "severe form of trafficking in persons." As defined by the U.S. TVPA, a "severe form of trafficking in persons" is:

> (A) the recruitment, harboring, transportation, provision, or obtaining of a person for the purpose of a commercial sex act in which that act is induced by force, fraud, or coercion; or in which the person induced to perform such act has not attained 18 years of age; or
>
> (B) the recruitment, harboring, transportation, provision, or obtaining of a person for labor or services, through the use of force, fraud, or coercion for the purpose of subjection to involuntary servitude, peonage, debt bondage, or slavery.

Because the term "trafficking" implies movement, human trafficking is often confused with human smuggling. However, these crimes are different.

The Department of Homeland Security (formerly the U.S. Immigration and Customs Enforcement, or ICE) defines human smuggling as "the importation of people into the United States involving deliberate evasion of immigration laws. This offense includes bringing illegal aliens into the United States as well as the unlawful transportation and harboring of aliens already in the United States."[3]

Human trafficking, however, does not require movement across a border. A person can be trafficked for the purpose of a commercial sex act or forced labor within a single country, state, or city, and even within a single dwelling (e.g., his or her own home). Although images, especially films and documentaries, often depict human trafficking happening in other countries to foreign victims, this crime is also happening within the United States to foreign national and U.S. citizen victims alike. Keep in mind that a smuggled person can *become* a victim of human trafficking if the smugglers use force, fraud, and/or coercion against that person for the purpose of labor or commercial sex.[4]

WHAT IS CHILD SEX TRAFFICKING? AS INDICATED above in section (A) of the definition for "a severe form of trafficking in persons," anyone under age eighteen who is induced to perform a commercial sex act is considered a victim of sex trafficking, with or without force, fraud, or coercion. A "commercial sex act" is defined by the TVPA as "any sex act on account of which anything of value is given to or received by any person." Erin Kulpa, Assistant Attorney General to the Commonwealth of Virginia, helped me to identify four types of child sex trafficking in America. These four types of trafficking are differentiated by the person or persons benefiting (financial or otherwise) from the use of a child[5] for commercial sex: pimp-controlled, family-controlled, gang-controlled, and organized crime–controlled sex trafficking. These categories are used here only as a way to organize and present common trafficking situations in America; they are not formally recognized categories in the study of child sex trafficking.

> *Pimp-Controlled:* The prologue is an example of pimp-controlled child sex trafficking.
>
> *Family-Controlled:* Minh Dang, former Executive Director of Don't Sell Bodies, is a survivor of family-controlled child sex trafficking in the San Francisco Bay area of California. Minh's parents groomed her via sexual abuse and then forced her to sign a contract to prostitute. "My parents began selling

me for sex at the age of ten after years of preparation," Minh explained, "My father raped me from the age of three until I left at the age of twenty."[6]

Gang-Controlled: Theresa Flores is a survivor of gang-controlled child sex trafficking in Detroit, Michigan. In her memoir, *The Slave Across the Street,* Theresa described how gang traffickers (including a fellow high school student) lured her in, sexually assaulted her, and then blackmailed her into cooperation.[7] The small organization of traffickers sought financial return as they sold Theresa to other male members in their ethnic community. Gang-controlled sex trafficking involving numerous types of gangs is growing across the country.

Organized Crime-Controlled: Shandra Woworuntu, a Survivor Advocate, Speaker, and member of Voices of Hope, is a survivor of organized crime-controlled sex trafficking.[8] In 2001, Shandra was lured from Indonesia to the United States with promises of work as a waitress in a major hotel. Upon arrival, the traffickers took Shandra's passport and forced her at gunpoint to work in a brothel. She was then transported and sold within the United States between traffickers working in the international organization's network.

Shandra and a minor managed to escape together through a second-story window. In a personal e-mail, Shandra described the minor as a fifteen-year-old girl who was also lured from Indonesia and trafficked for sex within the United States.[9] Shandra was a foreign national victim of adult sex trafficking within the United States; the fifteen-year-old girl was a foreign national victim of child sex trafficking within the United States. Adult and minor citizens can also fall victim to organized-crime controlled trafficking within and outside of the United States.

There are also a myriad of trafficking situations that overlap or fall in between these categories. For example, a self-proclaimed "pimp" controlling a child could also be his or her aunt, uncle, grandmother, grandfather, cousin, brother or sister, or any other family member; this same "pimp" could also be a member of an organized gang or crime network. Or, the person controlling a prostituted child could be an acquaintance who doesn't fit the profile of a pimp or gang member. This person may never before have sexually exploited anyone; however, upon identifying a child in a vulnerable situation, he or she may have seized the opportunity to sexually exploit that child for personal gain. There is no one profile for traffickers of children; traffickers can be and are of any age, gender, class, ethnicity, or race.

THE TVPA IS CLEAR THAT FORCE, FRAUD, AND COERcion are not necessary elements to constitute cases of child sex trafficking. However, there is one word in the TVPA definition that can be (and often is) debated: "induced." This word implies that someone or something is *compelling* the child to perform the commercial sex act, whether or not "force, fraud, or coercion" is involved. Some say that a controlling party (i.e., a trafficker) must be involved in order to constitute a case as "child sex trafficking." Others argue that a buyer or a situation (e.g., homelessness or drug addiction) can be the force that is *inducing* the commercial sex act. This difference in interpretation has caused some confusion between advocates and organizations when discussing child sex trafficking in the United States.

This brings up another term: the "commercial sexual exploitation of children," or CSEC. A community training curriculum funded by the U.S. Office of Juvenile Justice and Delinquency Program (OJJDP) defined CSEC as follows: sexual abuse and remuneration in money, goods, or services—or the promise of money, goods, or services—to the child or a third person or persons for the sexual use of that child.[10] Under this definition, the term CSEC covers all commercial sex acts involving children under the age of eighteen, whether or not a controlling party (i.e., a trafficker) is involved. For the purposes of this book, the term "child sex trafficking" will be used only to specify those cases of CSEC that involve a controlling party (i.e., a trafficker).

CSEC can occur in numerous ways, including but not limited to the following: street prostitution, hotel/motel prostitution, prostitution at truck stops, prostitution within houses or brothels, prostitution within massage parlors, phone sex, cybersex, exotic/topless/lap dancing, stripping, live-sex shows, child pornography, escort services, nude massages, nude modeling, child marriage, work as a "body shot girl" or "cantina girl," gang entry requirements, required ongoing sexual services in gangs, etc. The child, or a trafficker, may receive money, drugs, debt forgiveness, transportation, food, medicine, lodging, or other survival needs, or any other goods or favors in exchange for the sexual abuse or exploitation of that child.

Any child involved with any form of commercial sexual exploitation is a *victim* in need of services. The child is *not* a prostitute; the child has been commercially sexually exploited or trafficked. "When you talk about a young person being trafficked or exploited," explained Rachel Lloyd, Founder and Executive Director of Girls Educational & Mentoring Services (GEMS) in a 2012 interview with John Walsh, "the *ed* on the end makes it something that was done *to* that person; it's not who they are."[11] Lloyd makes an important point here. The word *prostitute* carries with it centuries of stigmatization. It implies choice and can cause society to project blame, shame, and/or ridicule onto the child. For those who insist on using this term to describe child victims, I wonder if they or their children have ever themselves been victims. News media often use the terms *child prostitute, teen prostitute,* or worse, *teen hooker,* in order to sensationalize their stories. When used in this way, the terms are derogatory, ignorant, and insulting.

"DOMESTIC TRAFFICKING" IS A TERM OFTEN USED TO describe human trafficking activity happening within U.S. borders; "domestic minor sex trafficking," or DMST, typically refers to child victims who are U.S. citizens and trafficked for commercial sex within U.S. borders. DMST victims are a subcategory of the total number of children in the United States (citizens and foreign nationals) trafficked within, into, or out of U.S. borders. It is also the category of children for whom the least number of resources are available. A foreign national child victim of trafficking is typically handled by the federal government. Federal legislation (i.e., the TVPA) stipulates for these victims to receive resources for placement and services. A U.S. citizen victim of commercial sexual exploitation, including child sex trafficking, however, is often handled by his or her home state or commonwealth. It is the state's law (not the TVPA), and the state's protocol and available resources (or lack thereof) that ultimately determine whether a U.S. citizen child victim is arrested, or offered placement or services or both—or neither.

"While the inducement of a child to engage in a commercial sex act is a form of human trafficking under U.S. federal law," states Polaris Project, an anti-trafficking organization based in Washington, D.C. (and which also oversees the National Human Trafficking Resource Center [NHTRC]), "many states still do not offer legal protections for minor [i.e., child] victims . . . or services to care for these severely victimized children. In many cases, these victims are treated as criminals or delinquents, which results in further harm to the child."[12] Polaris Project advocates for stronger legislation in every state and commonwealth of the country as do other organizations like Shared Hope International.

"Safe Harbor" laws are state laws that aim to protect all child victims of commercial sexual exploitation, regardless of gender, race, or class. This is accomplished by ensuring that a child protective response, as opposed to a criminal justice response, is in place when commercially sexually exploited children are identified by law enforcement officers. United Nations Ambassador and actress Mira Sorvino is an advocate for Safe Harbor laws. In a 2012 interview with John Walsh, Sorvino says that the Safe Harbor law "decriminalizes the child or the teenager, it gives them access to social services, and really establishes that the child in prostitution is the victim. . . ."[13]

"The real question that we, as a society, must ask ourselves is what kind of a country do we want to be?" says James Dold, former Senior Policy Analyst for Polaris Project. "Do we want to be a country that treats sexually exploited children as criminals, or do we want to be a country that sees these vulnerable young people as victims in need of our care, compassion, and understanding? It is our hope that, through the passage of Safe Harbor laws across the country . . . we will create a society that embraces this victim-centered, human rights approach to caring for child victims of commercial sexual exploitation."[14]

HOW MANY CHILDREN ARE TRAFFICKED FOR COMMERCIAL sex in the United States? The U.S. State Department examines the prevalence of human trafficking in every country across the globe, and then reports the results on an annual basis. The following excerpt is from Luis CdeBaca, Ambassador to the Office to Combat Trafficking in Persons (TIP), in his introductory statement to the 2013 TIP Report:

> Because reporting is uneven, we can't say for certain how many victims of trafficking are identified each year. This Report estimates that, based on the information governments have provided, only around 40,000 victims have been identified [globally] in the last year. In contrast, social scientists estimate that as many as 27 million men, women, and children are trafficking victims at any given time. That means we're bringing to light only a mere fraction of those who are exploited in modern slavery. That number, and the millions who remain unidentified, are the numbers that deserve our focus.[15]

In order to gather information about domestic trafficking in persons, the reauthorization of the TVPA (TVPRA) in 2005 mandated that the Attorney General submit statistical reports to Congress using available data from state and local authorities.[16] In response, the Department of Justice (DOJ) funded the creation of the Human Trafficking Reporting System (HTRS). In January 2009 and in April 2011, the DOJ issued two reports based on data collected from the HTRS, and results specific to child sex trafficking within the United States were as follows: the first report cited 375 potential cases of child sex trafficking between 2007 and 2008, as of September 30, 2008;[17] and the second report cited 248 confirmed cases of child sex trafficking (age seventeen and younger) between January 2008 and June 2010.[18]

Unfortunately, these statistics grossly underreport the issue. The authors of the first report say that "[b]ecause these task forces were not selected to be statistically representative, the data do not represent all incidents of human trafficking nationwide."[19] The second report included only that information provided by "high data quality task forces," which were defined as task forces that "regularly entered new cases into the system, provided individual-level information for at least one suspect or victim, and updated case information on a regular basis."[20] Only 18 of the 42 task forces during that period were considered to be "high data quality task forces."[21]

A 2001 University of Pennsylvania study estimated that about 326,000 children and teens in the United States were *at risk* each year of becoming victims of commercial sexual exploitation.[22] Ernie Allen, former President and CEO of the National Center for Missing and Exploited Children (NCMEC), testified in 2012 that NCMEC had estimated in the past "at least 100,000 kids were the victims of child prostitution and trafficking each year."[23] I have heard other guesstimates as well (some higher, some lower). Due to the lack of comprehensive government data regarding human trafficking, advocacy groups are extrapolating their own statistics. Needless to say, the numbers have been squashed, stretched, and questioned across the board.[24] But who is losing in this debate?

In May 2012, the *New York Daily News* reported the sentencing of a man named Sahim Lucas, age 34, who used the online classified advertisements site, Craigslist, to traffic a 13-year-old girl:

> Lucas met the teenage runaway from Delaware in late 2008 in Atlantic City. He promised to help her become a model and brought her to the Bronx, but when she arrived at his Prospect Ave. apartment, he ordered her to work as a prostitute, according to trial testimony.[25]

This article was written twenty years after my own victimization in 1992. The pimp trafficker in this story used almost exactly the same tactics as Greg used on me. How many times has this happened since this child sex trafficker was sentenced in 2012? How many times has this happened since you started reading this book?[26] Considering the concern for and the lack of concrete statistics, I wonder how many kids it will take for the issue of CSEC, including child sex trafficking, to warrant credibility, investigation, and action.

PART I

BEFORE ATLANTIC CITY

1

ARE YOUR CHILDREN AT RISK?

MANY PARENTS WANT TO BELIEVE THAT THEIR CHILdren are safe from the tactics of child sex traffickers; however, the truth is that *any* child can be susceptible. The very nature of *being* a child is a risk factor as youth often act on emotion and impulse. In a 2011 podcast, Sandra Morgan, R.N., discussed how brain maturation can effect the balance of power between children and traffickers. Morgan explained that a "brain develops from the back to the front" and that the prefrontal lobe, which is "where executive decision-making is housed" is "one of the last parts of [the] brain to develop. . . . You have a major advantage when you're a 26-year-old adult and she's a 14-year-old child," Morgan says, "This is . . . really important . . . to understand because executive decision-making is that ability to measure the consequences, to assess the risk, and [to ask oneself] *Is this a good choice? Is this responsible? Will this produce a good result for me?*"[1]

Daniel Romer, Ph.D., argues that adolescents are naturally prone to experiment with "novel (adult-like) behavior" and that their impulsivity and risk-taking is due to their lack of experience with such behavior as opposed to "a structural deficit" in brain maturation.[2] Regardless of the root cause, impulsivity and risky behavior are natural adolescent attributes, and such attributes are attractive to traffickers. Greg told me that he was 23 or 25; however, he was actually 31. Based on police records, I believe Nicki was 26 years old. At fourteen, I believed I was capable of making independent decisions. In reality, I was being manipulated and exploited by adults. It took many years for me to recognize that, though. I needed time to mature in order to understand how inexperienced and *immature* I was at age fourteen.

Along with impulsivity and lack of experience, there are other factors that might predispose a child to being more vulnerable to a trafficker's tactics. The greater the number (or severity) of these risk factors, the greater the risk is for that child if he or she encounters a trafficker. The following potential predisposing factors are often associated with the commercial sexual exploitation of children (CSEC); however, this list is non-exhaustive, and none of these factors predestine a child to become a victim of commercial sexual exploitation, including sex trafficking. However, any vulnerability puts a child at a greater risk for any type of exploitation.

ABUSE AND/OR NEGLECT IN CHILDHOOD

A 2012 Ohio Human Trafficking Commission report listed the following "early indicators" as "experiences of Ohio youth before involvement in the child sex trade: 41% were victims of neglect, 44% were victims of abuse, 40% were victims of sex abuse, 37% were victims of emotional abuse/psychological maltreatment, and 24% were victims of physical abuse."[3] These experiences happened to the youth at least one year or more "before entering the sex trade," and each of these indicators was listed as statistically significant.[4] Any type of unaddressed trauma in childhood can manifest in any number of negative ways, including self-loathing, depression, and anger. These manifestations are layers of additional risk factors.

Sexual abuse in childhood is by far the most common predisposing factor I've heard mentioned in discussions regarding CSEC within the United States. A 1983 study found that 60 percent of 200 subjects involved in commercial sex (adults and minors) were sexually exploited as juveniles.[5] A 2012 study found that 40.8 percent of 115 subjects who identify as "being involved in the sex trade before age 18" also report having been victims of "sex abuse."[6] Patricia Murphy cites two studies in her book, *Making the Connections,* that estimate that between 65 and 85 percent of prostituted women were the victims of "childhood rape."[7] In fact, some clinicians estimate this figure to be "nearer to 100 percent."[8] Many organizations that provide services to child victims of commercial sexual exploitation across the country have confirmed these higher statistics to me. Early childhood sexual abuse will be discussed more in depth in the following chapter.

POVERTY

Whether a child's family or entire community is impoverished, poverty can limit that child's options and resources. The National Center for Children in Poverty (NCCP) states that poverty can impede a child's ability to learn, can contribute to poor health and mental health, and can contribute to social, emotional, and behavioral problems.[9] Rachel Lloyd of Girls Educational & Mentoring Services (GEMS) works with child victims of commercial sexual exploitation in New York City. In her memoir, *Girls Like Us,* she describes the pervasive effects of poverty on children:

> Of course many children who grow up in challenging economic situations thrive, but the reality is that far too many don't, and too many children's futures can be determined by zip code. Children in poor neighborhoods frequently receive a substandard education, are often exposed to lead paint in poorly constructed buildings, have higher rates of asthma, and live in communities where there are little to no recreational or green spaces and where entire neighborhoods have been abandoned and forgotten by those in power. Children born into poverty are at risk for many things, including being recruited into the commercial sex industry.[10]

The story of Antonia "Neet" Childs, Founder of Market Your Mind Not Your Body and Neet's Sweets bakery, exemplifies the significance of this risk factor. As a child, Neet lived in New York where her mother struggled financially. "My mom worked hard to take care of us," Neet said, "and I always felt like I needed to help and support her."[11] Without resources to help her family, Neet began caring for her brother and sisters at an early age. "I always carry this habit of having to help everybody," Neet said in a 2013 interview with *Ebony* magazine. "I had seen my mother struggle and I didn't want that for her. I wanted to do everything in my power to help."[12]

At sixteen, Neet started working at an after-school job where she met a man. For several months, this man visited Neet and asked her questions about her life. Their conversations developed into a friendship, and Neet confided her family's struggles. This man, who posed as a friend, began to drive Neet home after her work shifts ended. "He would give me $100 bills at a time," Neet said, "As a teenager . . . a hundred dollars is a lot of money."[13] The man's monetary gifts ultimately led to requests for sex. Because she had accepted money from this man, Neet says she felt both responsible and obligated to concede. The man soon began trafficking Neet to other men within a high-profile fraternity. This man preyed on Neet's vulnerability for his own profit.

HISTORY OF FOSTER CARE/ CHILD PROTECTIVE SERVICES

Without a doubt, a history of foster care or child protective services is also a risk factor commonly discussed in child sex trafficking and other forms of CSEC within the United States. Tina Frundt, Founder and Executive Director of Courtney's House, cycled through more than twenty foster homes in Chicago, Illinois, before she was trafficked on her fourteenth birthday.[14] "I was adopted to a wonderful family when I was twelve years old," Tina says in a 2012 training video for AMBER Alert, "but because of prior sexual abuse . . . my trust on people was really low."[15] Tina was lured away from her adoptive family by a man who claimed to have also grown up in foster care. Tina later learned that this was a lie; it was a tactic the trafficker used to bond with Tina and to gain her trust.[16] The man then drove Tina to Cleveland, Ohio.[17]

"And that is when he brought two guys into the room and they 'seasoned' me," Tina explained in a 2010 interview with Free the Slaves.[18] "'Seasoned' is rape."

Withelma "T" Ortiz Walker Pettigrew, a trafficking survivor named 2011 Woman of the Year by *Glamour* magazine, described her early life in a 2013 Al Jazeera interview: "Like Tina [Frundt], [I] was raised in the foster care system . . . From the age of basically birth to ten years old, I endured various different multiple levels of abuse—verbal, sexual, physical—which made me really vulnerable [to a trafficker] at the age of 10 years old when I was used to being more mature than my age because of my circumstance[s] . . ."[19]

In November 2012, Abby Sewell wrote in the *Los Angeles Times* that "[o]f the 174 juveniles arrested on prostitution-related charges in Los Angeles County in 2010, 59% were in the foster care system, according to Probation Department statistics."[20] Melissa Snow, Child Sex Trafficking Program Specialist with the National Center for Missing & Exploited Children (NCMEC), stated that "[o]f the children reported missing to [NCMEC] who [were] likely child sex trafficking victims, 60 percent were in the care of social services or foster care when they ran."[21]

Kids living in foster care and other child protective services are not only vulnerable to exploitation—they are sometimes directly targeted by predators.

A *Miami Herald* article described a case in which four "alleged pimps" targeted children living in the foster care system. The article described how the men "[used] a teenage foster child as a recruiter" and then "plied [the] underage girls with cash, affection, and gifts." One of the victims, a 17-year-old girl, was stated to have "cognitive impairments." The article described how the girl was recruited by her peer and then sexually exploited by two of the alleged pimps. These men then sold her to other men; they would call her cell phone and pick her up from school or from the state facility.[22] Commercial sexual exploitation involving children with developmental disabilities is not uncommon, making this another risk factor.[23]

DIFFICULTY IN SCHOOL

The 2012 Ohio Human Trafficking Commission's report claimed that one of the three statistically significant factors for child victims of commercial sexual exploitation was "dropping out of school"; these factors occurred less than one year before victimization.[24] A 2002 research study, "Sisters Speak Out," found similar results; it was based on interviews with 222 women "representing various segments of the prostitution industry."[25] Of those women first commercially sexually exploited between the ages of twelve and fifteen, only one-fourth reported completion of a high school education or GED.[26] A child may struggle in school for any number of reasons: bullying, poor nutrition, lack of support with homework, etc. Dropping out of school can expose a child or teenager to many negative outcomes, including commercial sexual exploitation.

RUNNING AWAY

A child may run away from home for any number of reasons: to seek attention, to escape abuse or neglect, to seek acceptance, to seek opportunities for survival, etc. Running away is a risk factor; and the more times the child runs away, the greater the risk factor. Sergeant Byron Fassett with the Dallas Police Department recognized that children who ran away four or more times in a year were more likely to have been involved with commercial sex.[27] The story of author and attorney Carissa Phelps is an example of this vulnerability. In her memoir *Runaway Girl,* Phelps describes a childhood on the run:

> I decided I couldn't stay put for another minute. I bolted. Out the bathroom window, onto the roof, and over the back fence. I ran away. I left without any

> plans of coming back. A surge of adrenaline rushed through me. I was everything I wanted to be—out of the house, out from under my [stepfather's] roof, away from the voices and the mess, out on my own. I was free.[28]

A chronic runaway, Carissa attempted to flee her parents' dysfunctional homes, as well as detention centers and other youth facilities. She was ultimately trafficked by a brutal pimp at the age of twelve in Fresno, California. Staca Shehan, Director of the Case Analysis Division for NCMEC reports the following glaring statistic: *one out of eight endangered runaways reported missing to NCMEC in 2012 was likely [a] child sex trafficking victim.*[29] This is not surprising as traffickers, especially pimp and gang traffickers, will often hang around bus stations and youth shelters in search of young victims.

The U.S. Attorney's Office for the Eastern District of Virginia reports several cases of gang-controlled sex trafficking in which runaways were targeted. In July 2011, Alexander Rivas, an MS-13 gang member, was sentenced to ten years in prison for luring juvenile runaways into a sex trafficking ring with a majority of his activity happening in northern Virginia, including Woodbridge, Fairfax, and Alexandria.[30] Months later, Alonso Bruno Cornejo Ormeno, 22, was sentenced to 292 months in prison, followed by five years of supervised release, for sex trafficking girls who ranged in age from fifteen to seventeen.[31] Cornejo Ormeno targeted teenage girls who had run away from home and served them up to clients throughout northern Virginia, as well as Washington, D.C. and Maryland.[32]

MENTAL HEALTH ISSUES

The Ohio Human Trafficking Commission's 2012 study reports depression as an "early indicator" in 30 percent of Ohio youth "before involvement in the child sex trade."[33] Depression is often cited as a risk factor, and I strongly believe this is true. For me, signs of depression began as early as fourth or fifth grade and were severe by eighth grade, along with anxiety and impulsivity. Post-traumatic stress disorder (PTSD) is also gaining attention as a potential risk factor for and effect of commercial sexual exploitation.[34]

However, symptoms associated with *any* mental health issue may be a risk factor for any type of exploitation, including CSEC. The 2007 New York Study of Commercial Sexual Exploitation reports that 25 of 27 victims incarcerated in juvenile detention facilities for prostitution-related offenses had "records of previous mental health treatment."[35] Obviously, lack of efficacious mental health treatment is also a risk factor for exploitation.[36]

HAVING FAMILY MEMBERS OR FRIENDS INVOLVED IN COMMERCIAL SEX

NBC 5 Dallas-Fort Worth reported a story in January 2012 in which a "Houston-area man and his girlfriend [were] accused of forcing her 14-year-old daughter into prostitution at truck stops and apartments."[37] NBC 5 says that both adults were arrested "when a neighbor called police after noticing the girl near a street. The neighbor said the girl was barefoot and seemed hungry." The *Houston Chronicle* wrote: "Court documents show that the girl told investigators she initially accompanied her mother to apartments where the woman was prostituting herself. Customers began asking to have sex with the girl, who said she was then forced to act as a prostitute 'every day' during several weeks."[38]

Sadly, this story exemplifies the risk associated with having relatives or friends involved with illegal commercial sex, including sex trafficking. Sisters Speak Out says that "over half of the early starters grew up in a household with prostitution." "Early starters" are reported as those women participants who were first commercially sexually exploited between the ages twelve and fifteen. The study also reports that 87 percent of "early starters had someone suggest they engage in prostitution while they were growing up."[39] The Ohio Attorney General's 2012 report says that 33 percent of commercially sexually exploited youth have a close family member involved in the "sex trade." This report also says that 59 percent have friends involved with selling themselves and 30 percent have friends involved with selling others.[40]

LGBTQ[41] YOUTH

In March 2012, *Project Q Atlanta* reported that Atlanta drag queen personality Pasha Nicole received a fourteen-year prison sentence for "forcing a transgender teenager into prostitution," among other offenses related to sex trafficking.[42] Nicole, known legally as Christopher Thomas Lynch, was charged alongside 35-year-old roommate and gay bar "go-go dancer," Steven Donald Lemery. In September 2012, the *Atlanta Journal-Constitution* reported that Lemery was sentenced to 80 years in prison for human trafficking, aggravated child molestation, and enticing a child for indecent purposes and pandering by compulsion. The article quotes Assistant District Attorney Rachel Ackley:

> Two of Lemery's victims were 15 years old at the time of the offenses, and a third was 18 . . . One of the 15-year-olds and the 18-year-old were brought across state lines by Lemery and forced into prostitution . . . There was testimony how victims were held in the house, not allowed to leave, given drugs and alcohol . . . One of the victims testified at trial [about] being forced to prostitute and while being held at a client's house, he was held down and burned as they attempted to rape them.[43]

This case illustrates one of the many dangers faced by LGBTQ youth who are forced (or feel compelled) to seek support and solace outside their homes or communities. An anonymous survivor of child sex trafficking explained how her confusion over sexual orientation added to her vulnerability as an adolescent: "Even though I was often seeking romantic relationships with boys, I was physically attracted to girls in middle school. And I thought I was in love with someone, but I couldn't tell her. I felt like I couldn't tell anyone. Being gay or bisexual wasn't talked about; it was taboo. I didn't have anyone to help me sort through those feelings."[44]

Like many minority youth, LGBTQ youth often face and/or fear discrimination from their families and/or communities, leaving them open to predators posing as friends, role models, love interests, or caregivers. The Ohio Attorney General's 2012 report found the following statistics for "those who entered the sex trade before the age of eighteen": 52 percent were straight females, 22 percent were bisexual females, 3.5 percent were lesbian, 16.5 percent were straight males, 4.3 percent were bisexual males, and 0.9 percent were gay males.[45] Heterosexual boys and LGBTQ youth who are victims of commercial sexual exploitation seem to be the least studied population with the fewest available services specific to commercial sexual exploitation.

MISSING OR ABSENT PARENT

Katrina Owens, Founder of MPower and former Intervention Specialist with Georgia Care Connection, describes her childhood self as a tomboy with an "easy" and "normal" life. "I grew up in a middle class neighborhood with both parents," Katrina says, "[I] had tons of friends . . . and I've always been an 'A' student in school."[46] As with many children, life became more difficult as Katrina approached adolescence. She recalls missing a much-needed connection with her father.

"My father has always been a protector and the breadwinner, but he was not emotionally involved," Katrina says. "That's something that I always, always longed for from my father . . . Some of the things that I needed to learn and that I needed to receive as a younger girl—those needs [grew] as I became a teenager; and that was the turnaround."[47] Katrina's parents divorced, and the disconnection between Katrina and her father worsened.

Like Neet Childs, Katrina met a man while she was working at an after-school job; she was a hostess at the age of 16. This man used kindness, charm, gifts, and romance to build a relationship with Katrina before trafficking her for commercial sex in Atlanta. Katrina's story is not uncommon. I have met many survivors who grew up with one or both parents being physically, mentally, or emotionally absent due to various reasons, including death, divorce, physical or mental illness, substance abuse/addiction, a prison sentence, or abandonment. A missing parent is one of many common scenarios in America that can predispose a child to any number of exploitative situations. The 2007 New York Study of Commercial Sexual Exploitation reports that 68 percent of child victims from New York City who were incarcerated report "grief caused by the loss of or separation from a family member of significance."[48]

SUBSTANCE ABUSE IN THE HOME

Substance abuse in the home can cause a variety of additional risk factors, including parental abuse and/or parental neglect. Such conflict could cause a child to run away from home (or from placement in foster care) or to otherwise seek help outside the home, thereby increasing his or her risk of crossing paths with a trafficker. An anonymous survivor using the pseudonym "Alissa" fell victim to pimp-controlled sex trafficking at the age of sixteen. In a 2012 interview with *Marie Claire,* Alissa revealed her parents' substance abuse issues. Her mother was described as a "recovering drug addict who couldn't care for her;" and her father, "an alcoholic who wouldn't pay the bills." As a result, Alissa "ended up on the streets" and was lured into prostitution as a way to survive. "It was a high school reunion," the article quotes Alissa. "These were girls who had dropped out of school and disappeared."[49]

Children, especially young children, living with parents who suffer from severe addiction are in danger of many types of abuse or exploitation in the home, including sex trafficking. Family-controlled sex trafficking often involves parents selling their children for drugs or to pay off drug debts. In March 2012, the *New York Daily News* reported that a 35-year-old mother in Florida, Dalina Nicholas, was arrested for selling her six-year-old daughter for sex in exchange for drugs.[50] In January 2013, *The Florida Times-Union* reported that Nicholas pled guilty to four counts of child neglect. The author of the article wrote, "Jacksonville Beach police said Nicholas lived in subsidized housing and supported herself and her drug habit by selling her daughter for sex."[51]

Substance abuse in the home can also cross generations and cause a child or teen to experiment with drugs or alcohol. Regardless of why or how experimentation begins, addiction to drugs or alcohol is an even greater risk factor. Traffickers and buyers will exploit a child's addiction in order to coerce that child's compliance into commercial sex. An anonymous survivor of commercial sexual exploitation explained that, at age fifteen or sixteen, she exchanged a sex act with an adult male in order to gain money for drugs. Without her knowledge, the man videotaped the act. The man's cousin then used the tape in an attempt to blackmail her into trading sex for money.[52] This man is what I call an "opportunistic trafficker"; he recognized an exploitative situation and attempted to use it to his advantage. Pimp and gang traffickers will also target children who are addicted to drugs. One "ex-pimp" from a 2010 study says that he targeted "[w]hite girls from the bars who like to get high. . . . They were really a lot of profit," says the "ex-pimp," "but they didn't last long because they used too many drugs. Most were 16 to 17 years old."[53]

IT'S IMPOSSIBLE TO LIST EVERY INDIVIDUAL OR FAMILY circumstance that could present an opportunity for a trafficker to connect with a child; there are too many. Try to think of any and every situation that might leave a child vulnerable. Common situations include a lack of guidance or supervision; moving to a new neighborhood, state, or country; a friend moving away; difficulty making friends; death or illness within the family; conflict with parents and teachers; and bullying or the fear of being bullied. The severity of each circumstance and the child's ability to cope with it will determine the severity of that risk factor. If a child is well-supported and well-adjusted, perhaps it will be a slight risk factor. If a child is not well-supported (or if the child has additional risk factors), then it may become a more significant risk factor.

Although this chapter highlights those risk factors most *commonly* associated with CSEC, I must reiterate that *any* risk factor can predispose a child to being vulnerable to a trafficker's tactics. An "ex-pimp" was quoted in a 2010 report as saying, "It's impossible to protect all girls from guys like I was because that's what we do. We eat, drink, and sleep thinking of ways to trick young girls into doing what we want them to do."[54]

When I spoke to audiences about my testimony, I was often asked:

Why did you walk over to this man in the mall?

What compelled you to talk to a stranger?

I tried my best to answer these questions honestly. *Because I felt special,* I said, *because I was curious.* While there may be many imperfect answers for these questions, the perfectly plain truth is that I was a *child.* I was vulnerable and naïve. I may have appeared mature at age fourteen, but I wasn't. I may have smoked cigarettes, cursed, and dressed to look like an adult; but I wasn't an adult. The previous school year I ran up $300 in phone calls trying to win Vanilla Ice concert tickets. After watching Oliver Stone's movie *The Doors,* I strongly believed in the possibility that I was Jim Morrison in a former life. I also pretended to be tough in school, and I bullied weaker kids in order to hide my own fear of getting beat up. I was far from adulthood.

Try to think of how many times you, as a child or teen, ignored an adult's warning or an internal instinct to stop what you were doing; or how many times your child or niece or nephew failed to heed your advice. For many teens, such mistakes turned out to be simple lessons or close calls in which they were never in any real danger. For me, however, and for many other children like me, a seemingly benign interaction with a stranger ended up having severe and lifelong repercussions.

Why did this stranger call me over to him?

Why did he choose *me?*

These are the more important and appropriate questions. Instead of blaming a child victim of commercial sexual exploitation for his or her actions, or inactions, we must turn our attention to the perpetrators, including the buyers, and the risk factors associated with CSEC.

2

THE "WILLING VICTIM"

WHEN I FIRST BEGAN SPEAKING AT HUMAN TRAFFICKING awareness events, the prologue was all I shared of my story. Additional common questions included: *What were you thinking in the motel room? What was going through your mind? Why didn't you run away from the motel?* And, *why didn't you run away once you were on the street?* These last two questions are the most common questions posed to survivors; yet they are the most difficult to answer. These kinds of questions also left me feeling defensive, ashamed, and at-fault for my circumstances. Although the TVPA recognizes *all* persons under the age of eighteen as victims of child sex trafficking, regardless of their choices; I often wondered if I really qualified. I soon realized that, in order for audiences to understand, I had to go back further into my story.

Many victims of commercial sexual exploitation, including sex trafficking, are labeled "willing victims." A willing victim (or "willing participant") is someone who is deemed to have "chosen" to run away with or "chosen" to stay with a trafficker or buyer at any point, for any length of time. I am often referred to as a "willing victim" because I was not beaten, drugged, or abducted and because I didn't attempt to escape from Greg or Nicki. There may be any number of reasons a child "chooses" to stay with a trafficker, including fear, violence, and "trauma bonds" (e.g., Stockholm syndrome). A child may also "choose" to stay in a commercially sexually exploitative situation (with or without a trafficker) because he or she believes there are no other options.

I worry that images used in anti-trafficking advocacy are perpetuating the projection of blame onto certain victims. Many of the posters I see associated with anti-trafficking depict not just violence but also young children. I often see pictures of little girls crying, some in pigtails and some holding teddy bears with slogans overhead touting lost innocence. *This* was not me. By eighth grade middle school, I was angry, undisciplined, and sexually active. Did this make me less of a victim? What about many of today's victims who fail to match this picture of innocence? In a Wellesley Centers for Women Research & Action Report (Wellesley College), Kate Price, M.A., argues that children who do not fit the ideal for "innocence" are often seen as "bad kids" and blamed for their circumstances:

> As a society, we often seem to care more about protecting our cultural ideal of childhood innocence than about meeting the actual needs of real-life children—especially commercially sexually exploited children. To fit the ideal of purity, children require high levels of social capital; preferably, they're white, middle or upper class, and heterosexual. They have limited or no sexual experience, enjoy secure health care, housing, and education, and they live within a supportive nuclear family.[1]

In her memoir, *Girls Like Us,* Rachel Lloyd describes her young teen self as "a flashing neon sign for danger, for abuse, for a tragic ending. A perfect conflation of risk factors, a statistic waiting to happen."[2] This describes the early life for many "willing victims" of commercial sexual exploitation as many have experienced numerous layers of abuse as well as multiple risk factors. Without appropriate resources, such children often live on the outskirts of society's ideal for innocence. They then become walking prey, or "flashing neon signs," to many predators, including sex traffickers.

As discussed in chapter 1, abuse in childhood is a common factor among commercially sexually exploited youth. However, when it comes to "willing victims," sexual abuse is often that first layer of victimization. If you are looking for proof, talk to survivors. Keisha Head, Founder of Project 360 Degrees and former Program Associate at youthSpark (formerly Juvenile Justice Fund), was lured into prostitution at the age of sixteen by Charles Pipkins (a.k.a. Sir Charles), a notorious pimp trafficker in Atlanta.[3] From age four to twelve, Keisha lived with an aunt; she never knew her father and her mother suffered from schizophrenia. While living with her aunt, Keisha says she suffered sexual abuse at the hands of two other relatives.[4]

Survivor advocate Savannah Sanders, formerly known by the pseudonym Amira Birger, was also lured into prostitution by an adult at the age of sixteen in Phoenix, Arizona.[5] After her parents divorced; Savannah says she temporarily stayed with a family member. While living there, at the age of six, she was raped by an older cousin.[6] She was then molested until age thirteen.[7] Barbara Amaya, author of the graphic novel, *The Destiny of Zoe Carpenter,* was lured into prostitution at age thirteen by an adult couple in Washington, D.C. In an interview with *Fox 5 News,* Barbara described her family life before she ran away. "It looked really good from the outside," she said, "but it wasn't good; I was sexually abused by family members."[8]

Sexual abuse can also occur to children while outside of the home. Perpetrators can be pedophiles within the neighborhood, pedophiles working with youth,[9] or older children in the home or neighborhood. Jes Richardson, CEO of One Dream Movement, was lured into pimp-controlled prostitution at age seventeen in Portland, Oregon. In a personal e-mail, Jes described her parents as "loving and nurturing" but unaware of the sexual abuse that was happening to her as a child. "Without my parents' knowledge," Jes says, "I was repeatedly raped and sexually molested by three neighborhood teenage boys; I was four and five years old."[10]

Greg Bucceroni is also a survivor of commercial sexual exploitation, including organized crime-controlled child pornography. Greg says he was first sexually abused at age twelve by Ed Savitz, a notorious serial pedophile who abused many boys in the Philadelphia area. This abuse and exploitation continued as Savitz arranged for Greg to meet with other men in the pedophile ring; oftentimes these arrangements were to allow for an exchange of boys between overseeing pedophiles.[11] These stories are heartbreaking and difficult to read; however, it's imperative to understand a "willing victim's" early or initial abuse in order to understand what can predispose a child to being compliant to a trafficker or buyer.

Like many child victims of commercial sexual exploitation, I was also sexually molested under the age of ten by an older cousin. I was targeted by this older boy not just because I was often unsupervised in his home but also probably because of my timid and compliant nature. From a very early age, I lacked the assertion needed to escape potential abuse/exploitation.

My relative's home was tumultuous; my cousin and his sibling fist fought regularly and cursed at their parents (who often cursed at them in return). I often stood on the sidelines of their home hoping to avoid conflict. In my attempts to be invisible and appeasing, I eventually became a target for abuse by one of my cousins. (I don't think this cousin's intentions were to physically or emotionally harm me. I think he was an adolescent boy interested in sex and the female body, and he was exploiting my vulnerability to serve his own curiosity.) Instead of telling my parents about my cousin's "touching," I often begged them not to leave me at his house.

My parents belonged to a members-only bar that enforced an eight o'clock pm curfew for children. This was the reason I sometimes stayed with my cousin and his family on weekend nights. One afternoon, I begged my mother not to take me to their house. I begged until she promised to pick me up before bedtime, but she never showed. I lay awake in a makeshift bed on the dirty living room floor until my cousin fetched me in the middle of the night. He led me into the dark kitchen, and I stared at the fly tape hanging from the ceiling as he descended on me. This was the night in which two things happened: first, a "bad feeling" materialized inside me, a shameful feeling that would follow me for years; and second, a seed of anger and resentment toward my parents, but especially toward my mother, was planted inside me.

My constant complaining about my cousin's house eventually led to my cousin volunteering to babysit for me at *our* house. Even after this turn of events, I was reluctant to tell my parents about the abuse. Why do kids feel so incapable of revealing sexual abuse to adults? Why does it feel like a load that we must carry on our own? Some kids, like Jes Richardson, are threatened by their abusers, while others may not understand that what is being done to them is unjustified. Sexually abused children are often left feeling powerless, ashamed, or responsible.

"I really felt like it was something that I did, not that it was something done to me," explained Savannah Sanders. "I remember in first grade telling one of my friends at school [that] I had sex with somebody, not that I was molested or raped. I was 6, and he was 17. Every encounter after that felt like it was my own doing, never anyone else['s] fault."[12] In the Silbert & Pines study, 91 percent of the subjects who were sexually abused "believed that there was nothing they could do about the exploitation." Fifty-five percent reported that they "did not know what to do," while 36 percent stated that they "were too afraid of the repercussions or were too ashamed to do anything about it."[13]

I was in fourth grade when I finally conjured up the courage to reveal my cousin's "touching." It was a decision I made more out of desperation as I began experiencing nervous tics in elementary school. When I was alone I would tap my bedposts with my fingers and touch the floor with my toes in a methodical way. At school, I internalized my tics in order to hide them from others; I tensed the muscles in my ears and throat constantly to the point of exhaustion. I felt like I was going crazy, and I knew it was somehow related to my cousin. In retrospect, it was a stressful time for other reasons as well: my father lost his job; we had to move into a smaller house; I was approaching puberty; I was becoming increasingly self-aware and worried about bullying; and I was also becoming more aware of my parents' heavy drinking and arguing on the weekends, among other stressors.

Before dinner one night, I painstakingly told my mother about my cousin. While my mother assured me that I would not see him again (and that he would not babysit for me again),* she also discouraged me from ever speaking of it. Many parents fear the social stigma attached to early childhood sexual abuse. As a result, parents often deny it and/or discourage their children from discussing or exposing the abuse. It's an uncomfortable topic, and parents understandably want to move forward. For children, however, the shame associated with sexual abuse does not evaporate. It lingers and can erode their mental and emotional health.

I didn't receive proper counseling for the molestation, and I was left feeling confused. While I was happy that the touching would stop, I didn't understand whether or not it was my fault. I did, after all, pretend to be in a "boyfriend/girlfriend" relationship with this cousin when we were both too young to have devious intentions. Although the game involved only hugging and holding hands, I worried that I ultimately invited the abuse. Without counseling, the sense of shame worsened; and I felt my first pangs of depression.

My life changed for the second time in a year; we moved to a new house. This time we were in an entirely new neighborhood. As the new kid, I was bullied by a few of the older girls. I went to the same school though, so I still spent time with my classmates during the day. At some point, a social worker visited our school to give the "good touch, bad touch" talk. After her presentation, we

*While I will never know the full story, my cousin's troubles grew over time: He later commited suicide.

kids were invited into another room for follow-up questions or concerns. Many kids raised their hands in order to get out of class, and we gathered in the other room for lollipops and lollygagging. When it was my turn to have a private discussion with the social worker, I climbed into a chair and told the woman what a great idea all of this was.

"This used to happen to me," I explained. "It doesn't anymore, but it used to; so it's good you're talking to *other* kids about it."

Although I most certainly needed to talk about these experiences, I did not intend to seek help. I was looking to get a break from class with my friends. Despite any sense of relief I might have felt after exposing this to the social worker, I soon regretted it. The atmosphere in the room changed. Other adults were called in, and I realized I had made a big mistake. The social worker explained that not only did she have to confront my parents but that she had to visit my home right away. These words sent me into a panic. I begged the woman to keep it a secret, but she wouldn't budge. I felt dread and guilt that night as I told my parents what I had done. Secrecy was a virtue in our family, as it is in many families, and I had broken this unspoken rule. I felt pressured into concealment. I stood in the living room of my home, in front of my parents; and I told the social worker that I had lied. After this day, I became increasingly angry and resentful.

Keisha Head described similar effects when she finally exposed her abuse. "I tried to tell my aunt that it was happening," Keisha explained in a 2012 interview with *Kiss the Limit,* "[but] she just brushed it off as if it did not happen. . . . At the age of twelve I had reached my limit; I . . . was tired of being a victim—a victim of physical abuse, a victim of sexual abuse—and I lashed out. . . . I was a very angry child; all my childhood dreams and goals and aspirations, I think . . . went out the window that year, or that day."[14]

Early childhood sexual abuse is a tragedy, but I believe it's manageable if addressed. Kids are resilient, and with proper counseling, they can bounce back from many forms of abuse and neglect. Denying a child's cry for help or ignoring a child's need for treatment for any type of abuse is a greater tragedy. Lack of counseling and lack of validation can only lead to or worsen mental health issues related to the abuse. My resentment and distrust toward adults, including teachers, only deepened as I headed into middle school, as did the "bad feeling" I associated with my cousin.

Soon after the incident with the social worker, I befriended Crystal, who also seemed to battle with authority. Crystal could make me laugh until I doubled over in pain and peed my pants. She was the antidote to the "bad feeling"; naturally, I clung to our friendship as a distraction. However, my attachment to Crystal was increasingly unhealthy and symptomatic of underlying issues. More important though, as my story soon demonstrates, lack of counseling for sexual abuse can lead not only to mental health issues, but it can also position a child as an easy target for further victimization, including sexual exploitation and assault.

Growing up in a situation in which one is being abused not only normalizes the abuse, but it also breaks down the child's perception of personal rights and boundaries. It primes a child to be accepting of further sexual abuse/exploitation. Margaret Howard, Licensed Master Social Worker (MSW) and blogger for the *Huffington Post,* explained in a personal e-mail how this works:

> If a child's boundaries are violated early on, her sense [of] where [her rights stop] and others[' rights] begin can be compromised. Abuse teaches her that her rights to personal space and integrity—of body, or thoughts—are unimportant, and that she is not allowed the power to say no. Indeed, an abused child may not even be able to conceive of saying no, since her [past] attempts to say no were either ignored or punished.
>
> Importantly, there is emerging evidence that the trauma of abuse can create a kind of "off switch" that works like this: a cue related to the earlier trauma enters the person's conscious (or unconscious) awareness, the person dissociate[s] (i.e., checks out cognitively), and [does] not even process the threat as [being a threat]. During the earlier abuse it was necessary to dissociate (i.e., to [mentally] check out) in order to survive the horror of it. [Now, the disassociation is an innate reaction to threats.]
>
> It's important to understand that this is a mechanism entirely outside of conscious control. It happens in the autonomic nervous system. It's a protective mechanism, at root. [T]his is why we must never blame a victim of abuse of any kind. I have heard it said far too many times, *She should have seen the red flags.* Well, this evidence indicates that she may, literally, not be able to see the red flags.[15]

Without proper counseling, a sexually abused child may not be able to recognize sexual assaults or exploitations that occur later in adolescence. Without knowing their rights or personal boundaries, how can children or teens understand when these rights are being violated? Or, children may feel reluctant to report such violations if prior abuse failed to result in a proper response. With or without prior abuse, sexual assault/exploitation in adolescence is an additional risk factor for commercial sexual exploitation. The 2012 Ohio study reports statistics related to rape for the 115 subjects who identified as "being involved in the sex trade before age 18." Of these subjects, 47.4 percent report having been raped more than a year before being trafficked; 9.6 percent report having been raped less than a year before being trafficked.[16] Multiple instances of sexual abuse, assault, or exploitation are often seen in "willing victims" from all types of trafficking cases, but especially those controlled by pimps, family members, and gang members.

In a webinar titled "The Sexual Exploitation of Girls in Gangs," retired San Diego Deputy District Attorney Keith Burt says that girls (and boys) who join gangs or hang out with gang members are often seeking protection; a sense of power or respect; a sense of belonging; and/or an escape from abuse in the home; as well as access to material goods, fun, and/or excitement. Others may be following in the footsteps of older siblings or other family member(s). "Girls in gangs report a high prevalence of sexual and physical abuse," Burt says. "[They are often subjected to] a continuum of victimization out of the house and into the gang."[17]

This method of control via re-exploitation is not unique, and it's also not new. In his book, *Pimp,* the author, Iceberg Slim, describes how he victimized women and girls in the 1930s and '40s; and how he was inspired by and learned from other self-proclaimed "pimps" who began much earlier than him. In one scene, he describes a victim who recalls her childhood as "nothing but good" until, at age twelve, her mother died and her father began sexually abusing her. At age fifteen, pregnant and desperate, she fled. A pimp trafficker found her working as a waitress, and then he trafficked her until she miscarried. After the victim shared her sad background, the author offered her sympathy, protection, affection, and understanding, but only as a manipulative ploy to gain control over her.[18]

Although sexual abuse is common among predisposing factors in "willing victims," it is not a requisite. Consider Neet Childs's or Katrina Owens's story from chapter 1; neither survivor claims to have suffered sexual abuse, however, both were missing a father figure. Also, Carissa Phelps, author of *Runaway Girl,* did not report sexual abuse in early childhood; however, she had several other risk factors mentioned in her memoir: neglect, a missing parent, running away, and difficulty in school, among others. The story of Stacy Lundgren, Founder of The Stacy Project, is another example of multiple risk factors without sexual abuse.

Stacy's parents divorced when she was three years old, and her father struggled with alcoholism. In elementary school, Stacy was diagnosed with attention-deficit disorder (ADD) and dyslexia; and, in junior high school, she was bullied by classmates. "[I]n school I was tormented . . .to the point in Jr. high I tried to kill myself," Stacy writes. She turned to chat rooms online for conversation and companionship where she was first contacted by a trafficker at age fourteen. This man lured Stacy into a romantic relationship offline, and then he began trafficking her to other men. "I started to live 2 different lives," Stacy writes, "Everyone thought I was this . . . good girl . . . but no one [k]new about this secret life that I was living." The man was ultimately identified and arrested by federal law enforcement officers.[19]

Once you understand a "willing victim's" background, you can begin to see the dynamics behind his or her "choices." Children who have been abused in childhood and children with multiple risk factors are at a greater disadvantage when faced with commercially sexually exploitative situations. However, these are not the only kids at risk for sexual exploitation. There are also societal influences blurring the lines between personal boundaries, romance, and sexual exploitation, especially for girls and young women. Later chapters will expose how advertisers and popular culture promote misogynistic messages, causing many girls to accept, and even expect, exploitation. With additional media messages promoting materialism, consumerism, and the use of female sex appeal as a tool for advertising, the media influences girls to see themselves as commercial and sexual objects. As a result, many vulnerable girls in America accept and even initially embrace commercial sexual exploitation.

3

COMMUNITY RISK FACTORS

CERTAIN COMMUNITY RISK FACTORS CAN INCREASE the chances of a child crossing paths with a trafficker or buyer. These factors include: presence of a commercial sex industry, legal or illegal; tourist, sporting, and business attractions; proximity to military bases or other locations with transient populations of men; a high transit area; a subculture of homeless youth; a presence of gangs; and a proximity to national borders.[1] Education and awareness campaigns about commercial sexual exploitation of children (CSEC) and sex trafficking may curb crime against children in these areas, as well as training for professionals working within these communities. Outreach efforts to connect with potential victims may also be helpful.

As with individual and family risk factors, growing up under any one of these community risk factors does not predestine a child for commercial sexual exploitation; likewise, it is important to remember that CSEC can happen within *any* community, regardless of its characteristics and demographics. Theresa Flores, for example, was living in an affluent neighborhood when trafficked by gang members.[2] Middle- and high-income communities may not be watching for signs of CSEC, including child sex trafficking, if it is assumed that such crimes would not happen there; this alone creates a risk factor.

PRESENCE OF AN ILLEGAL COMMERCIAL SEX INDUSTRY

In an effort to revamp Atlantic City, New Jersey voters approved gambling in 1976. In May 1978, the first legal casino, Resorts, opened, just four months after

I was born, and several other hotels followed through the '80s. As the casino and hospitality industries grew in Atlantic City, a siren called to those in need of work. In 1980, my parents moved 60 miles away from their hometown of Riverside, New Jersey, to Mystic Islands, a waterfront community about 30 miles from Atlantic City. My dad started working in Atlantic City for Becker's Dry Cleaners and my mom got a job at the Atlantic City Medical Center. Even as a kid I knew that gambling, stripping, go-go dancing, and prostitution occurred in Atlantic City, but I didn't really understand these activities or give them much thought. To me, the city was a million miles away.

In reality, though, the city wasn't very far at all. The mall at which I first met the man who trafficked me was halfway between my home and Atlantic City; it was literally fifteen miles from the corner on which I was first sold. After meeting Greg for the first time, I didn't connect him to Atlantic City, nor did I associate him with pimps or prostitution. I thought pimps wore suits and hats like the bad guys in the cartoon movie *Who Framed Roger Rabbit?* Greg wore trendy brand-name clothes; and he looked the same age as any one of my friends' older brothers. Had I been educated about CSEC, including sex trafficking and the tactics of child sex traffickers, I may have picked up on warning signs in my conversations with Greg.

Locations that are known for illegal commercial sex are often surrounded by shopping malls, bus stops, arcades, skating rinks, movie theaters, and other neighborhoods all teeming with children and teens from various economic backgrounds. Any one of these kids could potentially cross paths with and be lured into a friendship or romanced by a pimp, gang member, or other trafficker or buyer looking to exploit children. However, children living within those neighborhoods known for illegal commercial sex activity are even more at risk; and they are likely to be living in poverty, an additional risk factor.

Illegal commercial sex is not unique to big cities; many cities in America have at least one impoverished area known for street or motel prostitution. These areas are commonly known by local residents, but the question is whether or not community members understand that these areas are also susceptible to CSEC, including child sex trafficking. Pimps and other traffickers are always looking for new victims, either within these neighborhoods or in the surrounding towns. In one 2010 study, the authors interviewed "ex-pimps" and found that "[r]ecruiting [of victims] was ongoing, not only because of turnover, but also because repeat customers wanted variety and new faces had to be continually supplied."[3]

Rachel Lloyd notes the difficulties of raising children in poor neighborhoods with such predators:

> Nationally, over thirteen million children live below the poverty line. Over half a million children in New York City live in poverty, concentrated in some of the most economically depressed communities, where most of the tracks [areas known for prostitution activity], unsurprisingly, are located: Hunts Point in the Bronx, East New York in Brooklyn, and Far Rockaway in Queens. Raising children, particularly girls, in areas where there's an existing sex industry, where johns are still driving around in the early mornings as children go to school, where pimps buy gifts for preteen girls with the intention of grooming and priming them, can be a constant struggle between the home that you try to create and the world outside your door.[4]

Poverty is an issue affecting families and communities across the nation in rural and urban areas alike. In January 2012, *MSN Money* reported the top fifteen poorest counties in the country were in the following states: Alabama, Texas, Kentucky, Louisiana, Tennessee, South Carolina, South Dakota, Mississippi, and North Dakota.[5] If illegal commercial sex and/or sex trafficking exists in these areas, then the risk for an already vulnerable child to meet a trafficker or buyer (i.e., a "john") on the street increases. Whether it's legal or illegal, however, the presence of a commercial sex industry and sex trafficking can normalize the activity to children living in those communities.

Brenda Myers-Powell, Executive Director of the Dreamcatcher Foundation in Chicago, is a survivor of commercial sexual exploitation. In an interview with the *Chicago Tribune,* Brenda described her life at age fourteen. She was a single mother with two children (a one-year-old and a six-week-old), and she was living in poverty with her grandmother. In 1973, days before Easter Sunday, Brenda and her grandmother were struggling to pay for rent and groceries. "[Brenda] decided to do what she'd seen the other women in her neighborhood do," says the author, "sell her body for money."

"Rent was about $110 a month," Brenda was quoted in the article, "and I made so much money that I was able to pay the rent, buy groceries, and buy my children good Easter clothes. . . . I even bought my baby a big ol' bunny rabbit."[6] Brenda continued to work on her own until two pimp traffickers abducted her and forced her to work under their control, all before she turned fifteen.[7]

Street outreach is one way to potentially connect with victims of CSEC, especially those involved with street prostitution. Courtney's House provides outreach to girls, boys, and adults on the streets of Washington, D.C.; their street outreach model is available for purchase to those interested in similar efforts within their own communities.[8]

PRESENCE OF A LEGAL COMMERCIAL SEX INDUSTRY

For children living in casino destinations like Las Vegas, the overwhelming normalization of commercial sex can be a risk factor; it can lower a child's inhibitions, thereby making him or her more vulnerable to CSEC. In a 2007 study, Shared Hope International notes:

> The culture of tolerance of the commercial sex industry in Las Vegas creates a high risk environment for children. The high-risk conditions of Las Vegas, such as easy access to alcohol and drugs, 24/7 gaming and the hyper-sexualized entertainment industry are not being addressed among the youth. Prevention programs in the community and/or schools working to mitigate the forces of the high risk environment are non-existent. Additionally, minimal media coverage is given to raising awareness of the issue of [domestic minor sex trafficking] in Las Vegas.[9]

Atlantic City, Las Vegas, and Reno, along with other casino destinations across the country, are not the only locations well known for legal commercial sex industries. Many other cities without gambling licenses are also known for their erotic dance clubs, peep shows, erotic massage parlors, escort agencies, pornography agencies, and more. Legal commercial sex establishments can be potential hosts for CSEC, including child sex trafficking. Audrey Morrissey (formerly Audrey Porter), Associate Director of My Life My Choice in Boston, and also a survivor of commercial sexual exploitation, says in an interview that "[a]nywhere there's an adult sex industry, there are always children in there. Always, always, always."[10]

I asked a former exotic dancer if she had ever known of underage girls working in strip clubs, and she replied: "Yes. There was a girl that was underage working at the strip club I had been dancing at [in Southwest Florida]. She had been working for almost a year at the same club when I had first started . . . She [later] told me she had started dancing in Georgia when she was 15. Moved to Fort Myers[, FL] within that year and started dancing here at about 16. I'm not sure if they never asked for her ID assuming she looked old enough or maybe because she had experience at another gentlemen's club. Maybe she had a personal relationship with management."[11]

I posed the same question to an anonymous survivor of adult sex trafficking who met her trafficker while working at a strip club: "Yes, I knew minors working at clubs I was at. After I got out, I actually had guilt for a while about this one once I realized so many of us had been victims of exploitation, and I wanted to go back and look for her. Last I had seen her, she'd gotten pregnant by her pimp and even then he let her keep no money and one time she was starving, we went and gave her $20 one time just so she could eat. She was a sweet girl and was determined to get off drugs for her baby, she really wanted to be a good mom and try to get back to school. I don't know what happened to her which makes me sad."[12]

The Courant reports another example of CSEC, specifically child sex trafficking, within strip clubs: a sex trafficker "found [a] 12-year-old [girl working] at a New York strip club and [then] recruited her to work for him in late 2004 or early 2005." The trafficker, 35-year-old Corey Davis, was "accused of driving [the girl and at least one other victim] to Connecticut, where they worked, among other places, at strip clubs called the Bishop Corner Cafe and Pleasant Moments in Bridgeport."[13]

Emily Tocci, law student, advocate, and IAHTI[14] consultant, urges for mandatory, survivor-informed training of club owners and staff, as well as regulations within the legal commercial sex industry in order to help prevent CSEC.[15] Providing outreach services to those working in legal commercial sex industries can also help to connect with potential victims. Jeanie Turner, Founder of One Way Out Ministries, in Fort Myers, Florida, for example, reaches out to women working in strips clubs. Her ministry provides services like life skills training, aid in continuing education, professional clothing, financial guidance, resume writing, drug and alcohol rehabilitation, and more.[16]

PRESENCE OF A TRANSIENT MALE POPULATION

Any location or event known for transient male populations will increase the likelihood of demand for commercial sex; these include casinos, bachelor party destinations, major sporting events, concert events, business conventions, motorcycle rallies, populations of immigrant workers, military bases, sports clubs, and fraternities. Numerous major cities are listed as top business, sporting, and bachelor destinations, including Orlando, Chicago, Boston, Phoenix, Dallas, New Orleans, Denver, St. Louis, and Washington, D.C.[17] In a 2007 study report, Shared Hope International explored the connection between business conventions and commercial sex:

> The city of Atlanta is home to large numbers of entertainment and media enterprises that feed the commercial sex industry and openly and visibly promote them. . . . Atlanta's commercial sex markets advertise sexual services in many brochures, newspapers, and magazines. Mainstream newspapers catering to young professionals regularly contain advertisements and photographs reflecting diversity in the prostituted girls marketed—Asian, Caucasian, and African-American . . .
>
> Marketing is specifically targeted at the conventions . . . advertisement cards are handed out to convention attendees promising VIP treatment at the various "Gentlemen's Clubs" in the area, as well as discount entry cards distributed at sporting events, concert and other events. One major hotel's courtesy guest shuttle was observed providing transportation for guests to a strip club, further facilitating the commercial sex markets.[18]

An increased demand for commercial sex may increase the chances of sex trafficking and CSEC. In an appearance on Dr. Phil's television show, Greg Bucceroni describes organized networks of pornography and sex trafficking of boys within the New Jersey, Pennsylvania, and New York tri-state area.[19] These networks involved members of organized crime and high-profile pedophiles like Jerry Sandusky and Ed Savitz. In a personal e-mail, Greg described how members of high-profile fraternities and members-only associations connected with local pedophile networks while on business trips and convention getaways.

"Serial pedophiles associated with Ed Savitz, including Jerry Sandusky, would often visit on business between NYC, Atlantic City, [and] Philadelphia in attending business meetings, conventions or business retreats," Greg says. "Many of these businessmen and some businesswomen would solicit Ed Savitz and/or Gambino mobsters associated with child sex trafficking in providing adolescent sexual entertainment. . . . Many times us kids . . . would be asked to either meet clients at a specific location or be transported to a specific location in sexually engaging the pedophile client. There was a lot of money available to kids that wanted to involve themselves in sex trafficking; there also were a lot of dangers."[20]

HIGH TRANSIT AREAS

Many cities and states are vulnerable to trafficking due to their location and multifaceted transportation systems. In a brochure, the members of the New Jersey Human Trafficking Task Force (HTTF) recognize that New Jersey is "ripe for human trafficking" due to the state's central location "between the northern portion of the East Coast and the tri-state metropolitan region of Philadelphia, Baltimore, and Washington, D.C.," as well as its ease of accessibility "by car, bus, truck, van, train, boat, and plane."[21] Traffickers will often travel between cities and states with their victims.[22] In the "From Victims to Victimizers" study, the researchers say the following:

> Eighty-eight percent of the sample [which was composed of 25 "ex-pimps"] transported the girls and women to the customer, unless they had installed the girl or woman in a hotel room in advance. However, in those instances the pimps moved the girls around so they didn't get known as regulars to law enforcement: "Nothing was permanent, we had to be a moving target[," stated a former pimp trafficker]. In some instances the pimps did the driving, and in others drivers were employed, or cab drivers paid. Some moved girls and women all over, from Springfield to the Gold Coast of Chicago, and to different states, including Indiana, Iowa, Nevada and Florida.[23]

In October 2012, Secretary of Homeland Security Janet Napolitano, Secretary of Transportation Ray LaHood, and Amtrak President and CEO Joseph Boardman announced a partnership among the Department of Homeland Security (DHS), the Department of Transportation (DOT), and Amtrak to combat human trafficking. Under this partnership, DHS and DOT worked with Amtrak to train over 8,000 frontline transportation employees and Amtrak Police Department officers to identify and recognize indicators of human trafficking, as well as how to report suspected cases of human trafficking. "We cannot let the American transportation system be an enabler in these criminal acts," says Secretary LaHood.[24] Although the success of this program is not yet known, it is encouraging to know that efforts are being made.

PROXIMITY TO TRUCK STOPS

Another organization working to bring awareness to the transportation industry is Truckers Against Trafficking (TAT). "Traffickers exploit our transportation system on a daily basis," says Kendis Paris, Executive Director of TAT. "Truck stops are one of the places in which they do this. Whether it is moving a victim to a more underground location and selling them along the way, or working a circuit that includes regular stops at lots, this is a crime that comes knocking on [truckers'] doors."[25] In a 2007 study, Shared Hope International discussed the dangers for children living close to truck stops:

> Trucking routes have been identified as "hot spots" for underage prostituted girls. Buyers seem to have little fear of intervention by police or fellow truckers. A recent example of truck stop trafficking is the case of over two dozen prostituted minors, the youngest just 12 years old, from Toledo, Ohio found at truck stops northeast of Harrisburg, Pennsylvania in December of 2005. The Gables of Harrisburg truck stop, just off the major highway I-81 in Linglestown, was popular with truck drivers looking for quick and cheap sex: about $40 for sex with one of these minor victims. Local Harrisburg police and FBI agents working with the Innocence Lost Initiative arrested sixteen pimps, many of them from Toledo, Ohio, who have been indicted as co-conspirators for trafficking in women and children, among other crimes. The pimps used violence and intimidation to recruit and control the women and girls.[26]

An anonymous survivor shared with me how she was trafficked for sex at local truck stops as a child:

> My trafficker, who was my father, took me to truck stops very late at night in either a pickup truck, which sometimes had a camper attached, or a van. He used CB radios to "advertise" my availability and to communicate when we would be arriving. We looked like a "typical" father and young daughter traveling. I was terrified and often drugged, which may have [given the appearance] I had just woken up. My father also used the same van to meet groups of truckers at truck stops and then transported groups of truckers to and from our house for parties where I was commercially sexually exploited.[27]

PROXIMITY TO INTERNATIONAL BORDERS

In June 2012, the *Las Cruces Sun-News* reported a sex trafficking case "in which women and underage girls were allegedly recruited from Juárez for prostitution in El Paso motels."[28] The traffickers "found girls from Juárez by putting ads in the newspaper." The ads implied that girls would be paid "big money" for domestic work and "discreet services."[29] Charles Marquez, 51, and Martha Jiménez Sánchez, 38, were charged with transporting the girls from Juárez, lodging them in El Paso motel rooms, and then forcing them into prostitution. If they escaped, the traffickers would find them in Juárez, and force them back to the motel room in El Paso.[30]

This case is one example among many involving foreign national women and girls smuggled across the Mexico-U.S. border and then trafficked for commercial sex. Half of the "top countries of origin identified for foreign victims of human trafficking in fiscal year (FY) 2012" were Mexico, Honduras, and Guatemala.[31] In a 2011 article, Jim Walters and Patricia H. Davis described some of the dynamics associated with sex trafficking across the southern border into the United States:

> Young girls often unwittingly become trafficking victims when they are singled out by their smugglers (or "coyotes") during the journey north. They are told they can travel at no cost, if they will agree to work later to pay off their debts. These smugglers/traffickers deceive and dupe the girls through false promises of jobs and other economic opportunities waiting for them in the United States. During their journeys, the girls are shown favoritism, and even given clothes, makeup, and gifts. Upon arriving at their destinations, however, they are informed that they owe a debt to their smugglers—and they will pay it off by working in the sex industry. In the United States, these girls are often held in slavery-like conditions and forced into prostitution, domestic service, or forced labor. They are terrorized emotionally, forced to take drugs, moved frequently, locked up, raped, beaten, deprived of sleep, and starved. The smugglers knew from the start that exploitation would be the cost of the "travel now, pay later" deal . . .
>
> Some victims of trafficking even possess the necessary documents to enter the United States legally. These women and children typically rely upon traffickers for transportation and sponsorship, only to discover that there is a

price for these services. Other victims are kidnapped, sold, and forced to come to the U.S.[32]

I believe there may also be cases of CSEC along the southern border involving U.S. victims, with some being taken to Mexico and beyond for the purpose of sex trafficking. Although such stories are scarce, I believe this may be due to the lack of recovery of such victims and/or the fear imposed on victims. Or, it may be due to the lack of awareness and investigation. In November 2011, NBC4 in Southern California reported a story in which an alleged sixteen-year-old American girl was offered up for sex in Tijuana to an undercover reporter.[33] The girl told the reporter that, as a child, she was "left largely on her own . . . hanging out with the wrong crowd.'" She said she was "flattered [by] the attention and companionship of men in the group" and that "[b]y the time she learned their true intentions it was too late." The reporter continued:

> [The girl] is afraid to run away. Her pimp, she said, has told her what happens to the bodies of runaways.
>
> "The morgue comes by the hospital and incinerates it before anybody can be alerted that an American died," she said. "That struck fear in my heart."
>
> She continued: "I don't have the power or the ability to do that."
>
> Then she told me: "There's been times when I have been wishing that somebody like you or some people [would] come down, inquiring about it."[34]

GANGS

The U.S. Attorney's Office for the Eastern District of Virginia reported several cases of gang-controlled sex trafficking in 2011 and 2012. In October 2011, José Ciro Juárez-Santamaria, 24, an MS-13 gang member, was sentenced to life in prison for prostituting a twelve-year-old girl to clients throughout northern Virginia, Maryland, and Washington, D.C.[35] U.S. Attorney Neil H. MacBride says, "With today's sentence Mr. Juárez-Santamaria will spend the rest of his life behind bars, while his child victim will spend the rest of her life working through the pain he inflicted."[36]

In June 2012, Rances Ulices Amaya, 23, an MS-13 gang leader, was sentenced to 50 years in prison "for recruiting girls as young as 14 from middle schools, high schools, and homeless shelters in Northern Virginia and forcing them to engage commercial sex acts on behalf of MS-13." Amaya is reported to have prostituted five victims who were between the ages of 14 and 17 years old. He reportedly used underage girls not only because they were preferred by buyers but because they were considered easier to manipulate and control.[37]

According to a 2011 FBI report, many gangs are using "prostitution," including "child prostitution," as "a major source of income," including Asian gangs, Bloods, Crips, Gangster Disciples, Mara Salvatrucha (MS-13), Sureños, Vice Lords, and members of outlaw motorcycle gangs (OMGs). The report states that "gang members often operate as pimps, luring or forcing at-risk, young females into prostitution and controlling them through violence and psychological abuse." It also estimates "[t]here are approximately 1.4 million active street, prison, and OMG gang members comprising more than 33,000 gangs in the United States."[38]

In a webinar titled "The Sexual Exploitation of Girls in Gangs," retired San Diego Deputy District Attorney Keith Burt explained that female gang members, as well as female friends of gang members (a.k.a. "gang groupies") are also at risk for sex trafficking.[39] In other words, gangs are not only targeting girls at random, but they will also exploit current members and they will recruit members for the purpose of sexual exploitation. "Gangs throughout the United States vary greatly[, but they] are found in almost every kind of community," Burt says in the webinar, "and gang members are not kids flown in from Mars; they're our kids, and they reflect the youth of their respective communities."

HOMELESS YOUTH CULTURE

Many kids who run away wind up homeless and living with other youth on the streets. The National Alliance to End Homelessness (NAEH) "estimates that there are 50,000 youth sleeping on the streets in the United States."[40] Estes and Weiner of the 2001 University of Pennsylvania study say that their "field research, indicates that, among runaway and homeless youth, approximately 30% of shelter youth and 70% of street youth engaged in prostitution in order to meet their daily needs for food, shelter, drugs and the like."[41] The 2001 University of Pennsylvania study reports that "[c]hildren and youth older than 12 years are prime targets for sexual exploitation by organized crime units. Most of the children recruited by organized crime groups come from among runaway and homeless youth. And most [are] recruited by same-sex peers, albeit adults play a very active role in managing the peer recruiters."[42]

"[T]here were a variety of kids that were runaways on the streets with me," states Greg Bucceroni. "[M]any of them came from dysfunctional homes where parents were alcoholics, drug addicts, control freaks, [trapped in cycles of] domestic violence, [and/or] physically abusive. . . . While on the streets, in an effort to survive day to day, many of the kids that were associated with me turned to child prostitution and 'kiddie porn' . . . some did it on their own and others were recruited by kids like myself."[43]

The researchers of the 2001 study state that adult exploiters (i.e., traffickers and/or buyers) often use "financial and drug incentives to the [peer] recruiters for each [new] child brought into the group."[44] Greg confirms these tactics: "[If the new,] troubled kid had caught the eye of pedophile types or mobsters, [it meant] the targeted kid had sexual value and appeal," Greg states. "[T]he mobsters or pedophile[s] . . . would pay us $50.00 to make a connection for them or $100.00 if we talked the kid into dabbling with child prostitution or 'kiddie porn.' Some of the kids would do it once and decide not to do it again, while others would discover a new avenue in making easy money on the tough streets."[45]

Male child victims of commercial sexual exploitation, including sex trafficking, do not always identify as gay, bisexual, or transgender. Estes and Weiner report that "a disproportionate number of boys involved in commercial sex, about 25%–35%, self identify as sexual minorities, e.g., as gay, bisexual, or as transgender/transsexual."[46] It is a matter of survival for many heterosexual boys, as it is for boys and girls of all sexual identities and orientations. Male survivors, like Greg, often refer to it as "hustling." Growing up in South Philadelphia, Greg was raised by a single parent, his mother, who struggled to pay the bills. "Living day to day on welfare . . . my mom [worked] two jobs with very little money left," Greg said, "Yes, life was much to do with self survival."[47]

WHILE THE RISK FACTORS MENTIONED IN THIS CHAPter may be associated with only certain communities, there is one last risk factor that can affect children living in *all* communities. Regardless of demographics, all children with unsupervised access to the Internet can be contacted by a trafficker. Pimp and gang traffickers especially have taken to social media as a way to connect with vulnerable children. Justin Strom, leader of the Underground Gangster Crips (UGC) in Virginia, was indicted by a federal grand jury in 2012 on charges of luring "at least seven high school girls to engage in commercial sex for his prostitution business."[48] Strom and his gang associates used social media sites like Facebook and MySpace to connect with potential victims.[49]

One victim who was sixteen when she met Strom "told the courtroom that she was a normal high school student[; she] had friends and enjoyed soccer, but Justin Strom 'brainwashed' her into believing that having sex with men for money was normal." The victim continued, stating that "she would eat dinner at home with her parents and then turn tricks at night. She slid into addiction, dropped out of school, attempted suicide and had a child. Now, at 20, her life is upside down." Strom was ultimately sentenced to 40 years in prison.[50]

Just to be clear, this case occurred in suburban northern Virginia, one of the most affluent areas in the country.[51] Audrey Morrissey (formerly Audrey Porter), Associate Director of My Life My Choice (MLMC) in Boston, Massachusetts offers the following warning to parents: "It can happen to all children," she says, "[Just b]ecause you live in the suburbs does not mean that it will not happen to your child. All of our children are sitting on the Internet."[52]

4

ADVERTISING TO CHILDREN AND TEENS

IN CHAPTER 1, I PRESENTED SEVERAL PREDISPOSING factors commonly associated with child victims of commercial sexual exploitation; however, one factor was missing: an unsupervised, overexposure to media. I believe an overexposure to media is a powerful predisposing factor often missed in discussions on the commercial sexual exploitation of children (CSEC). The media is loaded with negative messages that can be especially harmful to children because, by nature, children depend on their surroundings for social cues on behavior and values.

As a girl who spent the majority of her childhood watching TV, reading magazines, and listening to music, I consider myself an expert on the media's potential influences on children, especially on girls. This chapter will focus on advertising. Within most media is advertising; and without the balance of better judgment, advertising can promote unadulterated consumerism and materialism, among other misplaced values. Why is this important in CSEC? The connection will be clearer by the end of the chapter.

CHILDREN'S ADVERTISING

Long before a pimp spotted me in a South Jersey shopping mall, there were other strangers scheming for my attention. Anonymous and inconspicuous, advertisers and marketers used the media to build a commercial relationship with me in childhood. Although I was unaware of their presence, they were certainly aware of mine.

In 1978, the same year I was born, the Federal Trade Commission (FTC) proposed a ban on children's advertising. An article from the FTC described how the proposal was spurred by several advocacy organizations. The Action for Children's Television, the Center for Science in the Public Interest, and the Consumers Union, with support from the Commissioner of the Food and Drug Administration (FDA), all petitioned the FTC to regulate children's advertising. As a result, the FTC opened a proceeding to address advertisements for "highly sugared foods to children—particularly those too young to understand either the nature of commercial advertising or the health risks of excessive sugar consumption."[1]

The FTC's proposal was met with heated controversy. Those industries most likely to be affected by such a ban petitioned Congress to put an end to the proceeding. A clip from the documentary *Consuming Kids* depicts a lawyer for the Kellogg Company stating, "[T]he last thing we need [over] the next twenty years is a national nanny."[2] When I was two years old, Congress passed the Federal Trade Commission Improvements Act of 1980, which removed the FTC's authority over children's advertising.[3] As a kid, I watched cartoons and other programs with little standing in the way between me and advertisers.

Under President Ronald Reagan's administration in the 1980s, advertising was further deregulated and it became an open season for marketers to advertise to kids like me. Children's advertising apparently exploded in the mid- to late '80s. *Consuming Kids* reports that kids' spending (and kids' influence over parental spending) rose from $4.2 billion in 1984 to $40 billion in 2008. The documentary attributes this to the fact that advertisers could now create television shows and movies with the sole purpose of selling character-inspired products.[4] Indeed, pictures of me from my childhood are laden with paraphernalia from my favorite TV shows and movies: *Strawberry Shortcake* and *My Little Pony* bed sheets, *Dukes of Hazzard* and *Growing Pains* posters, Disney books, E.T. and Garfield dolls, Care Bears and Cabbage Patch dolls, and much more.

While I acknowledge the value of advertising in American society, I question the ethics behind children's advertising. Advertisers and marketers not only target the "children's market," but they do so using stealthy and manipulative means. The documentary *Consuming Kids* illustrates several ways in which companies "fine-tune" their marketing strategies, including the recruitment of child psychologists and other scientists. These professionals conduct focus groups, behavior analyses, and MRI imaging, among other studies, to tap into child psyches.[5] The goal is not to enhance the learning experience for kids but to create children's programming and advertisements that produce lovable characters and successful tactics to sell products.

Moreover, advertisers aim to incorporate these tactics into every media facet of a child's life. Why is this immoral? For children under the age of eight, advertising is not seen as "advertising" but as simply part of their social landscape.[6] A report from the American Academy of Pediatrics states that "[r]esearch has shown that young children—younger than 8 years—are cognitively and psychologically defenseless against advertising. They do not understand the notion of intent to sell and frequently accept advertising claims at face value."[7] Why do marketers want to surround children with their ads? One reason is to imprint their brands into children's lives.

"Marketers plant the seeds of brand recognition in very young children, in the hopes that the seeds will grow into lifetime relationships," says MediaSmarts in a 2010 article, "According to the Center for a New American Dream, babies as young as six months of age can form mental images of corporate logos and mascots. Brand loyalties can be established as early as age two, and by the time children head off to school most can recognize hundreds of brand logos."[8] The more media to which a child is exposed, the more likely these tactics will be effective.

Advertisers also target children most at risk and most in need of positive guidance and influence: those raised in lower-class economies. "It's really hard to find baby paraphernalia that's not plastered with media characters," states Susan Linn in *Consuming Kids.* "You can find unbranded baby stuff, but you can find it in high-end toy stores. . . . If you go to just places where poor or middle-class families shop, it's all branded, so the babies start out life with the notion of consumption."[9] Susan Linn, an Instructor in Psychiatry at Harvard Medical School, explains in her book, also titled *Consuming Kids,* how heavy children's advertising especially affects lower- and middle-class children and minority youth:

> Children, including very young children, often watch television by themselves, meaning that no adult is present to help them process marketing messages. Poor children, a population in which children of color are disproportionately represented, watch even more television than their middle- and upper-class

counterparts. However, regardless of class, African American and Latino children watch more TV than Caucasian children.[10]

In order to gauge how many advertisements children see, let's consider how many are seen by adults. With the advent of DVR and Netflix, television viewers are able to bypass commercials; therefore, advertising has increasingly moved into television programming via "product placement." Think of TV shows like *American Idol, The Voice,* and *The Biggest Loser.* Each of the judges on *American Idol* drinks from a big red cup labeled with the Coca-Cola logo. Contestants on *The Voice* are typically drinking Starbucks coffee alongside host Carson Daly with the logo often visible in the background. Perhaps, the most obvious product placements are the mini-infomercials seen on *The Biggest Loser* as contestants rave over the quality of Subway sandwiches or Brita-filtered water.

But advertising doesn't end when television programs are turned off. You've got product placement in movies, music, video games, and books as well. You've also got clever banner ads that cover everything from billboards to buses to entire buildings; as well as logos and brand names stitched into everything from t-shirts to sneakers. Advertisers expose you to a brand, logo, or commercial multiple times in order to build familiarity, interest, and trust.

Advertising can also be subtle as it blends in with the landscape of your life. Think of corporate sponsorships like the Lincoln Financial Field, Wells Fargo Center, and Citizens Bank Park, all of which are stadiums located in the Philadelphia Sports Complex. Consider product tie-ins; for instance, iPhones were initially only available to AT&T customers. And, of course, online advertising is in abundance. When reading the news online, almost every click now prompts a pop-up ad, and every news and YouTube video seems bookended with short advertisements. I'm even seeing ads in my online Bank of America statement.

And it isn't always clear when a celebrity endorsement is a paid commercial. In a 2013 *New York Times* article, reporter Nick Bilton exposed several celebrities promoting companies on social media:

> Take Miley Cyrus, the 20-year-old pop star who was traveling around America last week promoting her new album. One morning she posted on Twitter: "Thanks @blackjet for the flight to Silicon Valley!" The details of the arrangement between BlackJet, a Silicon Valley start-up that arranges for private jet travel, and Ms. Cyrus are unclear. But Dean Rotchin, chief executive of

> BlackJet, said "she was given some consideration for her tweet." Ms. Cyrus did not respond to a request for comment. . . .
>
> According to talent agency employees, who spoke on the condition that they not be named because they are not allowed to divulge private dealings with clients, some A-list celebrities can be paid as much as $20,000 for a Twitter post or Facebook update.[11]

Advertising is pervasive in our consumer-driven culture, and it's expanding as technology grows. Jay Walker-Smith, President of the marketing firm Yankelovich, Inc., estimates that we may be exposed to "as many as 5,000" ads per day.[12] Marketers are studying the habits of children in order to get a brand in front of them at all times, including while they're in school. *USA Today* reporter Trevor Hughes writes: "School administrators say that with a public unwilling to adequately fund K-12 education, they're obligated to find new ways to keep teachers in classrooms." Hughes notes examples of advertisements in school, at football games, and on report cards.[13]

But what is the long-term effect of constantly manipulating children into believing they *must* have *this* or *that* product to be content? If a child is "defenseless" against advertising tactics, as asserted by the American Academy of Pediatrics, then that child is taking in this message of materialism at face value. Children who view multiple commercial messages over time, without any adults interpreting those messages, may equate materialism and consumerism with social values and personal success. Many child victims of commercial sexual exploitation who have been "rescued" by police or social services run away from services and return to those exploitative situations. Why? I have met with many such victims, and one of the most common reasons given was "for the money."

THE COOL FACTOR

As a child approaches puberty, advertisers change their tactics and focus their efforts toward exploiting an adolescent's natural desire to fit in.[14] The result is that older children and teens are inundated with messages promoting the idea that certain products—not family, community, personal goals, or achievements—will lead to being *cool.* So, the values being passed from the commercial to the child are that popularity is important, popularity is dependent on having certain products, and lacking these product means you are unpopular, or a social outcast.

This theme is equally relevant in adult advertising as advertisers often appeal to a viewer's fears or emotional needs, including the need for acceptance, love, attraction, family, health, safety, and excitement. What's troubling about these kinds of commercials is that the images used often depict narrow or unattainable interpretations to what that need looks like. Think about car commercials that portray a certain level of success, or food products that portray family togetherness, or liquor commercials that depict fun and excitement among singles.

Ever watch a commercial and feel like your life is less adequate afterward? That's what the ad *wants* you to feel like; it is implying that you can attain that level of happiness or success *if* you buy or use that product. One recent college graduate told me she felt unsuccessful because her salary couldn't cover a big house on a hill and a new car. Too often we compare ourselves and our lives to the models and concepts we see in the media. For those who aren't informed about advertising tactics, life can appear bleak. Without the ability to purchase more and more products or without the ability to look like the people in the advertisements, a viewer may feel like he or she isn't measuring up to society's expectations.

If the average adolescent child is exposed to a limited amount of advertising each day, then it's possible these tactics would be obvious. But everywhere we turn, we see commercials and advertisements. We are inundated with images telling us what we should look like, what we should dress like, what products we should own, and how much fun we should be having. It can sometimes be difficult to differentiate reality from fantasy even for the most balanced adults, but what about adolescents? What effects are such advertising tactics having on them?

IDEAL FEMALE BEAUTY

By sixth grade, I was an avid reader of teen fashion magazines like *YM, Teen, Seventeen, Elle, Vogue,* and *Mademoiselle.* I would stand in the grocery store line flipping through the pages of pictures, articles, and quizzes. As an overly ambitious kid, I was trying to pick the magazine with the most relevant topics to make me *cool,* to make me *popular,* to make me *hot!*

Once home, I sprawled across my bed to study every single page. I dog-eared any article, advertisement, or beauty tip promising to make me over. I scooped mayonnaise from the jar and onto my head in order to tame my frizzy hair, and I poured peroxide and baking soda over my toothbrush to whiten my teeth (which I did only once because it burned like hell). I ordered painful hair-removal products, wasted money on bronzing lotions that turned my skin orange, and I stole pockets full of products from Rite-Aid, including foundation, nail polish, and facial cleansing oils.

But it was never enough. Nothing ever gave me smooth hair or glowing skin like the models pictured in the advertisements. The products didn't seem to work on me, and I thought this meant that I was unequivocally ugly. Even through the hottest summer heat waves, I wore sneakers and jeans to hide my legs and feet. I believed I had beauty flaws all over my body, a notion that fostered my already growing sense of low self-esteem and depression.

Former fashion model Nicole Clark interviewed several girls in her documentary *Cover Girl Culture,* which exposed the negative effects of selling beauty and fame to children and teens. Many of these girls responded that they would like to change their appearance:

"I would change the way I look," said Ava, age 10.

"I'd probably change my face," said Kailey, age 11.

"[I would] be skinnier," said Courtney, age 11.

"I would change my face," said Leslie, age 12. "I don't know, I don't like my face."

"If I could change one thing," says Chloe, age 12, "it would probably be my figure."[15]

From drugstores to grocery stores all across America, there are images up and down the checkout aisles of women who are predominantly thin, light-skinned, and blond. Some magazines portray celebrities as beautiful while other magazines highlight their physical flaws. The message is clear: you have to be perfect lest you face ridicule. For those girls and young women who fail to fit this narrow image of ideal beauty, the result may be eating disorders, body shame, low self-esteem, and depression, among other issues.

You're too mature for high school, my trafficker told me. *You're pretty enough to be a model.*

My story is far from unique. Pimps and other traffickers use these same lines on girls and young women all across the country and beyond. Like advertisers, they are looking to play on emotions. "Most girls are insecure," says nineteen-year-old Mycah Maurice Johnson, a member of the Seattle-based gang West Side Street Mobb, as he describes tactics to gain control over girls.[16] Johnson was convicted in 2009 for his involvement in gang-controlled prostitution of minors.[17]

USE OF CELEBRITIES

The media is saturated with images of celebrities as a tool to sell products. Sadly, many of these celebrities are famous not for recent accomplishments, but for recent scandals like drunk driving arrests, hospitalizations for drug addiction, and sex tapes.[18] Also, many of these figures thrown into the spotlight are famous not for talent but for wealth, sex appeal, or shock value. So not only are teens learning the importance of fame, but they are learning that beauty, wealth, and a disregard for society are the means to that end.

Those celebrities who are portrayed in a positive light are limited to Hollywood personalities: models, movie stars, television actors, singers, rappers, dancers, and designers. Materialistic values are reinforced when teens and preteens see celebrities endorsing brands or advertising their own lines of products in the media. In *Cover Girl Culture,* Nicole Clark explores the effects of selling fame and beauty to children. She asks girls what they would like to be when they grow up; one interview with a six-year-old girl unfolds as follows:

"I would like to be a model," says six-year-old Megan.

"Why?" Nicole asks.

"Because, well, I want to become famous," Megan answers.

"Why?"

"Because you make a lot of money."[19]

The documentary *What a Girl Wants* explores the effects of pop culture on middle and high school students. In 2003, kids from two different classrooms identified role models like Britney Spears, Christina Aguilera, Jessica Simpson, and Mandy Moore, all of whom are entertainers who were and still are commonly seen in teen magazines and advertisements.[20] "I like her hair," says one eleven-year-old girl. "I like her, um, her eyes, and her lips . . . I think most girls would want to be Britney Spears, [would want] to be in that exact position that she's in."

Pushing celebrities onto kids is shortening their list of long-term goals. In elementary school, I wanted to be an archaeologist like Indiana Jones or a gymnast like Mary Lou Retton. By intermediate and middle school, however, I was enamored with Hollywood. I wanted to be an actor like Julia Roberts or a singer or songwriter like the idols I saw on MTV. In response to an article about my experience in 1992, one reader commented that, at age fourteen, I was old enough to know that an offer for fame and fortune was a ploy. I beg to differ. The world created by the media for young teens, *especially* today's teens, is saturated with stories about reality TV stars and other celebrities. The idea of being famous or becoming famous is pushed on teen-targeted TV and popular primetime programming. From *16 and Pregnant* to *American Idol,* teens are watching girls transform from being peers to becoming household names almost overnight. They see and hear these teens on all kinds of media like MTV, the radio, and fashion magazines.

In a 2010 study, authors Jody Raphael and Brenda Myers-Powell questioned ex-pimps about recruitment methods used to lure girls. More than one mentioned pretending to be in show business or the fashion industry. "I had many games to cop a girl," says one ex-pimp. "I would tell them I was an agent. I would say I designed clothes. I even told them I sang with certain bands and managed different people."[21]

DESIGNER BRANDS

Advertising companies associate their brands or logos with teen-targeted events (e.g., the X Games) and teen role models (e.g., athletes, singers, actors). Many brands incorporate their products or logos into commercials on teen-driven media. But it's not just brand-name corporations targeting teens and preteens in advertisements, it's also *designer* brand names. Several recent G, PG, and PG-13 movies featured product placement for designer brands like Louis Vuitton, Gucci, Polo Ralph Lauren, Bloomingdale's, Tommy Hilfiger, Calvin Klein, Saks Fifth Ave., Versace, Tiffany & Co., Prada, Dolce & Gabbana, and Armani. Designer brands aren't limited to fashion either; they can include high-end hotels and luxury cars. *Transformers: Dark of the Moon* alone featured Ferrari, Hummer, and Mercedes-Benz.[22]

In a 2007 *Wall Street Journal* article, Vanessa O'Connell discussed the effects of advertising designer brands to teens. "[G]uidance counselors and psychologists say, fashion bullying is reaching a new level of intensity as more designers launch collections targeted at kids," states O'Connell. " . . .The greater focus on fashion in teen magazines and on TV has increased girls' awareness of designer labels."[23] Dorothy Espelage, a professor of educational psychology at the University of Illinois who "has studied teenage behavior for 14 years . . . attributes [the rise of fashion-related bullying] to the proliferation of designer brands and the display of labels in ads," writes O'Connell. "In the more than 20 states where she has studied teens, [Espelage] has been surprised by how kids revere those they perceive to have the best clothes. Having access to designer clothing affords some kids 'the opportunity to become popular—and that protects you and gives you social power and leverage over others.'"[24]

In her book *Consuming Kids,* Susan Linn notes:

> Marketing succeeds by purposely exploiting children's vulnerabilities. Therefore, what you see as its "worst" effect will depend on your child's weaknesses or predilections. For example, if your child is vulnerable to overeating and poor nutrition habits, then marketing of unhealthy foods (linked to childhood obesity) seems the worst. If your child is vulnerable to eating disorders, then body-image marketing is what gets your attention. If your child is susceptible to violent messages, then you might see marketing of violent media and toys (linked to violent behavior) as the worst potential effect of marketing to children. The same is true for materialism, decreased creativity, family stress, and so on.[25]

As a preteen, my greatest vulnerability was my lack of a strong sense of self and my disposition toward being easily influenced by others. "Holly needs to work on her self-confidence," wrote my sixth grade teacher on a student evaluation report card, "She is bright enough to be a leader not a follower." This disposition followed me into middle school, where I continued to be influenced not just by my peers but by popular culture. I did not think critically when it came to messages in the media. Without consistent, constructive guidance from adult role models in my life, I adopted the following values from the media: materialism, consumerism, and the importance of popularity. Without the balance of positive values (e.g., hard work, philanthropy, family, etc.), I had a growing sense of emptiness in middle school.

CRYSTAL AND I STARTED STEALING CLOTHES FROM DEpartment stores in middle school. We preferred Macy's because it had the least number of visible cameras, and the dressing rooms were always messy with piles of pants and tops on the floor. We figured we weren't the only ones using our "five-finger discount" there. Crystal and I yanked price tags from shirtsleeves and walked out of these stores wearing multiple layers of stolen clothes. We soon learned to buy a few small items in order to gain some shopping bags and appear less suspicious.

Through the winter and spring of eighth grade, Crystal and I were regular customers in the juniors' section of Macy's and other stores. We carried designer clothes by the armload into dressing rooms and then loaded our shopping bags with the clothes we liked most. This wasn't something I did for the thrill of possibly getting caught. I didn't want to get caught; I *wanted* new clothes.

Each piece of clothing that I stole seemed to fill a little piece of that empty black hole growing inside of me. I believed that new clothes would make me a new person, that they would give me a new identity. You know that feeling you got in the first week of school with your new wardrobe? Your clothes felt fresh and bright; you were a different person. It felt like anything was possible that school year. You could be voted cutest girl in the yearbook, or you could become a cheerleader. I was chasing a new identity with greater possibilities on a weekly basis. I wanted a new me, a better me. I wanted to be like the girls and women on the covers of magazines.

One weekend, Crystal and I went to the Ocean County Mall in Toms River, New Jersey. We didn't usually go to this mall because of the higher-end stores, most of which used sophisticated security tags. Crystal and I walked into Dillard's, and I spotted a shelf of Calvin Klein jeans. It was as if a ray of sunshine shone down on those piles of stonewashed blue jeans. I fingered the tan logo on the waist: the letters "CK" stood for more than Calvin Klein—they stood for possibilities. They represented a life that I wanted. I picked out a pair in my size and tried them on in the dressing room. Instantly, I could feel a difference. I turned to look at myself in the mirror and slid my hands down my hips. *My life would change if I had these jeans,* I thought, *my life would be so much better.*

I was *not* walking out of the mall without those jeans.

I stepped out of the dressing room and saw the same look on Crystal's face. She clenched the handle of her fake shopping bag, and we headed toward the door. But I knew it didn't feel right; the black bubbles in the ceiling of the store loomed over us. I knew there were cameras hidden in those bubbles, but a force greater than ourselves pulled us forward toward the exit. We reached the main part of the mall, and we pretended to carry on a conversation. I could see the anxiety on Crystal's face. And then I heard the footsteps behind us. A hand landed on my shoulder and a man's voice said, "Come with us, ladies."

Dillard's diligently followed through with the signs posted in their dressing rooms: *Shoplifters will be prosecuted to the fullest extent of the law.* The police picked us up and placed us into two separate jail cells. Crystal was surprisingly calm; she looked sad and defeated. I, on the other hand, roared at my captors. I spat insults and gestured at the camera in my cell. My mother told me later how she watched, stunned, as I raged in my cell.

I was consumed with anger and hatred toward the officers. It has taken me years to deconstruct this scene, but I now understand what was happening here. From television commercials to fashion magazine advertisements, society told me that I needed those jeans in order to *be somebody.* The problem was that my family couldn't afford an $80 pair of jeans, just as they couldn't afford a black suede fringe jacket, which had been necessary to be cool back in seventh grade.

Sitting in that jail cell, I felt like society was pushing its trendy black boot against my face. I felt as though those officers were telling me that I was a nobody, and that I *deserved* to be a nobody. In the summer of 1992, when that old man placed $200 into the palm of my hand in that Atlantic City hotel room, my first and only thought was this: *I can buy at least two pairs of Calvin Klein jeans with this money.*

5

NEGATIVE MESSAGES IN POPULAR CULTURE

IN 2010, THE KAISER FAMILY FOUNDATION ISSUED A REport titled "Generation M^2: Media in the Lives of 8- to 18-Year-Olds." Children between these ages are estimated to view media at "an average of more than 7 1/2 hours a day, seven days a week." This includes "watching television and movies, playing video games, listening to music, using computers, and reading newspapers, magazines and books."[1] This is a significant amount of time during which children are exposed to influences generated outside of their homes and communities. In addition to consumerism and materialism, what other lessons or values are being relayed to children?

EMPHASIS ON LOVE AND ROMANCE

In intermediate school, I listened to singers like Paula Abdul, Debbie Gibson, and Tiffany. The following song titles are a sampling of those from Paula Abdul's 1988 album *Forever Your Girl,* which I owned and memorized: "The Way That You Love Me," "Opposites Attract," "State of Attraction," "I Need You," "Forever Your Girl," and "Next to You." Debbie Gibson's hits included "Only in My Dreams," "Shake Your Love," and "Foolish Beat," while Tiffany's most well-known song was her rendition of "I Think We're Alone Now." These and many other songs from popular artists at the time were all about love, dating, or breaking up. I wanted *so badly* to experience these things. Like many girls approaching puberty, I fantasized about being in love.

Girls this age are naturally more interested in love and relationships, but teen-driven media shoves this concern front and center. Girls fall into a frenzy over boy bands who sing about being devoted to a girl. "You Got It (The Right Stuff)," "Please Don't Go Girl," "I'll Be Loving You (Forever)," and "Cover Girl" are a sampling of the song titles from the hit 1988 New Kids on the Block (NKOTB) album, *Hangin' Tough.* Of course today's songs from teen idols are similar in content. Justin Bieber's musical hits include "One Less Lonely Girl," "Baby," "Somebody to Love," "U Smile," and "Boyfriend." Female artists like Taylor Swift, Mandy Moore, and Jessica Simpson also emphasize love and romance in their songs. Even the products promoted by teen idols often sell romance. The following ad for Bieber's perfume, Someday, promises the following on Target's website:

> Someday by Justin Bieber is more than just a fragrance: It's energy with a state-of-mind that inspires. It is a personal gift straight from his heart, giving fans a chance to get one step closer to Justin. It's a fragrance he can't get enough of and can't stay away from, making those who wear it irrisitable [*sic*]. So take the experience past the music, beyond the performer, and journey deep into the world of possibilities [*sic*]. Someday is a flirty fruity, inviting floral and hopeful vanilla musk scent.[2]

Yes, to an adult this sounds silly; but to an eleven-year-old girl, Justin Bieber holds all the answers to being in love and being loved. From commercials to music to movies, girls are hearing over and over again that life isn't complete without a boyfriend. All of this emphasis on love leaves little room for teen media to address other real-life issues. In *Girls Like Us,* Rachel Lloyd discusses a common misconception that child victims of sex trafficking are very often addicted to drugs. The truth, Lloyd points out, is that the girls are more often addicted to love and affection:

> [E]ven in the initial years, and in over a decade that has followed, I've found very few girls who are addicted to "hard" drugs and for whom the addiction came prior to the exploitation. To see not just community members but sometimes family members so strung out, so desperate, so scorned does not induce many young people to try a drug with such visibly horrifying effects, and with such a strong stigma attached. Girls weren't drug addicted, they were love addicted, and that, I'll learn, is far harder to treat.[3]

In the Showtime documentary *Very Young Girls,* several girls who were victimized by sex trafficking and other forms of commercial sexual exploitation are interviewed. One girl, S——, describes a pimp trafficker who posed as a boyfriend. This man romanced S—— with compliments and devotion before trafficking her to other men. "*I like you; you cute, you sweet,*" said S——, recounting the words of the trafficker. "I was only twelve years old . . . at the time he was like, what, 29, 30; I didn't really care, I felt like it was cool for me to be twelve years old and for a older dude to be interested in me . . . I was like *I'm sexy,* like I had it going on. . . . He was like *I love you, you my baby; and we gonna be together.* . . . I thought that was the best thing that ever happened to me."

DATING VALUES

Considering the emphasis placed on love and romance, let's consider what popular culture is telling preteens and adolescents about dating and relationships. One of my favorite movies at age eleven or twelve was *Earth Girls Are Easy,* a PG-rated movie about aliens that land on Earth. The aliens land in the backyard pool of the main character, Valerie, who is played by Geena Davis. Valerie is a fashionable manicurist who just caught her fiancé attempting to have sex with another woman. Valerie takes the aliens to her boss, Candy (played by MTV personality Julie Brown), who shaves off their multicolored fur to discover *hot*-looking human guys. Upon this amazing discovery, Candy and Valerie take the *hot* aliens to dance clubs in Los Angeles. As every girl in the club begs to have sex with the two sidekick aliens, Valerie is torn between forgiving her cheating fiancé or loving the main alien, Mac, played by Jeff Goldblum.

The movie is undeniably silly with juvenile sound effects and behavior that would appeal to a PG audience. But it also is based on the premise that Valerie must not only be in a romantic relationship but that she must immediately choose between a cheating fiancé and a virtual stranger. Jeff Goldblum's character pushes Valerie to have sex with him despite her attempts to refuse and her expressed uncertainty about love, life, and their compatible anatomy. She ultimately gives in but has a nightmare about her decision afterward. The following day, Valerie abandons her job, her pet cat, and her planet in order to join Mac in another solar system.

I didn't choose this movie as an example because of its blatantly misdirected morals; I chose it because Crystal and I literally watched it over and over again. After we became friends in fourth or fifth grade, Crystal slept over on a regular basis and we watched many teen movies. *Earth Girls Are Easy* not only occupied our intermediate school-age attention, but it also offered us glimpses into womanhood. Like a sponge, I sucked in every message from this movie and I accepted them at face value as behaviors to adopt as my own—from the importance of beauty makeovers to the demand to be in a relationship to the linkage of sex and casual attraction.

I watched many other teen movies with female characters that taught me the following: a girl's value is based on her appeal to a popular guy or "bad boy;" a girl's value is based on her level of beauty and need for help, especially from a guy; sex feels amazing, especially with a well-endowed guy; passionate relationships between *cool* people often have an element of dysfunction, even violence, and that's desired; the need for a girl to be rescued by a guy; and the notion that girls should be attracted to *bad* boys, and that *bad* boys should be attracted to pretty, sexy, or mature girls. Think today's teen movies are different? Try watching *Twilight* (2008), *Prom* (2011), or Miley Cyrus's movie *LOL* (2012), among many others.

Some teen movies imply that an "ugly" or "nerdy" girl can be made over or made relevant by a *cool* or popular guy: *She's All That, Sixteen Candles, The Breakfast Club, Pretty in Pink, Dirty Dancing, A Walk to Remember, 10 Things I Hate About You,* etc. Many of these movies are dear to the hearts of those who watched them as teenagers, and my intentions are not to discredit teen movies. The problem is that, for preteen and young teen girls, an *overexposure* to multiple media messages that emphasize or promote distorted values related to love and dating can be detrimental. They are vulnerable enough to predators seeking to exploit their naïveté and desire for affection.

We need to take a hard look at the current rating system for movies by the Motion Picture Association of America. *Zoolander* (2001) is a playful PG-13 movie about competitive male models that features a group sex scene in which the main female character, Matilda, is pleasured by several characters. Yes, I realize this scene is meant to be humorous; however, I question whether a thirteen-year-old girl (or boy) has enough information and experience to realize that the scene is an exaggeration. This would imply that a thirteen-year-old has a firm understanding about sexuality and about positive and healthy romantic and sexual relationships between two people, let alone a group of people.

OBJECTIFICATION AND SEXUAL OBJECTIFICATION

As a preteen growing up in the '80s, my TV was always tuned to MTV. I studied music videos like Aerosmith's "Rag Doll," Alice Cooper's "Poison," Poison's "Every Rose Has its Thorn," and Billy Idol's "Cradle of Love." "Rag Doll" featured a pig-tailed girl who stripped out of her dress and abandoned her baby doll to join women in lingerie and black thigh-high stockings dancing in lit windows, reminiscent of the red light district in Amsterdam. Video cameras panned over women's bodies in Alice Cooper's "Poison." And the band Poison's "Every Rose Has its Thorn" featured a sexy girl in bed wearing thong-like underwear. I sat on the floor before my television and literally studied these girls and women as they stripped and danced before my rock star idols. The girl from Billy Idol's "Cradle of Love" video made the biggest impression on me as she writhed in a stranger's bed and crawled across his floor.

By the end of sixth grade, I was emulating the girls in these videos. I curled my hair and puckered my lips in the mirror. I squeezed into tight jeans and wore half-shirts to show off my belly. By summertime, cars began honking at me along my way to and from the local Rite-Aid. At first I was surprised by it, turning wide-eyed to see the long-haired boys waving from inside their Corvettes and Monte Carlos. I started buying Stewart's root beer and Mistic Mango Mania sodas from Wawa because they looked like beer and wine cooler bottles. On the way back home, I would dramatically swig from one of the bottles each time a car passed by, hoping to get a honk.

I began to judge myself based on the evidence of beauty and sex appeal as seen through *other* people's eyes, particularly older boys. Boys my age were usually uninterested in dating, or they were only interested in dating really popular and pretty girls. It was older boys who often paid attention to me and my friends. Attention from an older boy confirmed that I was desired, that I was worthy; and it produced a short-lived feeling of self-esteem.

A 2010 report from the American Psychological Association (APA) described how the objectification of women in the media often results in the self-objectification or self-sexualization of girls: "In self-objectification, girls internalize an observer's perspective on their physical selves. . . . [Girls] learn to treat themselves as objects to be looked at and evaluated for their appearance."[4] In his 2007 documentary, *Dreamworlds 3,* Sut Jhally explored how women are constantly objectified in music videos:

> [Women] are presented as wanting to be watched, inviting it, desiring the look, enjoying being on display. . . . In music video, the person being watched is regarded as a passive thing. . . . The assumption behind this way of looking at someone is that it is perfectly legitimate to watch in this fashion. Women's bodies are surveyed . . . analyzed in the same way that one might examine a landscape or an object. Their function in the videos is to be . . . desired by men.[5]

The sexual objectification of women in music videos continues across the Billboard music charts today, including within country music, rap, rock, R&B, pop, and more. The sexualization of idols in teen-driven media adds to a teen's self-objectification and self-sexualization. Female artists like Britney Spears, Christina Aguilera, and Miley Cyrus were all portrayed as sexualized objects on stage as they transitioned from adolescent pop stardom to reach a more mature audience. "Teen artists exploit their sexuality to establish a more mature and 'edgier' version of their former selves as they cross the threshold from teenage icon to adult musician," notes the APA in their 2010 report.[6] The message from the music industry to young teen girls is that sex appeal is a tool and that hypersexuality equals maturity. Male teen artists are also sexualized in the media while still reaching out to teen audiences. In order to connect with a celebrity like Justin Bieber, wouldn't a girl feel the need to meet him at the same level of sexualization at which he is portrayed?

SEX AS A VEHICLE FOR ADVERTISING

"The hyper-sexualization of our culture . . . [supports an environment in which gang members can] lure impressionable and vulnerable girls from all walks of life," says San Diego District Attorney Gretchen Dahlinger Means in a 2012 *America's Most Wanted* article.[7] I have read cases involving girls from low-income city blocks to upper-class suburbs, and every place in between. Former San Diego District Attorney Keith Burt agreed: "We live in a society [in which] a child cannot avoid constant exposure to sex as a vehicle for selling something."[8]

Burt notes that hypersexualization in the media (e.g., music videos, commercials, movies, etc.) is a contributing factor to the commercial sexual exploitation of girls. He points to certain music lyrics, movies, and TV shows (e.g., the 2012 TV series *Client List*) that even glamorize prostitution. Burt also mentions a top 5 finalist (Miss Ohio) in the 2012 Miss USA pageant who was asked about positive portrayals of women in the movies; her answer was Julia Roberts' character, Vivian, from *Pretty Woman*.[9] Considering *Pretty Woman* grossed nearly half a billion dollars in profit, Burt and I both agree that many young women probably share Miss Ohio's sentiments, as I did at age fourteen.[10] Even actress and singer Miley Cyrus dressed as Vivian and posted the photo to her 27 million Facebook fans in June 2013.

"The reason I mention this," says Burt, "is because it helps us understand the mindset of young women as they deal with the pressures put on them to cooperate with gang members." Another influence Burt brings up is the glamorization of the pimp culture in music videos and music lyrics, as well as the online promotion of pimp culture by gang traffickers. "Gang pimps use YouTube, Facebook, Twitter, Craigslist, BackPage[, and all other] manner of social media to glorify the pimp-prostitute lifestyle," Burt says, "[they then] lure impressionable, vulnerable girls. . . . But once they get them; [the girls] are trapped."[11]

Sex traffickers are not the only exploiters looking to capitalize on the vulnerability of children in our hypersexualized, consumer-driven society. As far back as 2003, *Newsweek* published an article about "teen prostitution" involving more and more kids from suburbia.[12] One seventeen-year-old girl said she was first approached by a man as she walked through the mall:

> Like many teenage girls in Minneapolis, 17-year-old Stacey liked to hang out after school at the Mall of America, Minnesota's vast shopping megaplex. Cute, blond and chatty, she flirted with boys and tried on the latest Gap fashions. One day last summer, Stacey, which isn't her real name, says she was approached by a man who told her how pretty she was, and asked if he could buy her some clothes. "He was an older guy, dressed really well," she recalls. "He said he just wanted to see me in the clothes." Stacey agreed, and went home that night with a $250 outfit.[13]

After this initial exchange, *The Daily Beast* quotes as follows from the original story:

> The encounter taught Stacey a lesson: "Potentially good sex is a small price to pay for the freedom to spend money on what I want." The easiest way, she discovered, was to offer her body in trade. Stacey, who lives with her parents in an upscale neighborhood, gets good grades in high school and plans to try out for the tennis team, began stripping for men in hotel rooms in exchange for money

> to buy clothes—then went on to more intimate activities. She placed ads on a local telephone personals service, offering "wealthy, generous" men "an evening of fun" for $400. All the while, she told her parents she was out with friends or at the mall, and was careful to be home before her midnight curfew.[14]

Sex and sexuality are constantly used by companies and artists as vehicles to sell products, from TV commercials to magazine advertisements to music albums. In our media-saturated, consumer-driven, hypersexualized, sexually exploitative society, how can we project the blame onto girls like Stacey? We tell her she *needs* this or that expensive brand-name product, and then we normalize the sexual objectification of women in the media. On top of that, we saturate her pop culture world with sexualized images as sales pitches. Is Stacey's story really so far-fetched?

SEXUAL EXPLOITATION

I studied lyrics to songs like "Sticky Sweet" by Motley Crüe, "Talk Dirty to Me" by Poison, and "Seventeen" by Winger. Many songs from mainstream rock bands in the late '80s and early '90s were about having sex with women and girls and/or partying. The lyrics to "So Damn Pretty" by Warrant mention the idea of being in love with "hookers," "whores," and a "teenage slut." The lyrics to Alice Cooper's song "Trash" idealize a woman for her wild and "tramp" style in bed, while Mötley Crüe's "She Goes Down" romanticizes girls who give oral sex to the singer and his friends. Oversexualized girls and women were clearly preferred, and these values are still relevant in today's music lyrics.

But what first got me hooked on this genre of music were not the songs about sex, but the songs about love: Warrant's "Heaven," Mötley Crüe's "Without You," Poison's "Every Rose Has its Thorn," and Alice Cooper's "Hell Is Living Without You" and "Only My Heart Talkin'." These musicians, whom MTV played in my bedroom every single night, were my idols. I played these love songs over and over again, and when I bought the bands' albums, I studied the lyrics to the other songs as well, most of which were completely degrading to women and girls. But I didn't question the ethics behind them at the time; I accepted them at face value as instructions on how I could be "relationship material" for guys who can love a girl as deeply as depicted in love songs.

One of the teenage DJs at the Tuckerton Skateway was a full-fledged rock star in my eyes. Like many other eleven- and twelve-year-old girls, I sought his attention at the skating rink. I used to request songs from him, not only for the chance to talk to him, but also to peek inside the booth, which I considered to be part of the MTV world. It was essentially a cubbyhole at the top of some stairs, and Crystal and I envied anyone who was privileged to be inside of it. One day, this seventeen- or eighteen-year-old invited me up into the booth.

I climbed the steps and turned inside the booth; immediately, I saw a box of records and I wanted to reach out and touch the sleeves. The guy pulled me toward him, and I held my breath thinking he was going to kiss me. I hoped that Crystal or another friend was watching to see how absolutely lucky I was. But he didn't kiss me—he put his hand on my shoulder and pushed me down to the floor. I was confused until he unzipped his pants. Although I had never performed oral sex, I had heard it described in music lyrics and had seen it implied in music videos and movies.

While I understood what was happening, I had neither intended for nor foreseen this. It wasn't that I *didn't* want to perform oral sex. I had *no idea* if I wanted to; he didn't ask me. What concerned me was that I didn't understand what it meant. *Was he asking me out?* I wondered, *did this mean we were going out?* It never occurred to me that I was being sexually assaulted. Moments later, I walked away disheveled yet hopeful that I was in a relationship with the coolest guy in the skating rink.

After a few days or weeks had passed without the DJ acknowledging me again, I understood that I had been "used," a term that became common among us girls by middle school. So-and-so was "used" for sex by so-and-so. The person being "used" was viewed as stupid, "slutty," or otherwise undesirable. Nobody I knew used the words "rape" or "sexual assault;" I believe we all thought those experiences involved extreme violence by strangers. I didn't want to be seen as undesirable, so I told no one that the DJ had "used" me.

I also told no one in authority when I was "used" by another local teenage boy the following year inside an abandoned apartment building that was still under construction. I snuck out of my house in the middle of the night to meet him; I had a crush on him, and he knew it. When he pulled me into a vacant bedroom of the apartment, I whispered into his ear in a very teen-romance-movie-kind-of-way that this was my first time. I couldn't wait to try sex. Not only were my hormones raging and my curiosity piqued, but music videos and movies made the act look like it felt *amazing.*

The experience that followed, however, was not amazing; it was degrading and painful. At the time, however, I again thought it was an act of dating.

Although I had to grit my teeth through the pain, I had hoped it meant I was finally, officially, in a relationship. Even when I learned he was making fun of me to others, I *still* hoped he would change his mind about me. He was a bad boy, I thought; he just needed to come around.

I realize that negative messages in the media might sound trivial to an adult, but to a twelve-year-old girl, movies and other media are not only entertainment, they are keyholes to society. And these keyholes have multiplied with cell phones, video games, and the Internet. Without supervision and interpretation, media messages can be channeled unfiltered into a teen's value system. My TV told me secrets about the world and about my place within the world. Instead of filing sexual assault charges, I waited for these guys to express how much they liked me.

6

VIOLENCE AGAINST WOMEN

IN AN ONLINE FORUM FOR MY HOMETOWN, SOMEONE started a thread a few years ago for people to post nostalgic memories about the Tuckerton Skateway. Some posted comments about the Ellio's pizza slices and "suicide" soda drinks, which were all the soda flavors mixed together. Others talked about the limbo contests, the skate races, and the shuffle skating. But one person posted fond memories for the "skating rink sluts." The comment was later removed or deleted. I wonder now if that commenter realized that these so-called sluts were literally *children*. They were teen and preteen girls emulating the women they saw in videos for the same music that played inside that skating rink every weekend.

The 2012 Ohio Human Trafficking Commission's study says that Ohio youth who were victimized via sex trafficking report the following statistically significant factors *less than one year* before being trafficked: knowing "people who purchase sex," "having dropped out of school," and having "a much older boyfriend."[1] Having a much older boyfriend is relevant not only to my own story, but also to the stories of most of my friends in adolescence. I have memories of older guys asking my twelve-year-old friends to lean over and show their cleavage, and of older guys leading my thirteen-year-old friends into bedrooms behind closed doors.

Like many middle school girls, I believed my self-worth was dependent on having a boyfriend and/or having sexual appeal to boys and older guys.[2] This naturally led to romantic rejections. Each rejection left me feeling more desperate for attention, which also led to further sexual exploitations. One guy drove his Camaro to the skating rink and flirted with several of us young girls. When he shoved his hand down my pants and probed with his fingers, I pretended to enjoy it, thinking this would make him like me.

He later drove me out to the woods and laid a blanket on the ground. I could see sticks poking up through the blanket, and it was chilly outside. My first experience with sex had been in a dark room in the middle of the night; so I was uncomfortable with the idea of being naked outside in daylight. I stood, feeling awkward, until he finally rolled the blanket up and drove me back to his house. "That's OK," he said, "we can do it next time." He then flirted on the telephone with another girl from my school until I asked him to take me home. I was twelve, maybe thirteen; I believe he was 21 at the time, maybe 22.

I was confused, and I began to feel duped by all of my rock star heroes. *Guys don't care about love at all,* I thought, *guys only care about sex.* I stopped "'liking" boys and older guys. I knew they would either break up with me or want to use me. This realization endorsed my worries over being ugly or stupid. Just as my self-esteem took a nosedive, Crystal began making new friends and I became increasingly paranoid about losing her friendship. Crystal was drawn to a "tough crowd," so I often found myself among aggressive and/or overeager guys. At a time when I needed supervision and guidance the most, I was frequently on my own.

Crystal and I once slept over at a girl's house, and I woke up with the girl's older brother pushing his tongue into my mouth. I pretended to kiss him back while kicking at the couch to wake the others up. Another time I stood on the stoop of a girlfriend's house and the girl's older cousin yanked me into the house and forced me to the floor. I managed to pry myself away from him. On a different day, I found myself on the floor of a friend's bedroom with an older boy. What probably began as flirting ended with sex on the floor. I did *not* like this guy; but once it went too far I thought I was obligated to concede. And I hated myself for it.

There was a high school guy who had broken teeth and a criminal record. I didn't like him either, but I didn't stop him from flirting because the attention made me feel good; it eased the idea that I was unworthy of being in a romantic relationship. However, when the boy pushed for sex, I felt obligated to cooperate because I had encouraged his flirting. Instead of saying no, I used stall tactics: *Maybe later. Not right now. No, I'm not a tease.* When he pushed hard enough, though, I simply gave in. I waited for it to be over, and then I avoided contact with him again.

Why didn't I say no? Because I didn't know I could. No matter how much I did not want to follow through with a sexual act, I had *no idea* that saying *no* was a real and viable option. As a teenager, I felt like I was surrounded by messages about sex, especially on the radio, which became my strongest media influence in middle school. Sex was not a message unique to rock music; many dance and hip hop songs were about love and sex, including Salt-n-Pepa's "Let's Talk about Sex," Color Me Badd's "I Wanna Sex You Up," and Bell Biv DeVoe's "Do Me!" The messages I heard were loud and clear: *You should be sexy, you should be dating, you should be having sex,* and *you should be enjoying sex.*

Nobody was telling me that it was OK *not* to have sex, at least not anybody in the realm of popular culture. There were no songs telling me that if I felt confused about sex, I could say no or that I *should* say no. There were also no songs telling me that I didn't *need* a boyfriend. My self-esteem fell further and further with each rejection and with each undesired sexual act. Each of these guys ranged in age from high school to early twenties. I tried hard to date, but none of the guys I really liked were interested. I tried hard to be sexy, but I didn't enjoy sex. I hated it. And, the contrast between what I was hearing and what I was feeling made me believe that something was physically wrong with me.

I was becoming severely depressed and stressed, and my parents noticed. I would later learn that my parents had allowed me to spend a lot of time with friends because my mother had been diagnosed with an advanced stage of cancer, and they wanted to protect me from the realities of chemotherapy. Although I knew my mother had been diagnosed, I was ignorant to the seriousness of her illness. Unfortunately, my time away from home only deepened the divide between my parents and me, and my resentment toward them grew.

By the time my parents noticed my growing state of distress, it was too late. Our relationship had been too strained for them to reach me. After the social worker visited our house in elementary school, my cousin's abuse was never brought up again. My parents' drinking continued, though. When they stumbled through the door at night, I would look up from my homework and I would narrow my eyes, especially at my mother. She would rarely make eye contact with me as she leaned against the couch for support. Even when she looked my way, her eyes were rarely in focus. She often smiled in an attempt to seem normal. She would lean against my father or slide her hand along the wall, trying to appear less tipsy. This made me even angrier. To me, the pretending to be sober confirmed that she knew her drinking was wrong.

The constant conflict between my parents and me often resulted in arguments and punishment. If I was grounded and kept from going to the skating rink with Crystal, I would become enraged. I dreaded the idea of Crystal having fun without me; to me, this meant that she would find other friends and leave me behind. The "bad feeling," which I associated with my cousin, returned as I struggled to keep Crystal's friendship and make sense of sex and dating. I often felt like I was unraveling at the seams. Without understanding what was wrong with me, I couldn't communicate my feelings to anyone. I didn't know where to begin, and I didn't know what was normal or abnormal.

My parents moved to a neighborhood that was about five miles away from Crystal, which exacerbated my anxiety. Crystal started dating an older guy, Chad, which was good at the time because he would pick me up in his car so we could all hang out at the mall on the weekends.

And then there was Rich, a high school grad who also had his own car. Rich and I kissed and held hands as we drove around town, but he never tried to have sex with me. I thought this meant he *really* liked me until I learned he had a *real* girlfriend in high school. I was devastated. Rich and I stopped talking, and I worried that the friends of Rich's *real* girlfriend would beat me up in high school the following year.

Something broke inside me after Rich.

It feels stupid to write all of this as an adult, but as a fourteen-year-old girl who'd been dumped and "used" several times through middle school, I felt lost and overwhelmed. Something finally broke inside me, and I was numb. This was when I started hitchhiking. Outside of school, I rarely saw Crystal after we were both arrested at Dillard's. Toward the end of the school year, I started walking down Route 539 alone. Sometimes I walked the five miles to Mystic and sometimes I only walked to the Wawa in Tuckerton. It was on one of these long and lonely walks that I met Mike.

"Want some candy, little girl," Mike had hissed from behind the dirty screen door of his father's house as I walked past.

Mike was scary. He shaved his head, wore combat boots, and shot a rifle in his basement for target practice. I often left the safety, but heavy silence, of my bedroom to visit Mike, who once held a knife to my throat during sex. By that point, though, I was so far removed from myself that I had regarded the knife with only mild concern. I visited Mike simply because I knew nobody else would be expecting me. When I knocked, he opened his door; and that at least was *something.*

It was in this state that I met Greg at the mall, shortly after graduating middle school. *This* was the reason I searched the faces of strangers; I was hoping to make a connection with someone and to find a way out of my life. I was fourteen, and I was in desperate need of help. Unfortunately, nobody except Greg seemed to notice and offer help. So let's rewind to that motel room and those questions I'm so often asked: *What were you thinking? What was going through your mind?* Without hearing all of this back story, how can my audience understand that I really wasn't thinking very much at all? If I felt anything, it was mostly disappointment. I thought Greg was different; but like all the others, he only wanted to "use" me.

When I first started speaking publicly about my experience, I felt pressured to tell audience members that I was *scared* in order to satisfy their confusion about my compliance to a trafficker's demands; this was exactly what I told Dr. Oz and *Cosmopolitan* magazine when interviewed in 2011. But the truth is . . . I wasn't scared. I was not *happy* about the fact that I had just been tricked into running away. I felt stupid, duped, and disappointed, even sad and apprehensive; but I was not cowering in a corner as many images of sex trafficking convey.

On that summer day in 1992, Greg was looking for a particular girl with particular qualities that he could exploit for personal gain. Greg knew that, once I was under his control, I would become a "willing victim." Why didn't I run away when it was clear that Greg intended to prostitute me? By that point, prostitution didn't seem so preposterous. There is a detail I left out of the prologue because, without context, this detail would make no sense. The day I ran away, I had causally handed my body over to that eighteen-year-old high school guy in order to secure a ride to the mall. I already saw my body as a form of currency even before I arrived at that motel room. And, I was serious about starting a new life. When it became clear I was expected to prostitute myself, it didn't occur to me to scream and run for my life. I had already risked too much to return home. In my mind, going home meant returning to a mountain of mistakes and fears.

It is often said in the advocacy world of anti-trafficking that a girl does not wake up one day and say, *I wanna be a prostitute.* "Little girls don't grow up to want to give blowjobs for money," says Deputy District Attorney Gretchen Dahlinger Means in a 2012 AMBER Alert training video. "That takes a tremendous amount of breaking down of someone's character and soul."[3] Polaris Project lists several methods used by traffickers to "break" a girl down; they say it is a "systematic process . . .documented and replicated by pimps nationwide."[4] Polaris's list includes:

- Beating/Slapping/Whipping—With hands, fists, and kicking, as well as with objects such as bats, tools, chains, belts, hangers, canes, and cords
- Burning—Of personal items and items of meaning to foster hopelessness and demoralization or directly burning women and girls using cigarette/cigar butts
- Sexual assault—Rape or gang rape
- Confinement—Using torture practices such as confinement to lock women and girls in closets, trunks of cars, or rooms for indeterminate amounts of time
- Other torture techniques—Such as deprivation of food or water, or various forms of bondage such as chaining individuals to items or tying them up
- Emotional abuse—Direct verbal insults, name-calling, threats, mind control, brainwashing, cognitive re-programming
- Re-naming—Offering "nicknames" both for endearment and to erase former identity
- Creating dependencies—By instructing how to walk, how to talk, what to wear, when to eat, when to sleep, and where to sleep
- Removal from familiarity and support structures—By transporting a woman or minor to a new location where she knows no one
- Document confiscation—Of identification documents (identification, birth certificate, Social Security number)
- Forced sexual education—Inducement of viewing pornography to learn to have sex

Like many "willing victims," however, the process of breaking me down had begun long before I met my trafficker. I cringe when people refer to me in news articles as a "former sex slave" because if I was a sex slave to anyone, it was to popular culture. Advertisers, entertainment producers, and other moguls of the media were the ones who seasoned me to accept sexual exploitation and prostitution. My body was an object; its sole purpose, I believed by that point, was for sex.

Even if a teen or preteen girl is fortunate enough to dodge an experience of sexual abuse, assault, or exploitation in childhood, she is likely to have witnessed some form of violence against women if her family owns a radio or TV.[5] It appears in the most popular, chart-topping songs that bombard listeners daily. The following are select lyrics from those songs in the top 50 of the Billboard Hot 100 the week of August 17, 2013:

- "So hit me up when you passing through, I'll give you something big enough to tear your ass in two" (Robin Thicke, "Blurred Lines," #1 chart position)
- "You're a princess to the public, but a freak when it's time" (Ariana Grande feat. Mac Miller, "The Way," #20)
- "For Pete's sake, homie, pull it together, Just f*ck her one time and be through it forever" (J. Cole, "Power Trip," #26)
- "Put Molly all in her champagne, she ain't even know it; I took her home and I enjoyed that, she ain't even know it" (Rocko feat. Future and Rick Ross, "U.O.E.N.O," #38)
- "Is it bad that I never made love, no I never did it; But I sure know how to f*ck (Wale feat. Tiara Thomas, "Bad," #40)
- "She a trick for a dolla bill . . . Lead her to the bathroom, she askin' where you takin' me" (Sage the Gemini feat. IamSu, "Gas Pedal," #46)
- "I got smart, I got rich, and I got bitches still" (J. Cole feat. TLC, "Crooked Smile," #47)
- "She ride this d*ck, her ti**ies jiggle, that's my pillows; that's because I sleep in that ho" (Rich Gang feat. Lil Wayne, Birdman, Future, Mack Maine, Nicki Manaj, "Tapout," #48)

The culture of accepted and even encouraged sexual exploitation of women and girls extends far beyond the music industry. A 2013 study from the Parents Television Council reports the following regarding the sexual exploitation of girls on television:

> The study showed that primetime broadcast television programs routinely include sexually exploitative dialogue and depictions of females, as that term is defined by the United Nations. However, even more disturbing was the apparent relationship between age and sexual exploitation as well as the relationship between age, humor, and sexual exploitation. The findings potentially reveal a troubling media trend of: a) creating younger and younger sexually exploited female characters; and b) presenting sexually exploitative dialogue

> and depictions of these young girls through a comedic lens which allows the audience to laugh at what would otherwise generate a sobering social response. Consequently, if past research is correct that television can shape our attitudes towards social issues, and if media images communicate that sexual exploitation is neither serious nor harmful, the environment is being set for sexual exploitation to be viewed as trivial and acceptable.[6]

Many artists who glorify violence against women also glamorize pimp-controlled prostitution in their music lyrics and videos. The idea of being a pimp or "pimping" was glorified in music in the late 1990s and early 2000s. Examples include the following songs: "P.I.M.P." by 50 Cent, "Big Pimpin'" by Jay-Z, "Pimp Juice" by Nelly, and "Pimp Slap Dat Hoe" by Soulja Boy. Advertisers even used the word "pimp" as a way to draw attention to products and television shows: Pimp My Profile (a website for MySpace profile templates), *Pimp My Ride* (a television show on MTV), and Pimp Juice (an energy drink). The unfortunate result is a continued glorification of the "pimp culture" in popular culture today. Some female artists also glorify the idea of being a commercial sexual object; see Rihanna's video to her 2013 song, "Pour It Up."

Perhaps a "ho" or "bitch" was exactly what that skating rink DJ saw in me and my eleven- and twelve-year-old friends as we dressed like the girls in music videos. When he invited me into his booth that day, maybe he saw a "slut" who was "asking for it." Perhaps he thought it was OK because he was seeing and hearing the same media messages that I was. Or, perhaps he was being influenced by a father or an uncle who, like the commenter on that social media forum, had carried these projected ideals of women and girls into adulthood.

"Turning a human being into a thing is almost always the first step toward justifying violence against that person," says Jean Kilbourne in the documentary, *Killing Us Softly 4*. "We see this with racism, we see it with homophobia, we see it with terrorism; . . . the person is dehumanized and violence then becomes inevitable. And that step is already and constantly taken with women. The violence, the abuse, is [a] chilling but logical result of this kind of objectification."[7] If we as a society accept widespread images of women and children being treated as commercial and as sexual objects, why would a middle school girl, a high school boy, a grown man, or a trafficker feel any differently?

I did not grow up on the mean streets of any city. I grew up in Little Egg Harbor Township, New Jersey, an area known for fishing, clamming, decoy carving, and tourism. Tuckerton, my then hometown inside Little Egg Harbor

Township, was small. Even twenty years later, the population is estimated to be only 3,354. Other facts about Tuckerton: 93.8 percent of the population is white;[8] 89.2 percent graduated high school or higher; the median household income is $56,577; and 10 percent live below the poverty level.[9] Like many kids living in middle-income neighborhoods, I was raised on MTV, after-school specials, and commercials for Levi's jeans and the Easy Bake Oven. Welcome to the typical life of any misguided and media-overexposed American teenager living in suburbia and addicted to love. For those kids who aren't being noticed by anyone except predators, a pimp or other trafficker is likely to fall in line.

PART II

ATLANTIC CITY

7

THE BUYERS

WHEN I AM INTERVIEWED BY THE MEDIA, I'M VERY OFten asked about the "johns" or buyers. News reporters can be incredibly rude, blunt, and unapologetically invasive. *So, how many times were you forced to have sex?* I'm often asked, along with *How much money did you charge?* In her memoir, *The Road to Lost Innocence,* Somaly Mam describes her survival of human trafficking overseas. Following the scene of her sale to a Cambodian brothel, Somaly writes, "I am writing about this place now because I never want to have to talk about it again. I never want to remember this again."[1] I'd like to echo her words here as my own sentiments. I finally answer these questions here only as a way to shed light on the characteristics of those men who buy children for sex, and I hope to never have to speak of it again.

"JOHN" #2

The old man drove me back to Nicki on Pacific Avenue, and Nicki had already lined up another "date" for me. The next "john" was tall with dark, bushy hair and a beard. He looked like a porn star from the '70s. I knew this only because I had found old Playboy magazines in a public park once—I stuffed them into my pants and studied the pictures at home. This unfortunate yet brief exposure to pornography skewed my ideations and expectations about sex throughout my adolescence and beyond. In today's world, children are only a click away from being bombarded with pornographic images on the Internet.

This man wore a suit, and he got straight to the point in his Trop World casino hotel room.

"Take off your clothes," he instructed.

I pulled off Nicki's red dress as he laid each piece of his sharp-looking suit over a chair.

"Now," he said, "Suck my dick."

I moved toward him, but he held up his hand.

"No," he said, "use a condom first."

He spoke to me firmly like one would to a child.

"*Now* suck my dick," he said.

I kept quiet and followed his instructions.

"Now lay down," he said, "Not that way, *this* way . . . this is called the sixty-nine position."

I didn't have to tell this man that I didn't kiss on the mouth like Julia Roberts. I didn't have to tell him anything at all. He didn't ask me any questions, and I figured he could tell I didn't know what I was doing.

"Now, finger my ass," he said.

I looked at him, confused.

"It's ok," he said, "Just use your finger."

When I realized what he wanted me to do, I sat up quickly. He sat up and snatched my arm by the wrist. And then he smiled; it was the first time he smiled at me. I eyed the doorknob of the hotel room.

"It's OK," he said in a patient tone. He squeezed my wrist and unrolled my finger.

"It's OK," he repeated, "I'll do it to you, too."

This will end, this will end, I repeated to myself. This was what I thought as this man violated me in a way I had never known before. I closed my eyes and repeated to myself, *This will end, this will end . . . It's just business, it's just business, it's just business . . .*

When it was over, the man led me to the bathroom.

"Hold out your hands," he said.

He poured soap into the palms of my hands and told me to scrub.

"I can get you a better job in Vegas," he said to me. "You'll make more money there if you work for me."

I thought about this. In this new world, sex wasn't an act that left me confused and empty-handed. It was a business transaction. I realized I actually had value in this world. I suddenly felt like an adult. I could make money and I had options: I could stay or I could go to Las Vegas with this man. I began to consider myself lucky.

"No," I said, "thanks, though."

I felt a growing sense of gratitude and loyalty toward Greg and Nicki. I believed they were my friends because they were the first people to offer me an alternative to my life. I may not have thought all of this consciously at the time, but I know this was how I felt. The man paid me $100 and said it was no big deal. He ran his hands through his bushy hair and looked from the mirror to the door as if I was already gone.

"Let's go," he said.

Once on the street, I headed down Pacific Avenue. Other girls walked past me, older girls, in tight groups with chests and hips that filled in their dresses. They laughed out loud through red lipstick and a haze of hairspray. I was enamored with these exotic creatures; I wanted to collapse into a crevice and just watch them like an episode of *21 Jump Street.* The walk back to Nicki's corner felt long, and the size-seven heels flopped on my feet and blistered my skin. I slipped them off and carried them with me down the crumbling sidewalk. Most of the buildings between the casinos were vacant, broken, and barricaded. I passed a group of women dressed like me, but they didn't look friendly.

"Beetch," one of them yelled as I walked past.

I looked around to see who she was addressing and realized it was me.

"Beetch," another one screamed, "you better put yer fuckin' shoes on, beetch."

They filed behind me as I picked up my pace.

"Who da fuck you think you are?" another one of them shouted. "I'll beat yer ass, beetch."

I really didn't think they would sympathize with my shoe-size problem, so I shoved them back on my feet and flopped across the street. They stopped at the corner and shouted at me from the curb, as if a force field blocked them from moving on. Two young white guys stumbled toward me, giggling and slapping each other on the back. "You ask," said one holding a brown bag in the shape of a six-pack of beer. The other said, "Naw, man, you ask." They didn't seem to notice the women shouting behind me.

"You wanna date?" I asked quickly.

"Umm," said the one with the beer, "OK."

I followed them into Sands casino in order to escape the women outside.

As we walked through the glass front, a man passed by us on the outside and frantically lipped to me, *Are you coming back?* I nodded, wondering who the hell he was, and turned back to the guys, relieved. Something else happened here. I felt . . . *pretty.* Amid all that confusion, I felt *desired.* I felt like I was in a music video. My first favorite music video about love was "The Way You Make Me Feel" by Michael Jackson. In the video, Jackson stalks a beautiful skinny model through the streets of a city. I would sit on the floor and watch the streetlights shine through this girl's mound of curly hair and highlight her long legs.

I'll never be that pretty, I thought back then.

Yet that's exactly how I felt at that moment. I was that girl in the high heels running from Michael Jackson's advancements in the dark streets. My transition into Stacy Combas (Greg's pseudonym for me) was quick; pretending to be another person was easier than being me. This identity change is often difficult for audience members to understand; but, says Dr. Lois Lee, Founder of Children of the Night in Los Angeles, for many child victims "entry into prostitution is more of a 'slide' than a gigantic step."[2]

"JOHNS" #3 AND #4

"It'll be two hundred each," I announced in the room.

They pulled bills from their pockets and counted their money together.

"We only got a hundred."

I said that was fine, and then they stood in the room looking at each other.

"I'll go first," said one.

"I'll wait in the hallway," said the other. They were giddy. The second guy grabbed two bottles of Budweiser and left.

Finally, I thought, *normal guys.*

I straddled the first guy and returned to my Julia Roberts character.

"I don't kiss on the mouth," I said mysteriously.

"Hey," he said, "you got that from *Pretty Woman.*"

"Yeah . . . well," I said, "it's a good rule."

I didn't play any role with the second guy; they both finished too quickly for me to find another role to play. I pulled a wad of crumpled bills from the purse Nicki gave me.

"Oh gawd," one of them shouted and they both threw their arms up.

"Don't count yer money in fron' of us."

"Sorry," I said, shoving the bills back into my purse with unused condoms. "This is my first night."

"Oh gawd," the guy said again and sat on the bed, "You gotta be kiddin' me."

The other flopped into a big chair and asked, "How old are you?"

"Seventeen," I lied.

"How did you get here?" he asked.

"Some guy is helping me," I said.

They both looked sad.

"Let me drive you back home to yer parents," said the one on the bed.

This struck me as asinine. The fact that this man offered to help me *after* he and his friend had just had sex with me was reminiscent of the guys who "used" me back at home. It made me angry.

"No, thanks," I said, "I'm OK."

It was right about here that something else happened: whatever last thread of fantasy I held inside that I might fall in love or be loved someday *snapped.* Not only did I no longer believe it, I no longer *wanted* it. I felt suddenly empowered by prostitution. It protected me against any feelings toward men. As a prostitute, I now understood exactly what was expected of me; and I understood exactly what I would be getting in return. There was no romance in question, only a business transaction. The money I earned would help me become *somebody.* I felt like I was finally in control.

In the elevator, an old lady stood next to me as we descended to the casino floor. I could tell she had money and lived a fancy life. When I looked at her, she clutched her pocketbook and pursed her lips at me. I let my yellow hair fall over my face. I knew I didn't fit in there; it was in *her* world that I did *not* have control over my life. It was bright and loud on the casino floor, and I felt very out of place. I spotted a door and pushed through it. I found myself outside with some bellboys who looked surprised to see me. They watched in silence as I hurried toward Pacific Avenue, painfully aware of my flopping high heels and their eyes on my back.

I have been asked why I wouldn't accept help from these two "johns," and I can understand why this might be difficult to conceive. But I must reiterate here a sentiment from chapter 1: as a society, we must stop blaming children for their actions, or lack of actions. No child victimized through sexual exploitation or commercial sexual exploitation should be blamed for his or her circumstances. For those who believe these men *really* sought to help me, I want to know why then didn't they call the police? Why didn't they ask for my age *before* paying me for sex? We need to stop placing responsibility on those children and teenagers who are so obviously broken that they believe prostitution is their only viable option.

NICKI STOOD WAITING FOR ME ACROSS FROM THE JULIUS Caesar statue. She seemed annoyed.

"Where you been?" she said.

I told her about the girls who chased me, and she sighed as if frustrated.

"You can't take yuh' clothes awff on the street," she said. "You gotta wait until you get in the room."

This was one of many rules of which I was not aware. Today, there seems to be even more rules in prostitution, especially pimp-controlled street prostitution. Girls aren't allowed to walk on the sidewalk, especially if a pimp is walking on the sidewalk. Girls aren't allowed to look a pimp in the eye; otherwise, a pimp considers this to be an act of "choosing up," which means choosing a different pimp. Such an act of treason can result in violence from the original pimp. Pimp traffickers will often brand girls and women with tattoos in a proactive attempt to show ownership over them.

"Don' worry, baby," Nicki said, "I'll tawk to 'em—just don't do it again."

"My feet really hurt," I said. "These shoes are too big."

"We'll get ya' a new pair tomorrow," she said, "How much money you got?"

"Two hundred," I said.

"Damn, shooga," she softened up. "We gotta' drop awff afta' every john."

Nicki took me to a pizza place and introduced me to a few girls.

"She a good girl," Nicki said to the others, "she good."

I smiled as they nodded and made room for me. After a year of falling short in Crystal's crowd, I felt like these women accepted me without judgment. I felt lucky. I felt like I was finally good at something. I sprinkled parmesan cheese and crushed red pepper on my cheese slice, and I swung my leg. I felt like one of them. *I was born to be a prostitute,* I thought. This isn't an exaggeration; I actually thought these words. This is why it's difficult for me to identify with terms like "sex slave" and "modern day slavery." I saw Greg and Nicki as my *liberators* from the sexual slavery imposed on me by popular culture and by boys and men in my community. While I could hardly form this into words at age fourteen, I knew that everything about this new life just *felt* right.

If an anti-trafficking advocate had reached out to me on the street and used the words "trafficking" or "slavery," I would have turned up my nose. If someone offering street outreach showed me pictures of kids in chains, I would have told them they were talking to the wrong person. At this point, I didn't think I needed help; I thought Greg and Nicki had already rescued me. In fact, Nicki pointed out a group of undercover female officers patrolling the street, and I stayed away from them.

When Greg showed up outside of the pizza shop, we had to walk past him, as if we didn't know him, and pass him our cash. I did as Nicki said. I handed Greg my money, and he just kept walking. He didn't look at me or talk to me. I was glad to have all that money off of me, but then I had the sudden intuition that this meant it wasn't my money anymore. I wondered when, or *if,* I would get any of it back from him.

"JOHN" #5

Nicki and I returned to The Corner. A car pulled over and Nicki asked the driver if he wanted a date. She climbed in, and I watched as the car pulled away. Although still nervous about being on the street alone, I felt safe from other aggressive women so long as I stayed on Nicki's corner. A police car suddenly pulled the car over. Nicki nonchalantly stepped out of the car and stepped onto the sidewalk as if she had just stepped into the wrong car. She swung her purse and headed in the opposite direction of the police car; if I wasn't so horrified, I would have been in awe of her. Officers jumped from their cars and ran toward her.

I shrunk into the shadows as Nicki was handcuffed and escorted to the police car; the driver of the car was let go. Apparently this is a common scenario. In their report, *Demand. A Comparative Examination of Sex Tourism and Trafficking in Jamaica, Japan, the Netherlands, and the United States,* Shared Hope International writes:

> Statistically, it is clear that political and societal will and resources to bring the buyer and trafficker to justice is lacking. For example, in 2006, according to statistics collected in one county in Nevada, 153 minors were arrested for prostitution, but only two pimps were arrested in these cases. Furthermore, Congressional findings in the End Demand for Sex Trafficking Bill issued April 28, 2005, stated that 11 females used in commercial sex acts were arrested in Boston for every one arrest of a male purchaser; 9 females to every one male purchaser in Chicago; and 6 females to every one male purchaser in New York City.[3]

I was worried I would never see Nicki again, and I didn't know what to do. And then a car pulled up in front of me. A man waved at me to jump in. It was the same man from outside of Bally's—the one who had lipped, *Are you coming back?* I jumped into his car.

"Oh my God I found you," the man exclaimed, "I found you; I've been waiting all night."

"Let's go," I said.

He hit the accelerator, and I tried to see Nicki through the window of the police car.

"You are so beautiful," the man blabbered as he drove, "I've been waiting all night for you."

I worried this man might be a police officer; I was worried it might be some sort of a set up.

"What's your name?" the man asked.

"Natasha," I said.

He quickly calmed down.

"That's not your name," he said.

I stared in the rearview mirror at the blue lights now behind us.

"What's your real name?" the man pleaded, "I really wanna know your real name; I bet it's long, like sing-song long."

I thought of Crystal and me sitting on a curb in Mystic Islands singing TKA's song, "Maria." It was my favorite song. It was about a boy who loves a girl named Maria so much that he vows to take her away from the ghetto and away from her drug-dealing boyfriend. I so badly wanted a boyfriend who wanted to save me like that. The thought of Crystal and of Mystic Islands was weird; they both seemed like visions from a past life.

"You're right, it's Maria," I lied. "I'm out of condoms. Can you stop somewhere?"

This guy looked like any ordinary balding white guy in a crappy suit. He seemed too meek to be a cop, but I wanted to be sure. While he was in 7–11 buying rubbers, I rummaged through his glove compartment looking for evidence. I only found car manuals. He exited 7–11, and I slammed the glove box shut. He was wearing the same bashful smile as he got back in the car.

"Is your name really Maria?" he asked.

I stared back at him.

"I really want to know your real name," he said.

"OK, OK," I said, "it's Jennifer."

"*Jennifer,*" he whispered it, as if he had unlocked some secret door to my soul.

I wanted to say my name was Crystal, but I figured that wasn't sing-song long enough for him. He took me to The Lodge hotel. His room was dark. The blanket felt thin and hard. I was lying flat on my back with his face between my legs. I tried to get things over with when we first arrived, but he begged to please me instead. It was awkward. I didn't know what he wanted me to do. He kept saying that he wanted to make me feel good. But it *didn't* feel good to me; it didn't feel like anything at all. He said he would do it all night—that it *turned him on.*

"I charge by the hour," I said.

"I don't care," he said.

I moaned and moved my hips, pretending to feel something. When this didn't prompt him to finish, I just lay there, watching a dim light grow around the curtains. I told him I had to leave, but he pleaded to take me home with him.

"I'll take care of you," he begged.

Somehow I knew that if I went to this man's home, I might never see the light of day again. I met a guy like this once while hitchhiking to school. He was the same kind of man—older, Caucasian, and wearing a suit that said he had a boring job. That man had also asked to take me home with him; he said he wanted to "keep me safe."

"Naw," I had said to the man in the car, "I should go inside."

We sat in his cramped car outside my middle school.

"Yeah," he said, squeezing the steering wheel with white knuckles.

Both the man in the car and the man in the hotel room had the same look of reluctant self-restraint. Looking back, I'm pretty sure both of these men were casebook pedophiles, along with the first man who bought me and possibly the businessman with the bushy hair. My gut says the businessman started out with adult women, but developed a taste for teenage girls. I also suspect Nicki purposely took me to a corner that was known for juvenile prostitution.

People often ask me for my opinions about "john schools," which are diversion programs for those caught buying sex (similar, say, to "driving schools" for those caught driving under the influence). "John schools" aim to educate buyers about sexually transmitted diseases and the violence and coercion involved with sex trafficking and commercial sexual exploitation of children (CSEC). Pedophiles cannot be diverted with "john schools;" pedophiles are psychologically coded to prey on children. My thoughts are that two out of five of the men who bought me that night *might* have had a different perspective on illegal commercial sex if they had gone to an effective "john school." However, there were other men interested in having sex with me as a child even before that night.

As I have mentioned, I started hitchhiking in middle school. It happened on an impulse as I walked to the bus stop one winter morning. I slipped behind some pine trees and waited until the school bus came and went, and then I sprinted toward the highway, crossing over Route 539 just past the Garden State Parkway exit ramp. I turned around, and the oncoming traffic roared past me. A Mack truck barreled down the hill and gritted its bare teeth at me. I sucked in car exhaust and tar fumes and stuck out my right thumb.

This was how I spent many school mornings: walking backward on the highway, wind in my face, jean jacket unbuttoned, left thumb hooked in the pocket of my ripped jeans, and right thumb in the air. *This* is the sight of a child in distress. While many bypassers may have seen me as a hoodlum or even a homeless person, others saw me as *interesting.* Pickup drivers, good ol' boys, and businessmen alike pulled over for me *every single morning.* They threw open their passenger doors, eager to get a closer look at me. I turned and ran toward each one, kicking gravel and dust up behind my size-five sneakers. I knew it was dangerous, but I also knew it was the only thing that enabled me to walk through the front doors of my middle school each morning.

"Where ya' headed?" I'd hear.

"To Frog Pond Road," I'd say, "not far."

I would sit in the passenger seat and eye the contents of the car around me; I knew each of the drivers was also watching me. I figured some of them picked me up for one reason only; they hoped something, anything, would derail the car into a cabin in the woods where we could "get to know each other better." It was during these rides that I first developed my indifference and disgust toward "johns," although I knew them then only as men who, if chance allowed, wanted to have sex with a teen girl. Why did I hitchhike? I liked colliding against other people's worlds, and I liked the danger of it. Sometimes I'd wonder what it would be like to pick a different final destination, like New York City.

My point? I worry the issue runs much deeper than any "john school" can fix. There are men and older boys looking to sexually exploit women and girls in every city and suburb across America. There needs to be a diversion program that begins in high school, middle school, even elementary school. It begins with media literacy. Kids must be raised with the understanding that images of objectified and exploited women and girls create a climate that supports violence against women and children. We cannot stop advertisers and artists from creating these images; it's their right to freedom of speech. However, we can refuse to purchase their products; and we can educate our youth about the power of images and their effects on society.

8

CONTROL AND VIOLENCE

JULY 2, 1992

The man in the hotel room paid me $400 and finally let me leave. The morning light was gray and foggy, and I stuck out on Pacific Avenue with my white legs and red dress. I did not belong there, and yet it had been only a few hours since I had. The last time I saw Nicki she was in a police car, so I used a payphone to call Greg. When we connected, he was angry and demanded to know where I had been.

"You said to work 'til six," I said.

He hung up the phone. I did not understand Greg; I wanted Nicki. When he showed up in a cab, Greg made me squat on the floor.

"Get down!" he yelled and shoved my head down with his huge hand. I watched him frantically look around, and I understood he was worried about the police. Once we got back to the room and he saw how much money I had, though, he was nicer.

"You did real good," he said.

Traffickers will oscillate between praise and anger, or love and violence; it is a tactic that can leave a victim craving the positive attention. A violent trafficker will cause his victims to live in a constant state of fear. I have read news reports and heard survivors' testimonies detailing beatings, whippings, and even waterboarding by traffickers. Although Greg intimidated me, he did not beat me. There was no reason for him to abuse me in this way; I was easily influenced and compliant at age fourteen. I believe minors who are trafficked over longer periods of time are more in danger of experiencing violence from a trafficker.

Greg's praise made me feel better. I had made $800 that first night, and I felt proud; that amount of money seemed like thousands of dollars to me. But it wasn't just the money, it was the sense of approval and belonging, and really feeling like I was good at something. In school, I didn't seem to fit in anywhere; I had no talents or sports abilities. I couldn't wait to see Hollywood and New Orleans, like Greg had promised over the phone. Nicki had to see a judge and pay a fine for getting arrested the night before. I was relieved to know she would be coming back. *It's just business,* I thought, *it's all just business.* Greg gave me a shirt to wear, and I slept on the pull-out couch. It was only a few hours later when I felt a heavy weight on the cot. I opened my eyes, and the sun glared behind the curtains. Greg leaned over me.

"I gotta test my goods," he said.

"Huh?" I said.

Greg slid his hand up my leg, and I grabbed at the shirt I was wearing. I did not want to have sex with Greg. Having sex with "johns" was easy because it felt like nothing; I was almost absent in the act. I became a different person; I was Vivian from *Pretty Woman,* or I was Stacy Combas. Having sex with someone I knew or liked was different, though. It was awkward; and with too many feelings invested, I always felt bad afterward. I hated it. It reminded me of the "bad feelings" from childhood.

I *liked* Greg. I didn't want to start hating the person who helped me. But it didn't seem to matter to Greg that I didn't want to have sex; he said I had to do it sooner or later. In the Guns N' Roses' album *Appetite for Destruction,* the album insert depicted the controversial drawing of a woman who had obviously just been raped. The culprit appeared to be a bony robot that had clamps for hands and binoculars for eyes. In the air leapt another robot attempting to defend her. The other robot spewed sweat in the shape of skulls and crossbones.

It was undoubtedly a disturbing picture, but what was so compelling about the image was the seductive quality of the raped woman. There she lay on the sidewalk with disheveled blond hair and a saddle shoe missing from her left foot. Her white panties were wrapped around her knees, her neck was arched back, and her shirt was ripped open to expose a breast and one dark brown pointed nipple. As a viewer, you don't know whether you should root for the heavy metal hero in the sky to save her; or if you should push aside the binocular robot to finish pulling off the girl's panties. Although I never actually use the word "panties," it is the only fitting word to describe the undergarments in this picture.

This was the image I thought about with Greg over me. Even though it was painful, and even though I begged Greg to stop; I didn't *judge* Greg for having sex with me against my will. I figured he couldn't help it. I figured all guys couldn't help it, just as I couldn't help leering over that drawing in my bedroom. Greg said he was going to break me in slowly, and I thought that was his way of being nice.

Greg was gone when I woke up. I fumbled with the knobs of the shower, and I scrubbed. I scrubbed my skin and my sorry-ass hair. I understood two things in this moment: (1) I understood that I was *not* in control of what was happening to me after all, and (2) I believed that I had brought all of this on myself. Because I had chosen to run away with this man, I believed that I deserved what was happening to me. Did I cry? Crying would imply the presence of an emotion, of which I had none. I had only skin and teeth and bones.

"HEY, BABY!" NICKI SAID WHEN SHE RETURNED FROM court.

I was relieved to see her. She flipped the television on and turned to MTV. The female singers of En Vogue appeared on a stage wearing long red dresses and black gloves.

"These are my girls!" Nicki said and turned up the volume. She sang the lyrics to their song, "Giving Him Something He Can Feel." She swung her hips and shimmied as she moved around the room picking up her clothes. I lay on the bed with my head in my hand, and I watched her. Nicki was young and sexy and tough and real. I imagined her growing up and working the streets in New York City as a teenager. She was beautiful. With Greg gone, I fell under Nicki's spell. I even began talking like her, mimicking her accent. Later that day, Nicki took me to the mall to get new shoes; I wanted tall black suede boots like Crystal had in seventh grade. Nicki talked as we walked through the Pier Mall.

"How old are you?" she asked me.

"Seventeen," I lied.

"Yeah?" she said.

"No," I said, "I'm fifteen."

She raised her eyebrows as if to question me.

"I'm fourteen," I said.

She laughed. "I thawt so," she said. "That's OK, but don't tell anyone else."

I was glad she didn't mind my age.

"Did you have sex wit' Greg?" she asked.

The question stopped me. *What if she loved him?* I thought. *Should I say I didn't want to, that I asked him to stop?* She turned back to look at me, and I nodded.

"He's big ain't he?" she said.

"Yeah," I blurted, "it hurt."

"I know," she said, "but that's the only time I really like it; I like it when it hurts."

"You do?" I said. "I don't like it at all."

She was so easy to talk to.

"Nicki," I said, "some guy asked me to do something really weird last night."

"Oh yeah," she said, "dat happens."

"What's the weirdest thing you ever had to do?" I asked.

"Some guy made me wear a cheerleading outfit," she laughed, "pawm-pawms and all."

I laughed.

"Another guy made me pee on his stomach," she said.

I followed behind Nicki as she browsed through the mall. She wanted to buy Greg an outfit and was looking at different nylon jumpsuits. This struck me as really odd that a woman would buy an outfit for a man. Buying a tie or something was one thing, but a whole outfit seemed strange. I asked her about the money I had made. She explained that Greg kept all the money and that anytime we needed something we just had to ask. I didn't say anything, but somehow I knew I was getting cheated. I wondered why Nicki would want to buy anything at all for Greg.

We walked down to the boardwalk and leaned against the rail together. I knew Ripley's Believe it or Not was somewhere on the boardwalk, and I wanted to ask Nicki if we could go. But I didn't want her to think I was immature, so I leaned back on the rail of the boardwalk like she was doing. I felt a very strong bond with Nicki. Even after only hours of knowing her, I didn't want to leave her. "Trauma bonds" are often formed in sex trafficking; perhaps that's what I was feeling.

I listened to the ocean waves crashing behind us. It was broad daylight, and the boardwalk was full of families and vendors with hot dogs and cotton candy. I felt like we didn't belong there; we belonged on the street at night after the families went home. Nicki and I went back to the motel room and took our time getting ready. It was still early when we returned to the strip in a cab, so Nicki took me to a corner bar. We sat at a booth with some other girls who were drinking beer. I waited to be carded, but the beer glasses were slapped down in front of us without hesitation. I wiped foam from my lips and listened to the girls as they talked.

In seventh grade, I befriended a Latina girl named Luz. She took me to Vineland, New Jersey, where I met her friends and extended family. I was enamored by their culture. Her family's neighbors played music through open windows with fans blowing shreds of curtains; and the girls wore giant gold necklaces with the lettering of boys' names. As much as I loved being in this environment, I was also intimidated. The older boys hollered as we walked by and the girls sneered at me when Luz wasn't looking. I never went back again; I knew I couldn't stand up for myself to any of them if Luz wasn't there.

But Nicki was looking out for me on the street. If she said I was good, then I was good. The women accepted this. I could tell there were rules on the street. Even though I wasn't aware of what all these rules meant; I liked knowing there were rules in place. The one rule that I didn't like, though, was that I had to be available sexually to Greg. And, I worried about being alone with him again.

NICKI "TURNED A TRICK" BEFORE ME THAT NIGHT SO I stood alone waiting by the fountain. A man walked up and stood beside me, eyeing me.

"What's your name?" he asked.

"You wanna date?" I asked.

"I'm a detective," he said.

I turned away.

"I'm not gonna arrest you," he said, "I just wanna warn you we've had a guy killing prostitutes."

I turned back, wide-eyed.

"He's white and his head is shaved," the detective said, "And he has a spider web tattoo on the side of his head."

He handed me his card and said, "Call me if you see anything."

Women and girls exploited through commercial sex often face violence not just from traffickers but also from other girls and from "johns." Jes Richardson, CEO of One Dream Movement, was brutally raped, beaten, and held by three men for multiple days: "I didn't see it coming. The room was dark as he stepped in behind me, the moment the door closed two other tricks jumped out and started beating me. I didn't stand a chance."[1] Barbara Amaya, author of the graphic novel, *The Destiny of Zoe Carpenter,* also describes violence from buyers: "I've been shot, I've been stabbed; I have cuts; I have wounds," says Barbara in a *Fox 5 News* interview, "I have battle scars from top to bottom of my whole body. . . . I just think it's a miracle that I'm alive."[2]

Survivors of commercial sexual exploitation have described to me scenes in which "johns" pulled knives on them and raped them; "johns" who threw them from moving cars; "johns" who robbed them; and "johns" who beat them and left them for dead. I have heard people blame these girls and women for these acts of violence, but this only perpetuates the abuse. Blaming these girls and women only reinforces the very reasons why many victims of sex trafficking do not seek help. Girls and women in "the life" know they will likely be judged, and they will likely be condemned.

In a closing ceremony for the 2012 Department of Justice's Trafficking in Persons Symposium in Salt Lake City, Utah, Keisha Head described an experience in which she sought help from police after having been raped by a "john." "I remember . . . the police officer . . . pulled over and arrested me," Keisha stated. "I told him I've just been raped, and he laughed at me and [said] . . . *you weren't raped, you're a prostitute.*"[3]

"JOHN" #6

My first date of the night was with a nervous college-type guy. He got a room at the Martini Martinique Hotel. Once inside, he obviously didn't know what to do next.

"Is this your first time doing this," I asked, "I mean in A.C. like this?"

"Yeah," he said.

I felt experienced and mature as I went over my prices with him. When I went to work, he was stiff and awkward underneath me. He reminded me of the eighteen-year-old with whom I had traded sex for a ride to the mall the day before. That guy's name was Jordan, and he worked at a restaurant in the Shore mall. I knew his shift started about the time I needed to be at the mall, so I called him and asked for a ride. He agreed and picked me up. Before going to the mall, he took me back to his house. He led me into his room and sat on the bed. I thought I understood what this meant; I thought he was implying that he wanted something in return for driving me to the mall.

Reluctantly, I climbed on top of him and pulled off my shirt. Jordan was a high school senior, but he wasn't as *cool* as the guys who drove Monte Carlos. He drove a rusty car, and he worked as a dishwasher. Despite these drawbacks, Jordan was a senior and had a car, so I assumed he was experienced at sex. And so I also pretended to be really experienced and sexy. I oohed and aahed, stroking my sides like I'd seen in music videos. I was quite in my own world of acting when he jerked forward and squeezed me. The closeness made me uncomfortable, and I pushed away from him.

"Wait," he said, "I just lost eighteen years of my life."

I thought about this now with the college guy underneath me. I wondered to myself, if Jordan was a virgin, then he couldn't have *expected* to have sex with me. He could have obviously *hoped* for it; but without any experience, why would he *expect* that from me. And if that was the case, why did I feel so obligated? I didn't want to have sex with him. He had acne on his back and his dog farted on the floor. Yet, I thought I *had* to. This was my very first glimpse of the concept of personal rights and boundaries; unfortunately, it was fleeting and confusing.

"Are you enjoying this?" asked the college guy underneath me.

I was immediately pulled from my thoughts.

"Huh?" I said.

"Does this feel good to you?" he asked.

"It never feels good to me," I said.

"Never?"

"No."

"I think it would feel better," he said, "if it felt good to you."

I put on an act, and he finished quickly. *Another job well done,* I thought. I returned to the strip and stood waiting for Nicki against the fountain wall. A car pulled up next to me and I could hear guys inside laughing over music. I kept my face turned away from the car. I never looked inside any of the passing cars in fear of someone recognizing me. The following day we were going to New York City, and I thought I might feel relieved to get away from South Jersey.

"If you're gonna be a hooker," a boy hissed from inside the car, "then get a tan."

Passersby often made fun of girls on the street. One time a carload of girls drove by in a convertible, and one of the girls stood up and screamed, "Hookers!" She screamed it like she hated us. I left the corner to look for Nicki and found her walking with an enormous black woman in skin-tight pants. The woman strolled right into traffic shaking her huge chest in the windows of single men.

"C'mon honey," she yelled, "you wanna date?"

The woman ran alongside the cars and the rolls on her stomach jiggled as she whooped and cackled. Nicki egged her on shouting, "Go on, girl!" and "Look out now!" I preferred the company of these women over the pretty girls in the convertible. I wished I had tomatoes to launch back at the hecklers who drove past us. The large woman pulled a roll of toilet paper out of her purse.

"I'll be right back," she said and headed down an alley.

A rundown sporty car pulled up to the corner, and Nicki took long strides toward it. She swung her hips and leaned into the passenger window. A moment later she was inside and driving away. This scene is broken into pieces of memories now. I remember the large woman running from the alley, and I remember a police car. The sporty car pulled over, and Nicki casually stepped out. Then, there were police all around her, and she was yelling *I was just giving him directions.* And then I remember standing very still, waiting. I think I *wanted* to be spotted. I watched an officer turn and look my way; and then I saw his resolve. He headed toward me.

"How old are you?" he asked as he got closer.

"Eighteen," I said.

He narrowed his eyes at me.

"When's yer birthday?" he said.

I thought back to Greg's instructions from the day before.

"June nineteenth," I hesitated, "nineteen seventy . . . three?"

Math wasn't my best subject, especially under pressure. Plus, I wasn't convinced I wanted to lie, but I knew Nicki was watching; and I was pretty sure Greg was watching, too. Somehow I always sensed his presence around us.

"Don't you lie to me," he said.

I panicked and screamed, "Wutch you messin' wit' me fo'?"

I waved my arms around like Nicki had told me.

"All dees bitches out here and you gotta' fuck wit' me," I shouted, "Fuck this sheet, go fuck with some udda' ho."

The cop looked me up and down, snorted, and walked away. I was stunned. I got away with it. *I did it,* I thought, *I really will be able to go to California and Las Vegas. I really can have a new life.* And then I thought about Greg and being alone with him again.

"Wait," I yelled.

The officer turned around, but I wasn't sure what to say.

"What would happen if I *was* under eighteen?" I asked.

This was a sincere question. What I meant by this was *What are my options? Do I have any options? Is there anywhere else for me to go?* I knew I didn't want to be alone with Greg again, but I also knew that I didn't want to go home.

"That's it," the officer yelled, "I don't have time for this shit."

I was handcuffed and placed inside a police car heading to the Atlantic City police station. The officer shouted words like *hooker* and *whore,* and I knew I had a made a big mistake. I was so angry, but I was mostly angry with myself. I stared out the window and piled the full blame of my circumstances onto my own head. This was how I was "rescued" from the streets.

9

TRAFFICKERS AND THE RULES OF TRAFFICKING

WHEN IT COMES TO THE TRAFFICKING OF CHILDREN for commercial sex in America, the only rule is that there are no rules. A trafficker can be anyone: a family member, a friend, a boyfriend or girlfriend, a stranger, an acquaintance, a known criminal or upstanding citizen, a U.S. citizen or foreign national, a male or female, an adult or minor, an extended family member or a member of one's community, and even someone who is trusted to work with and protect children. And, there are a myriad of ways in which children can be obtained and trafficked for sex.

Some children may be kidnapped, drugged, and/or threatened in any number of ways; while others may be lured via romance, friendship, addiction, glamorization, obligation, or lack of other options. Children can be sold in homes, on the street, in cars, via online ads, at truck stops, in strip clubs and other licensed commercial sex clubs or bars, in restaurants, and any other establishment. Child sex trafficking requires only an individual looking to sexually exploit a child for commercial gain.

PIMP-CONTROLLED CHILD SEX TRAFFICKING

In general, there are two types of pimp traffickers often discussed in this field: Romeo (a.k.a. finesse) pimps and gorilla pimps. Romeo pimps will lure and/or control their victims with romance or other romantic ideations. Gorilla pimps, on the other hand, will use intimidation and violence as a means to obtain and/ or control victims. A period during which a pimp is building a relationship or trust with a victim is called "grooming;" this can look like courting or a gradual exposure to commercial sex. The same process applies with pedophiles. Pedophiles will often gain a child's trust with gifts and friendship, and then they will chip away at the child's boundaries through various means (e.g., tickling, sharing sexually graphic material). Likewise, a trafficker will spend days, weeks, even months developing a relationship with a child and chipping away at his or her boundaries. The man who gained my trust over the phone spent two weeks talking with me before honing in on my obsession with music and fame; only then did he encourage the idea of running away with him to Hollywood.

Pimp traffickers may try to create an atmosphere of family and belonging, especially if they target victims who come from broken or troubled homes. Pimp traffickers will often require their victims to call them "daddy," and many will require each victim to refer to each other as "wife-in-law," "wifey," "family," or "folks." Some survivors have described sit-down dinners with traffickers and their "folks" in private homes or apartments; for some victims, this family atmosphere is difficult to leave. "It became the family I never had," says Alissa (an anonymous survivor using a pseudonym) in a 2012 interview with *Marie Claire,* "until I realized how violent pimps could be."[1]

As described earlier, traffickers will often break their victims down into a state of submission. This may involve drugging, beating, raping, or other forms of degradation. Alissa indicated a moment when her trafficker suddenly became violent. The author of the article described the scene: "One night, her [trafficker], suspicious that she was trying to leave him, choked, punched, and hit her on her stomach and the back of her neck—places that wouldn't be visible to customers. On another occasion he carved her face with a potato peeler."[2]

Another means of control for pimp traffickers is to father children with their victims, thereby literally forming a familial bond with them. Traffickers will sometimes leave these babies to live with a family member in order to gain even more control over their victims. Traffickers may also pit girls against one another, using psychologically manipulative tactics. The relationship between a trafficker and a victim can resemble intimate partner violence/ domestic violence.

Pimps and other traffickers will also project blame and responsibility onto victims. "The pimp and the customer [both] convince the victim of prostitution it is her/his decision to prostitute and that the pimp or customer is only a facilitator of the act," says Dr. Lois Lee of Children of the Night. "The pimp does this to avoid prosecution—if the victim blames [him- or her]self then the victim is unlikely to aid the police; the customer does it to eliminate guilt."[3]

Pimp traffickers will also often appoint one girl as his "bottom." A bottom is often described as the woman/girl who has been with the trafficker the longest, and she is the one most trusted by the trafficker. The bottom often instructs new girls, collects money, and handles other transactions and duties within the business. Traffickers will often set nightly quotas for victims; a common quota is $500 to $1,000. Victims are often terrorized in a number of ways if they fail to meet their quotas.

In July 2012, the Los Angeles Police Department (LAPD) reported the arrest of a gorilla pimp named James Grady III. Grady allegedly recruited a fifteen-year-old girl and then forced her into prostitution for four months. The following excerpt describes the violence this pimp used as a means to control and terrorize the victim into compliance:

> During the four months that 27-year-old Grady forced her to work for him as a prostitute, he continually degraded her and forced her to perform sexual acts upon him. On two separate occasions, Grady intensified the violence on the victim. Both incidents stemmed from Grady setting financial quotas the female minor was to earn for him daily. When the young female did not meet her "quota," Grady forced her to take off all of her clothing and enter the shower with the water running. He then brandished an electrical taser and held it to her skin. Grady cycled the Taser several times and told her that if she did not earn her "quota," the next time he would electrocute her in the shower. The second incident involved Grady forcing a rifle underneath the young woman's chin and telling her that if she did not earn her "quota," he would kill her and her family.[4]

Another method used by traffickers to control their victims is "branding." Traffickers will often tattoo their names or somehow mark a symbol signifying ownership over the victim. I have seen pictures of branding on girls' chests, backs, legs, necks, and even inside the inner lip of one girl who said she was first trafficked in San Diego at age sixteen.[5] An extreme case of this was reported by CBS Miami in March 2013. A thirteen-year-old runaway was trafficked via online advertisements with Backpage.com. After the girl threatened to leave, the trafficker allegedly forced the girl to a tattoo shop where he had his street name tattooed on her eyelids. He and a woman were both charged with human trafficking, false imprisonment, lewd and lascivious exhibition, and delivery of a controlled substance to a child.[6]

Polaris Project offers the following "sample glossary of terms" in their guide, "Domestic Sex Trafficking: The Criminal Operations of the American Pimp." Law enforcement should be familiar with these terms in order to identify potential situations of trafficking. It is also necessary to understand this culture in order to communicate with potential victims; however, keep in mind that not all pimp traffickers insist on using the following language. Also, I recommend using this language only when necessary; use of this language might only reinforce the reality of this world created by traffickers.

- "Daddy"—another term for "pimp," evoking images of fatherhood.
- "Bottom" or "Bottom Bitch"—the woman who's been with the pimp the longest and often takes on a mid-level controlling role to keep other victims in line.
- "Dates," "Johns," and "Tricks"—terms used to describe buyers of commercial sex.
- "Square"—a term used that describes trying to go straight and get out of the life, or that describes law enforcement and those that don't understand "the game."
- "The life" is a term used to describe a life in prostitution/trafficking.
- The "Stroll," "Track," or "Blade"—the common area or cross-streets where street prostitution is known to occur on a nightly basis. A "kiddie track" is known for the sale of minors.
- "Pimp circle"—the process of multiple pimps swarming and surrounding one woman or girl . . . for the purposes of humiliation and intimidation.
- "Wife in Law"—each individual in a group of women or girls that are [controlled by] the same pimp. "Family" and "folks" also are synonyms. [By using terms like "wife in law" or "wifey"; pimp and gang traffickers often intentionally create a sense of family, especially for those recruiting victims from broken homes.]
- "Stable"—refers to the group of women and girls under a pimp's control (i.e., a pimp's stable).

- "Out of Pocket"—a term used to describe when a woman or girl breaks "the rules" [created by the pimp trafficker].[7]

Pimp-controlled sex trafficking is often (but not always) structured around a set of rules. These rules may apply to other forms of trafficking as well, especially if the traffickers self-identify as pimps. Polaris Project offers the following examples of formal rules that are sometimes imposed on victims by pimp traffickers, especially in street-based sex trafficking:

- Women and girls under a pimp's control must never know his real name or identity and refer to him exclusively as "daddy."
- A woman or girl may not ever make eye contact with another pimp. If this rule is broken, the woman or girl suffers serious physical violence.
- As indicated by the term "Pimps Up, Ho's Down," women and girls must always exist in "lower" ways than the pimp, including by standing only on the street during street prostitution. A woman or girl who ventures onto the sidewalk is severely reprimanded or forced into what is known as a "pimp circle."
- Pimps set nightly monetary quotas that the women or girls must reach through providing commercial sex or theft.[8]

There are many other rules, terms, and tactics in pimp-controlled sex trafficking; however, as indicated earlier, these rules are not universal. For example, some pimp traffickers intentionally pit victims against one another as a means to prevent alliances, while others will reprimand victims for conflicting with each other. In his book, *Pimpology: The 48 Laws of the Game,* author Pimpin' Ken explains the differences in tactics from pimp to pimp: "In the game we're all competing for the same spot. No one wants to share their secrets or their game, because they don't want to give another player an advantage. The less your opponent knows, the better."[9]

In "From Victims to Victimizers: Interviews with 25 Ex-Pimps in Chicago," Jody Raphael and Brenda Myers-Powell explore the backgrounds of pimp traffickers and identify several predisposing factors. The authors report that an "overwhelming majority" claim early childhood physical and sexual abuse influenced their eventual involvement with trafficking, while 60 percent report pimping or prostitution as a "family business." Of those interviewed,

68 percent report involvement in commercial sex before switching to pimping, while others report a gradual association with managing women or girls. Some say they were coerced via gang involvement, and others report pimping as a means to survival. Others explained that it gave them a sense of "power and control"; the report points out that this was especially true for those from abusive homes.[10]

FAMILY-CONTROLLED CHILD SEX TRAFFICKING

Minh Dang, former Executive Director of Don't Sell Bodies, offers the following dynamics of family-controlled sex trafficking based on her own victimization and similar testimonies:

1. *Incest is a major component.* Trafficking is an extension to the overall environment of childhood sexual abuse. Incest will often happen within extended families as well, so that extended families are trading children. You could call this a pedophile ring. [Parental traffickers may also sell children to non-related pedophiles within local pedophile rings as a way to gain sexual access to other children or to fuel an addiction (e.g., drugs, alcohol, gambling).] The trading can start as "favors" for fixing a car, obtaining drugs, etc.; and then it can become monetary. "I have heard few stories like mine in which families sell their children to brothels," Minh says. "Many are doing more 'individual trading.' What is VERY important to acknowledge is that mothers are often part of this abuse both actively and indirectly. They are often complicit with their husbands doing this and many are also sexually abusing their child(ren)."
2. *Children are vulnerable due to dependency.* Many children who are trafficked for sex are targeted due to their situations of vulnerability; however, children who are trafficked by family members are literally born into a state of vulnerability. They are fundamentally dependent on their parents and other family both physically and emotionally. Because of their very nature, children will follow their parents' instruction and desire their parents' love and affection. "By the time children realize they are being abused," Minh says, "they may be torn between the bad guys 'out there' and the bad guys at home. Also by

nature, children will try to justify and idealize their parents as the 'good guys.'"

3. *Victims may feel shameful and obligated to secrecy.* In their need to see their parents as good and loving, children may feel forced into secrecy, silence, and shame. "They may want to 'save face,'" Minh says. "Although this is traditionally discussed in Asian families, I believe all children want to protect their families from being seen as bad."
4. *Victims may be physically or emotionally isolated.* "Isolation can happen in different ways," Minh says. "My family lived 45 minutes away from my school, and they restricted me from leaving or developing attachments with other adults. They kept me very busy, which prevented me from developing friendships with others." Sexually abused children may not only feel compelled to secrecy; but they may be taught to distrust teachers and other adults. They may also be held out of school or forced to work in a family business. "I worked at my mom's nail salon," Minh writes, "which seemed socially acceptable."[11]

As far as prevention, Minh recommends therapy and parenting education for adults. "[Parents must] heal their own trauma so they don't pass it down," she says.[12]

As discussed in chapter 1, another common scenario of family-controlled sex trafficking involves parents selling their children for drugs or to pay off drug debts. A tragic and infamous case of family-controlled child sex trafficking began in 2009 when five-year-old Shaniya Davis was reported missing in North Carolina; her body was found days later. CBS News reported that Shaniya's mother, Antoinette Davis, was accused of selling her daughter to pay off a drug debt; she was charged with felony sexual servitude and human trafficking, among a slew of other charges. In May 2013, CBS also reported that Mario Andrette McNeill, 33, was convicted of first-degree murder, first-degree kidnapping, sexual offense of a child, indecent liberties with a child, human trafficking, and sexual servitude in connection with Shaniya's death.[13]

Procuring drugs or settlement of drug debts is not always the motive for family-controlled sex trafficking, however. ABC News reported in May 2011 that a Utah mother, Felicia McClure, allegedly attempted "to sell her 13-year-old daughter's virginity for $10,000." She was charged with "multiple counts of sexual abuse of a minor and sexual exploitation of a minor."[14] In March 2013, NBC News reported that an Indiana mother, Natasha Hillard, 24, was "charged in a federal indictment with selling her 1 ½-year-old daughter to a man . . . for child pornography." Christopher M. Bour, 39, of Indiana was the alleged buyer; he was reportedly "charged with production of child pornography, purchasing a child for production of child pornography and possession of child pornography."[15] A June 2013 CBS Chicago article reported additional charges against Hillard as a second child, between the ages of three and five years, was discovered to also have been sold to Bour.[16] Family-controlled child sex trafficking cases can include relatives other than parents, including a child's grandmother or grandfather, aunt or uncle, brother or sister, cousin, or any other family member or legal guardian.[17]

GANG-CONTROLLED CHILD SEX TRAFFICKING

A 2012 Intelligence Report "assesses with medium confidence that gang activity is expanding towards juvenile prostitution primarily for its steady financial rewards and perceived low risk of law enforcement interaction."[18] San Diego Deputy District Attorney Gretchen Dahlinger Means explains this trend in a 2012 interview with *America's Most Wanted:* gang members are moving away from selling guns and drugs because a gun and a bag of drugs can be sold only once; a girl, on the other hand, can be sold over and over again.[19]

Gang and pimp traffickers will often use similar recruitment methods. The 2012 Intelligence Report states that "[g]ang members and associates recruit and exploit juveniles at detention centers, public housing units, shopping malls, schools, flea markets, sporting events, and through telephone chat lines."[20] The report also confirms use of the Internet "to recruit, advertise and exploit victims. . . ."[21] These websites were specifically mentioned: MyRedBook.com, BackPage.com, PoshListings.com, MyProviderGuide.com, MyPreviews.com, CheatingBoards.com, and CityVibe.com.[22] Use of online advertising allows for child sex trafficking activity to occur within any community as children may be kept off the streets and held in hotel rooms. The following passage exemplifies how varied gang recruitment techniques may be:

> August 2011 FBI reporting indicates that gangs such as the Bloods, the Crips, the Latin Kings, and MS-13 control prostitution operations in different areas of New York City, and employ various operational tactics to recruit victims. Gangs recruiting members within their neighborhood, typically favor the

> "snatch and grab" technique. ["Snatch and grab" is described as "a recruitment technique where pimps kidnap victims of prostitution whom are already working 'the track,' have been groomed, and taught 'the game.'"] Whereas, Crips gang members recruit victims outside their neighborhood and use traditional grooming techniques.[23]

Tina Frundt, Founder of Courtney's House in Washington, D.C., has described scenarios in which gang members from northern Virginia invited school girls to "skip parties" (i.e., house parties held during school hours).[24] In the 2010 study "From Victims to Victimizers," the authors report that "[o]ne pimp said he gave parties, got young girls high on liquor and marijuana, and the girls never knew the guys at the party had paid for the pleasure of being there and having sex with them."[25]

While pimp traffickers often discourage drug use among victims, gang traffickers may encourage or even force drug use. Gangs have a greater access to drugs, and drug addiction may be used as a means of control. In a 2012 interview, San Diego Deputy District Attorney Gretchen Dahlinger Means explained how the dynamics of gang-controlled sex trafficking can have terroristic effects on victims.[26] Gang traffickers work in collaboration, she explained, so a victim is not just "owned" by a single pimp but an entire gang. "In some jurisdictions, criminal street gangs are over 400 members strong," Means says. Take the many manipulative and coercive methods used by pimps and "multiply that by 400," then add "all the layers of intimidation and violence that is inherent in a criminal street gang," and you have a snapshot of gang-controlled sex trafficking.[27]

Gang members will also employ female members to entice victims and conduct business. In August 2012, the *Los Angeles Times* reported a case of gang-controlled child sex trafficking in which high school teens were lured in with promises for "quick money to get their hair and nails done, [to] buy a house, [and] even [to] get their kids back from foster care."[28] A female recruiter for the Rolling 60s Crips gang told the girls, "us[e] what you got to get what you want."[29] The 2012 Intelligence Report says that "[a]s part of efforts by the [gang trafficker] to remove himself from direct prostitution operations and shift culpability away from himself, juvenile victims—some of them female gang members and associates—may be forced to advertise for the business, solicit customers, schedule appointments, and collect money for the gang."[30]

In *The Sexual Exploitation of Girls in Gangs*, former San Diego Deputy District Attorney Keith Burt explains that victims of gang-controlled sex trafficking often work on a part-time basis, and are sold through online advertisements or forced or compelled to walk the tracks at night or on the weekends.[31] In a 2012 press release, the U.S. Attorney's Office in the Eastern District of Virginia detailed an example of gang-controlled child sex trafficking. Rances Ulices Amaya, 23, aka "Murder" and "Blue," was convicted of conspiring to commit sex trafficking of a child and three counts of sex trafficking three girls. The following is an excerpt from that report:

> In 2009, Amaya joined forces with an MS-13 associate who was already prostituting underage girls. Amaya used the violent reputation of MS-13 to ensure that sex customers paid for the sex and did not lure the underage victims away. He also used his MS-13 contacts to find sex customers and would offer free sex with the victims and a cut of the profits for any gang member who provided customers or underage girls. Amaya and his co-conspirator sought out illegal aliens as customers because they believed illegal aliens were unlikely to call the police. Amaya would hand out his telephone number at construction sites and convenience stores frequented by day laborers from Latin America. . . .
>
> At night, after the paying customers were finished, Amaya would invite his fellow MS-13 members to have sex with the girls. Sometimes, to punish victims, the gang would "run a train" on a victim, which meant that multiple gang members would have sex with the victim in rapid succession. The jury heard that the defendant and other gang members raped the victims both for their enjoyment and to "groom" them for the sex trafficking scheme.
>
> Besides raping them, to keep the victims compliant, Amaya would provide them with cigarettes, alcohol, marijuana, and other drugs. The evidence showed that Amaya prostituted five victims who were between the ages of 14 and 17 years old. The jury heard that using underage girls had two advantages: customers preferred young girls and Amaya found them easier to manipulate and control. In addition, there was always an implicit threat of violence insofar as the victims knew that Amaya was MS-13 and he frequently carried a machete with him, MS-13's weapon of choice. . . .[32]

ORGANIZED CRIME–CONTROLLED CHILD SEX TRAFFICKING

The dynamics of organized crime–controlled sex trafficking are probably what most Americans associate with the term "sex trafficking" in America. The

National Human Trafficking Resource Center (NHTRC), a program offered by Polaris Project, created several webinars on topics related to human trafficking within the United States. "Working with Foreign National Child Victims of Trafficking" explains some of the dynamics associated with organized crime–controlled trafficking, including Latino residential brothels and Asian massage parlors.

The victims in Latino residential brothels are often Latina women and minors, while the victimizers are often Latino men and women. Victims are said to be recruited via false job promises, smuggling, boyfriends, and family members. The clientele typically consists of Latino males and the victims are trafficked in residential areas, rural trailers, and apartments. Other fronts include cantina bars and escort agencies. Advertising is typically via word of mouth and business cards. "Latino residential brothels frequently victimize undocumented Latina women and girls," says the narrator of the webinar. "It is not uncommon for a woman or child in this network to have sex with 25 clients per day."[33]

The victims in Asian massage parlors are primarily Asian women, and sometimes children, who are controlled by male and female Asian adults. Victims are said to be most often recruited via false job promises, promises of a better life, and smuggling. The clientele can consist of anyone, and locations of sex trafficking include legitimate businesses and storefronts, including health spas, nail salons, and massage parlors. "Victims are commonly moved every few weeks to various massage parlors," says the narrator of the webinar. " . . . [T]hey are confined and coerced into providing commercial sex seven days per week." Services are advertised via online and print advertising, and the victims are controlled via confinement, expanding debts, and other means. "Women in the massage parlors are coerced into providing commercial sex through a complex system of fees, debt bondage, shame, manipulation, threats, and isolation," says the narrator. "They are told that in order to pay off their debt, they must earn tips by providing commercial sex to customers."[34]

10

THE "RESCUE"

THE OFFICER WHO ARRESTED ME TOOK ME TO THE Atlantic City Police Department. He escorted me to a small window within the station and told me to empty my purse. As I spread money and condoms across the counter, the officer joked with another man behind the window. A female officer then took me into a separate room and checked to see if I was wearing any underwear, which I wasn't.

"Squat," she said, which I thought was weird.

I squatted.

"Cough," she said, which I thought was even weirder.

I coughed. She then led me back to the arresting officer.

"What's yer first name?" he asked me.

I was silent.

"If you refuse to answer our questions," he said, "I'll just throw your ass in juvie until someone comes to claim you. By then you'll probably get beat up."

I told him my first name. Getting beat up was one of the reasons I was running away from home in the first place. I was afraid of getting into a real fight in high school.

"What's yer last name?" he asked.

"Smith," I said.

"Gimme your real name," he hollered.

"That *is* my real name," I said.

The man insisted that I give him my real last name, and I continued to insist that I already had. Twenty years later, my mom and I briefly talked about this night. She said she had filed a missing person's report on me with our local police department but that the Atlantic City Police Department was not aware of it. Had they seen this file, they would have known I wasn't lying. I gave the officer my home number, and then I sat handcuffed to a bench. I squeezed my knees against my chest and didn't care that I was wearing a dress. I did *not* want to go back home, but nobody asked me what I wanted. Nobody asked me why I had run away from home either. An officer stopped in front of me with a Polaroid camera.

"Sit like a lady," he said.

I stared at him. He sighed and snapped my picture. This image is stained in my memory: the yellow hair, the red dress, the make-up smeared down to my cheeks, and the sunken, sullen look on my face. I just wanted to be left alone. I believed I had forsaken the only people who cared about me. I believed Greg and Nicki were the only adults who wouldn't judge me and who really wanted to help me. Without immediate support and understanding from law enforcement, child victims of sex trafficking are left only with the support and understanding offered by their traffickers. Law enforcement officers who work with child victims of commercial sexual exploitation must realize that they are often working with children and families in crisis. They must, at the very least, offer compassion and resources to victims and their families.

WHEN MY PARENTS ARRIVED AT THE POLICE STATION, my mom asked the arresting officer what she and my dad should do with me. The officer became angry. "I'm not a babysitter," he hollered, "Get her the hell out of my station." I was released to my parents wearing the same clothes Nicki had put on me hours earlier. I was emotionally paralyzed and probably dissociating because I remember very little about the remainder of this night. My memories are blurred and probably out of order. I vaguely remember riding in the back seat of my parents' car. I think my father sat in the back seat to ensure I didn't jump out.

My next memory is a hospital room filled with silence. I felt like nobody was talking to me, but I think one or both of my parents were in the room with me. We waited for what felt like a long time. I believe we were waiting for staff to perform a rape kit analysis, but they decided not to do this because I told them I had taken a shower. However, I don't remember telling anyone any details about Greg or the prior two days. I may not have done so until the following day; or this memory may have never taken place. I then remember sitting in a basement-like room of the Little Egg Harbor Township Police Department. Detectives and possibly social workers gathered around me in an effort to get me talking:

"Who was he, Holly?" they asked. "He's not your friend."

"He will do this to others," they said, "you're not the only one."

But I was stone silent. I folded my arms against any help. All I could hear were the words of the first officer who arrested me. One by one, everyone shrugged their shoulders, shook their heads, and sent me home. But, I began to doubt myself. *Didn't Greg and Nicki help me?* I thought. *Where were they? Why weren't they looking for me?*

My parents took me home. My mother and father sat long-faced at the dining room table. My mother was quiet and emotionally detached, which I expected. It was my father who unnerved me. He sat sober and empty-handed at the table; he didn't even light a cigarette. The dining room table was used most often by my parents when entertaining friends. It was meant for Jack and Cokes, cans of Miller High Life, and bottles of Rolling Rock; and for ashtrays surrounded by decks of cards and piles of poker chips and pennies. It wasn't meant for empty hands.

"She's a whore," my father said, "our daughter's a whore; that's all there is to it."

In my father's defense, he and my mother must have been equally turned upside down. We were all sent home with no counseling, no instructions for future action, and no understanding for what had just happened. All that my father knew was that I was refusing to identify the man who had prostituted me. I went to my bedroom. At some point, I must have slept; and at some other point the following day, I agreed to cooperate with police. Again, I remember very little about my time at home, but I know I agreed to cooperate for three reasons: (1) I didn't want my parents to be angry with me; (2) I wanted to escape the prison of my room; (3) I needed to know: *Did Greg and Nicki use me?*

My parents must have called the two local undercover detectives from Little Egg Harbor Township; they showed up at the curb outside my house. I climbed into the back seat of the police car, and my mom ran down the sidewalk. She handed me a ham and cheese sandwich through the window. Everything felt wrong and bad, empty and lonely, distant and hostile. I wouldn't know until many years later that they were probably symptoms of post-traumatic stress disorder (PTSD), which often accompany victims of sex trafficking. In that moment, I was overcome with this bad feeling, which was a more intense version of the feeling I associated with my cousin in childhood. The officer pulled the car away from the curb, and my only thought was *I know my mother's gonna throw my red dress away.*

As an advocate today, I am in touch with many officers and service providers who work with child victims, and many have confirmed a child's need for personal items that belonged to them in "the life." My mother did throw that red dress away, but I needed that dress in a way I couldn't explain at the time. It connected me to Nicki and to Stacy Combas; I needed to part with that dress on my own terms. I encourage law enforcement and service providers to allow victims to keep belongings from "the life," even if the items must be kept out of sight. A child's identity is torn away by traffickers, and other exploiters. Stripping a child of his or her few belongings from "the life" can be another loss of identity. I have heard stories of children weeping over trivial items kept for evidence or left behind.

The daylight stung through the police car windows that day, and I longed for the night. I longed for the sparkling, dizzying, drowning lights of Atlantic City. We drove for miles down the Black Horse Pike as I studied each passing motel. The only thing I knew about Greg and Nicki's motel was that it was on Route 42, otherwise known as the Black Horse Pike, and that the motel was shaped like a horseshoe.

"She's lying," the passenger cop muttered.

I was looking out of the backseat window when the second officer grew impatient.

"She's giving us the runaround," he said.

"No, she's not," said the driving officer. "She wouldn't lie to us."

"This is *bullshit,*" shouted the passenger cop.

I'm told today that playing a good cop/bad cop routine is typical when working with victims, but I was not only annoyed by it; I was angered. I was frustrated. I was offended because I really was trying to cooperate, but I sincerely didn't know the name of or directions to the motel.

"Jus' gimme a minute!" I shouted.

Finally, I recognized the U-shaped motel.

"There it is," I pointed.

The officers parked outside of room 115 and knocked on the door. I ducked behind the back seat and peered through the window. I felt like such a traitor. *How could I do this to Nicki?* I thought. *How could I do this to Greg? He saved me. He saved me from my life.* Nobody answered the door. I watched as the officers headed toward the management office. I leaned over and pulled on my door to give Greg and Nicki some warning, but the doors were locked. I was tempted to scream, but the officers were already heading back with the motel manager. The manager unlocked the door, and I ducked low in my seat, feeling like a coward. I waited, but nothing happened. The officers emerged from the room, nodded at the manager, and headed back toward me.

"They moved out overnight," said the driver, obviously frustrated with me for not cooperating with law enforcement sooner.

I thought about all of Nicki's makeup, all of Nicki's clothes, the TV, the bed sheets, all the stuff laying all over the floor. All that time they spent moving the night before was time they didn't spend trying to find me, I realized. And then I thought about my favorite pair of jeans, the pictures of Crystal, my favorite cassette tapes, and my diary. I imagined Greg and Nicki laughing over my diary entries, but I knew the truth. I knew my diary and other belongings were all at the bottom of some shitty dumpster. *They did use me,* I thought. I leaned back against the seat. *My father was right,* I thought, *everyone was fuckin' right!*

THERE WERE THREE CHAIRS, A TABLE, A TAPE RECORDER, and a video camera with one red eye glaring down at me. The only other thing I remember about the interrogation room was the light. I lowered my eyes, I crossed my legs, and I folded my arms against it, but the light was dogged in its pursuit. I felt like it exposed all my filth and shame. I stared at the dust pushed into the corners of the room. Sitting directly opposite from me was a new detective; another detective sat with folded arms to my left. Because the motel was located in a different district, I had to be interviewed by the Absecon Police Department. Following my "rescue," I had been handled by at least six different police officers in total.

The detective who sat opposite from me raised his finger and held it over the red button of the tape recorder. "Ready?" he asked me as if it really mattered. I knew it didn't matter if I was ready. I believed it didn't matter to anyone, including my father, who sat outside the interrogation room. The detective pressed the red button and started speaking.

"Time is 1947 hours. Today's date is 7–3–92. We're at the Absecon Police Department in the Interview Room next to the Detective Bureau. This interview is being conducted by Detective Sergeant [name withheld]. Statement is being taken from Holly Smith. This interview," he looked at his notes, "is taken with her consent and her father's consent. . . . It is concerning a rape investigation which occurred on 7–2–92 at 930 hours in the morning. At the Casino Inn Motel, room 115. The case number is [withheld]."

He looked at me.

"Miss Smith," he asked, "are you aware this interview is being taped?"

Nearly twenty years later, I obtained a copy of this interrogation and it still pains me to read it. I remember this officer questioning me, and I especially remember him addressing me as *Miss Smith.* Here are my problems with this scenario: I was a *child.* I was being interrogated in an unfriendly environment, by myself, with two unfamiliar male detectives, and one of them spoke to me like I was an adult. I'm often asked what would have helped here—a female detective? A different room? A victim advocate? And, my answer is *yes!* All of the above! Appointing one officer in charge of cases involving child victims of commercial sexual exploitation would be most helpful, though, especially one who is trained to handle such cases. This officer's matter-of-factness with me made me want to pick up my chair and throw it at him. Nobody *talked* to me like I was a person outside of a criminal case; I felt like an alien.

I answered his question: *Yes, I was aware the interview was being taped.*

"Is the interview being done with your consent?" he asked.

I wanted to smash the table with my fists and scream *No!* I was doing this because everyone *else* wanted me to do it. I believed my father wanted me to testify because he was embarrassed and wanted this to be over. I believed the officers wanted me to testify because they wanted their perpetrators. I felt like nobody was concerned with *me* or what I needed or wanted. And the fact is, what I needed was serious mental health treatment. I was so angry; I was so desperately disconnected that it wasn't just an emotional pain, but a physical pain, a physical presence.

These officers were questioning a child in crisis. Each and every child victim of commercial sexual exploitation needs immediate aftercare services in a program trained to work with such victims. Unfortunately, only one program existed at this time, and it was on the other side of the country. Children of the Night (COTN) in Los Angeles opened its doors in 1992, but nobody in the realm of my case had heard of them.

"Yes," I said, indicating that I was consenting to the interview.

"For the record, Miss Smith, could you tell me your full name?"

"Holly Austin Smith," I said.

"Your date of birth?"

"January 19th, 1978," I said.

"Your address?"

They wanted to know my phone number and my social security number as well, but I remember thinking that none of that had anything to do with me. Neither detective cared about me, I thought. I hated both of them. I hated the interrogation room, I hated my life, and I hated the questions they asked me.

When it comes to interrogating victims, officers must think like the very people who exploited the victims: child traffickers. The man who lured me away from home asked me questions about myself over the phone, but his questions were different. He asked about my friends, my family, and my school. He also asked about my favorite music, my favorite celebrities, my boyfriends, and my concerns and goals. In no time, I befriended this stranger because he *pretended* to actually care about me and my life outside of the immediate conversation.

"OK," the detective said, "could you tell me what occurred . . . approximately two weeks before this incident occurred?"

Both detectives leaned in close; they were quiet, steady, and eager to tweeze the plastic apple of testimony from my throat. Even then, even at age fourteen, I knew my story did *not* begin two weeks earlier. I knew that meeting Greg and running away had minimal meaning over the totality of my story, but I lacked the wherewithal to say as much. I answered this detective's questions with as little information as possible. He was relentless as he asked for specific details about sexual acts with Greg and with "johns." I described the events out of order as I tried to hold back as much information as possible. I felt ashamed, humiliated, and exposed.

My father sat outside the interrogation room. Upon seeing me exit, he smiled. I have pictures of my father and me in childhood. We were buddies; we often posed together in front of the camera. Dad stopped at a produce stand to pick farm fresh Jersey tomatoes and corn one day when I was under ten years old. My mom snapped pictures from inside the hot car. My dad's socks are pulled up halfway to his knees in these pictures; his smile is as bright as the sun glaring down on my face. I'm smiling and squinting, which makes my face look froggy. I'm still young enough that my smile is gummy instead of teethy. Inside the Absecon police station, my father's smile is not so bright. It's a tired smile. I lunged toward my father.

"Are you happy now?" I screamed at him, "Are you fuckin' happy!?"

Four days later, I attempted suicide, alone in my bedroom. I swallowed so many pills that I woke up vomiting and nearly deaf from a ringing in my ears. I later learned that a severe ringing in the ears is common after an overdose of ibuprofen. I lay my face against the cool tile of the bathroom floor in between bouts of sickness. There was a blurred commotion behind me when my parents first woke up to the noise. There were lights, muffled shouting, and then the lights went back out. Toilet, floor tile, sleep: this was all I knew for hours. A small glass of iced tea appeared now and then; and I knew my father was filling it for me.

I should have never been sent home with my parents in this way. Child victims desperately need a period of transition between commercial sexual exploitation and returning home. And, any program or facility that accepts child victims of commercial sexual exploitation must have staff trained to work with this population. Ideally, law enforcement or aftercare program staff should have working relationships with local survivors of commercial sexual exploitation who are healthy, empowered, and able to speak to child victims, especially those victims who fail to see themselves as such. It can be extremely difficult for victims, especially "willing victims," to relate to adult professionals who have not experienced commercial sexual exploitation. Unfortunately, there are few transitional or residential programs available in the country with such resources and training.[1]

I understand that catching criminals is a priority, but law enforcement must show equal, if not more, concern for a child's welfare. If a detective is working with a child victim of commercial sexual exploitation, especially an uncooperative victim, then the focus must be taken off of the potential traffickers and commercial sex crimes, and it must be placed on the child as a whole. If the child is a runaway, the detective must try to address why the child ran away in the first place. Even better, child runaways should be interviewed to determine reasons for running away *before* they become victims of commercial sexual exploitation, especially if they are chronic runaways. I know a case in which a teen victim of sex trafficking kept running away from home because a family member was trafficking her.

With that being said, I do realize that authorities want to catch the perpetrator(s) before another child is victimized. With or without testimony, and with or without an arrest, law enforcement must ensure proper aftercare placement for victims of commercial sexual exploitation. Despite the awful experience of this testimony I *am* glad that Greg was ultimately found and arrested, as were two other adults involved in my case. Nearly twenty years later, I drove to the Atlantic County Prosecutor's Office in Mays Landing, New Jersey, and obtained a copy of my testimony along with other police records for all three persons arrested in my case. It was at this meeting that I learned about the facilitator, Greg's cousin, who was the man on the phone. Although this man was initially arrested, there was no law in place at the time to charge him, and he was released. Today, this man would be liable under the TVPA if prosecuted in a federal court.

Greg and Nicki were both arrested and charged with second degree endangering the welfare of a child and third degree promoting prostitution. Greg was also charged with sexual assault of a minor between thirteen and sixteen years of age. Reading Nicki's testimony was more difficult than reading my own; she spoke of my fourteen-year-old self as though I was a nuisance to her. Although Nicki was arrested, she posted bond and fled. She is still a fugitive in the state of New Jersey today. Greg was caught in Tennessee in 1993. He was sentenced to 364 days in jail with five years' probation.

I often watched for Greg after Atlantic City; I even imagined him climbing through my window. Sometimes I didn't even care if he sought me out for revenge. I thought an act of revenge would at least mean *something.* I thought it would prove that my existence had mattered in some way to these people. But I never saw them again.

SERGEANT BYRON A. FASSETT AND HIS PARTNER, DEtective Catherine De La Paz, with the Dallas Police Department in Dallas, Texas, have witnessed the victimization of children via commercial sexual exploitation for over twenty years. Sergeant Fassett will be the first to tell you he wasn't always sympathetic to this population: "I thought a prostitute is a prostitute is a prostitute," Fassett said. "I figured they were choosing to be on the streets."[2] After a few years, however, Sergeant Fassett and Detective De La Paz began to realize these kids weren't *choosing* to be involved with prostitution; they were being manipulated, or they were isolated and out of options.

In 2005, Fassett and De La Paz developed an intervention, prevention, and suppression program within the Dallas P.D.'s Child Exploitation Squad. Today, this program is called the High Risk Victims and Trafficking (HRVT) Team. High Risk Victims (HRV) include runaway children (i.e., children over age twelve with multiple runaway episodes; children over age twelve who were sexually exploited in any way while running away; and children under the age of twelve with any number of runaway episodes); children who are repeat victims of child sexual abuse or sexual exploitation; and children who have experienced any form of commercial sexual exploitation. The HRVT team handles all cases within Dallas County involving HRVs and victims of child sex trafficking.

For those children who are not victims of commercial sexual exploitation, the goal of the HRVT team is to intervene *before* this victimization occurs. For child victims of commercial sexual exploitation, including sex trafficking, the goal is to stop the cycle of exploitation by focusing on the current victimization and identifying prior victimization. "Child sex trafficking is a symptom," Sergeant Fassett said, "it's a symptom of prior trauma that hasn't been addressed."[3] Sergeant Fassett and Detective De La Paz both stress that understanding the genesis of a child's pathway toward victimization is important not only for serving the child, but also for addressing gaps in the system and safeguarding children and society in general.

The HRVT team trains patrol and vice officers, child protective services, juvenile justice system personnel, youth shelter workers, and other stakeholders in the county on how to identify HRVs and victims of child sex trafficking. All cases are then referred to the HRVT program 24 hours a day, 7 days a week. Each HRV or trafficking case is assigned to one detective in the program, and this detective is responsible for interviewing the child, overseeing the case, and advocating on behalf of this child until he or she is at least age eighteen.

After interviewing hundreds of victims, Detective De La Paz realized traditional interview models were not working with this population. Many HRVs and victims of sex trafficking do not trust law enforcement and many are still under the influence of their traffickers or other exploiters. In accordance, Detective De La Paz created a unique interview model that recognizes that multiple interviews may be necessary in order to ensure the safety and security of a child, and to build a sense of trust between the officer and the child.

"Everyone wants to jump down to prosecution [of the child's assailant]," Sergeant Fassett said, "but we chew our victims up in the process; we end up destroying them. We re-victimize them. It's important to accept victims for who they are and where they're at. We don't measure our success on the number of traffickers arrested, we measure our success by the number of victims recovered; and, we focus on one kid at a time."[4]

And time is exactly what it takes for many victims to understand that they have been manipulated or exploited at the hands of traffickers who posed as boyfriends, caring family members, or friends. Because trust is built over time, the HRVT detective will schedule follow-up visits with the child victim. For those minors who are picked up on charges in Dallas County, especially on charges of prostitution, the HRVT team will often replace the prostitution or other offense with a lesser charge like running away, truancy, breaking curfew, or loitering. After the initial interview, any child with charges will typically be placed into the Letot Center, a program in Dallas County that offers immediate services specific for HRVs and victims of trafficking. The HRVT team recognizes the need to remove the child from the streets, to render aftercare services, and to hopefully break the cycle of exploitation and to stop the pathway toward criminal behavior.

"Without victim services, victims will become offenders," Sergeant Fassett said, "and being a victim doesn't give someone the right to victimize others."[5] Without proper intervention or treatment, child victims of sexual abuse and exploitation are often arrested later as perpetrators in various crimes. Mandi Lynn Bowman, 22, of West Palm Beach, Florida, was sentenced to four years in federal prison "for her role in helping an alleged pimp turn a 14-year-old runaway girl into a prostitute," says a *Sun Sentinel* article in July 2012. However, Bowman was also a victim in childhood, which is the reason she received a lesser sentence. The article notes:

> Bowman's own life was "horrible," her assistant federal public defender told the judge. She was tied to a chair and raped by a babysitter when she was 12 and was gang raped when she was 16, the lawyer said. She became a prostitute at 16, suffers from post traumatic stress disorder and bipolar mental illness, and attempted suicide three times between 2006 and 2010.[6]

When I first began advocating for child victims of commercial sexual exploitation, I vehemently opposed the incarceration of victims. However, I now recognize the need for some children to be removed from the streets for their own safety. Without programs in place, officers are often forced to incarcerate victims. Incarceration must be treated as a last resort, however. Every community across the country must actively seek better solutions for commercially sexually exploited children. If taken into custody, a child victim should be placed into a program where he or she will receive immediate services.

My experience with law enforcement was awful; however, what was most tragic was the lack of immediate and long-term aftercare. When I attempted suicide following my interview with police, it was no cry for help. My intention was to succeed. The Letot Center in Dallas offers a 24-hour intake process that includes risk assessments of all children referred and provides families with crisis intervention services. It also offers medical services; substance abuse treatment; and individual, group, and family counseling.

The Letot Center also offers a voluntary program to girls and their families called E.S.T.E.E.M. Court (Experiencing Success Through Empowerment, Encouragement, and Mentoring). The E.S.T.E.E.M Court program fosters prosocial development of the victim and his or her family through many means, including case management, group therapy, individualized counseling, mentorship, and life skills training. The mission of E.S.T.E.E.M Court is to provide positive experiences that will foster success and empowerment and thereby prevent further involvement in the legal system. This program also collaborates and works with other local organizations like Big Brothers Big Sisters (BBBS) to ensure long-term mentorship and community involvement for participants. Upon completion of this program, the juvenile justice system will drop the misdemeanor charges against the child.[7]

The HRVT program model, the Letot Center program model, and/or the model of collaboration between the two may or may not work for every community. Regardless of which models are used, there must be a program available to child victims of commercial sexual exploitation in all American communities. And these programs must have working, collaborative relationships with law enforcement and the juvenile justice system. Oftentimes, these victims are picked up by law enforcement in the middle of the night; without a protocol in place, these victims may wind up in juvenile detention or released back onto the streets. "Seeing a trafficking victim on the streets is like spotting a person stranded in the ocean," says Sergeant Byron Fassett, "Law enforcement is often the last boat to pass by. . . . What will you do?"[8]

To investigate protocols used in other cities and states, I recommend starting with an article titled, "Shifting the Paradigm from Prosecution to Protection of Child Victims of Prostitution." Authors Rami S. Badawy, J.D. and Toolsi Gowin Meisner detail programs offered in New York; Boston, Massachusetts; and Georgia. Any protocol implemented, however, should be reviewed and updated on a regular basis. This will allow for open discussions, ideas for changes and further collaborations, and continued improvements to the system.

PART III

AFTER ATLANTIC CITY

11

IMMEDIATE AFTERCARE FOR CHILD VICTIMS OF COMMERCIAL SEXUAL EXPLOITATION

A CHILD VICTIM OF COMMERCIAL SEXUAL EXPLOITATION should be placed into residential treatment immediately after his or her removal from exploitation, especially if law enforcement or social services suspects that the child's family cannot or will not seek aftercare services. Crisis stabilization (i.e., medical and psychiatric) should be first priority, followed by proper placement into an intermediate or long-term care program. Placement into a program whose staff are equipped and trained to work with child victims of commercial sexual exploitation is most ideal. However, I strongly believe that any and all programs designed to work with children (especially children in crisis) should require their employees to be educated on commercial sexual exploitation, including child sex trafficking, and expertly trained to work with such victims.[1]

There are few best practices currently available for mental health professionals working with this population of victims either in short or long-term treatment. However, there are professionals working on curricula to fill this void. As a way of contributing to these efforts, I'm including in this book my medical files and psychiatric evaluations from two placements in child psychiatric care after Atlantic City. In this chapter, I will discuss my mindset while under the care of these mental health professionals. With twenty years of insight into my own recovery, I hope to provide objective, victim-centered advice to those professionals working with child victims of commercial sexual exploitation today.

HOSPITALIZATION #1

The days at home following my "rescue" in Atlantic City were so dark that I'm able to recall very little from them. At some point, I was finally sent to a group home, Harbor House. During the intake at Harbor House, I remember feeling desperately isolated and alone. After disclosing the suicide attempt, I underwent a medical evaluation and a Psychiatric Emergency Screening Services (PESS) evaluation. I am including these evaluations (see Appendix G: PESS #1) as a reference for mental health professionals, and I'd like to point out a few inconsistencies in the interview.

The clinical social worker notes that I was "sexually active once prior to the prostitution." While it is possible that I misunderstood this question, it is more likely that I deliberately concealed prior sexual history. It is important for anyone working with victims of commercial sexual exploitation to realize that this population is usually very reluctant to reveal anything personal or sincere to adults, especially adults in professional positions. As I have said before, many victims have been in circumstances in which adults consistently let them down. But victims of commercial sexual exploitation are especially unlikely to share prior sexual activity.

Many victims have been conditioned to conceal early childhood sexual abuse; and many find it particularly painful to recall any sexual encounters before the commercial sexual exploitation. It will likely take several sessions with a victim, especially a "willing victim," before he or she even considers the idea of trusting a professional. It is for this reason that I recommend stabilizing a child in immediate aftercare treatment first, and then seeking intermediate/long-term care services coupled with therapy. I also recommend that intermediate/long-term care programs consider new arrivals to be in a possible state of crisis, and to respond accordingly. This should include a medical evaluation, a mental health assessment, extra attention, and restriction from leaving the premises, if necessary.

The social worker further notes under "Psychiatric History" on the PESS #1 form that I attempted suicide two years earlier "by scratching my arms." This is not true. If I did state that I attempted suicide, it was only because I didn't understand the difference between a suicide attempt and cutting. Also, I was not cutting as a direct way to deal with emotional pain, I was cutting as a way to gain attention and to express a need for help. "Nonsuperficial cutting" is a means to cope with emotions, and the wounds are often hidden. An act of self-mutilation (i.e., "nonsuperficial cutting") forces the brain to shift its focus from emotional pain to immediate physical pain. In sixth grade, I made *superficial* cuts on my arms and face in places that would be seen. I also painted bruises on my face in hopes of looking tough and/or gaining attention from friends and teachers. I probably didn't correct the therapist because I was too depressed to make myself understood. What I find concerning is that the social worker makes no note of asking me *why* I supposedly "attempted suicide" two years earlier.

Last, the social worker notes under "Aggressive Behavior" that I denied "any past or present ideation to hurt others." This also is not true. The truth is that I was so jealous of Crystal's new friends that I scared myself at the lengths to which these jealous ideations took me. Also, I kicked a classmate in the head. While I admittedly did not get along with this girl, the act of aggression was neither provoked nor premeditated. It was spontaneous and cruel. Like my prior sexual activity, I was reluctant to share details about aggressive feelings toward others. Other than that, I was generally straight-forward and honest in this interview; however, I didn't offer much information other than what was asked of me.

All I remember about this and most other interviews with mental health professionals is the clipboard between them and me. I believed they were only doing their jobs. I didn't think there was any real motivation to help me, which, in turn, inspired no real motivation in me to seek help. This may have been based on the lack of real help I received from authority figures in the past; or it may have been based on the lack of intimacy between the health professional and me. These questions were all clinical.

I was referred to a psychiatric hospital (Hampton Hospital, see Appendix H: Discharge Summary #1) where I stayed for twenty days. This was an opportunity for a psychiatric professional to evaluate me and then to recommend appropriate intermediate/long-term aftercare. I saw the psychiatrist periodically for private sessions, but I became angry and evasive when prodded about my past. Although I was asked about early sexual abuse, I denied it. I also initially denied prior sexual activity; I was ashamed at the number of times I had been "used" by older boys and men. I did not realize these boys and men exploited me. I didn't even know, let alone understand the meaning of, that word in middle school. In my mind, the number of times I'd been "used" only confirmed my fears of being ugly and unlovable. *This* was exactly what I was trying to keep hidden from the world. I wanted people to think I was "cooler" than what I really believed myself to be. I wanted people to love me.

It was easier for me to expose details about the prostitution than it was for me to recount anything from the time before Atlantic City. Speaking openly about prostitution and being hypersexual were both weapons of deflection for me. They also became weapons of retaliation. I spoke openly about prostitution as a way to make everyone uncomfortable partly because everyone seemed to think I chose to run away to "become a prostitute." You can see this attitude in my PESS #1 as the doctor notes that I "went away with a 'pimp'" and I "engaged in prostitution." There's no mention of manipulation or exploitation. In a later assessment of my history, the following was noted: *She met with her "pimp" at a local mall.*

I don't think my therapists understood that I did not willingly accompany a "pimp" to Atlantic City for the purpose of prostitution. I was led into running away with a man whom I *thought* was going to help me find adventure and opportunity. Although I understood that I had been tricked into running away, I didn't understand how I was *coerced* into prostitution. Since I didn't run away from Greg, I believed I must have chosen to prostitute. This sentiment is often expressed among young victims. And so, I talked openly about prostitution and sex acts as a way of thumbing my nose at society and as a way of controlling the conversation.

Patients in the juvenile and adult wards of the psychiatric hospital all ate lunch in the cafeteria. Although patients from different wards were not allowed to fraternize, I blatantly disobeyed this rule and flirted with a young guy in the adult ward. As discussed in chapter 5, victims of commercial sexual exploitation may be influenced by the pop culture illusion that a woman's sexual appeal is what validates her self-worth. The problem is that sexualization, especially in vulnerable girls, often leads to sexual exploitation. So it's a cycle: I wanted a boyfriend to validate my self-worth; I sexualized myself in order to appeal to boys; I felt good when I gained attention from older boys; I felt bad after being pushed into sex and then ignored by an older boy. Sexual attention became a drug; it was the only antidote to temporarily relieve the most recent rejection from a boy. It is for this reason that I do not recommend that men work with female victims of commercial sexual exploitation, unless they are educated on commercial sexual exploitation and well-prepared to work with these victims.

I was banned from the cafeteria for my behavior; and my meals were brought to the ward by orderlies who pushed carts of covered trays. One orderly in particular was an older man who talked with me privately when everyone was away at lunch. I sensed no attraction or desire from him, which disarmed my hypersexuality. If I didn't sense a sexual desire from a man, then I tentatively respected his authority. One day this man asked me why I behaved the way I did toward men. Without a clipboard between us, I wanted to answer him; but, I didn't know the answer. He asked me to write a list of every person I had any type of sexual encounter with before my arrival. I did this; and when I saw him again, he told me that the list was somehow connected to my current troubles. He didn't ask to see the list, he only told me to think about each person and the circumstances surrounding each encounter.

Although I never saw this man again, I kept the list and often thought about the people on it. Over time, this list did help me to understand my behavior in adolescence. The reason I opened up so easily to the orderly was because I sensed his genuine concern. It wasn't this man's job to ask me questions, and he didn't document my answers. Plus, he didn't ask me to recount my prior sexual activity out loud. I wrote it down, and I was in control of the list. I could write anything I wanted because it was private. Nobody would see the list unless I showed it to them.

I recommend this technique to therapists who work with child victims of commercial sexual exploitation, especially those victims who are unwilling to discuss their past histories. Ask the child to write a list of prior sexual encounters (or other forms of abuse or exploitation). If the child is not yet comfortable with disclosing or discussing the list, then offer some tools to help her or him think about it. For example, talk about the differences between dating and sexual exploitation or assault. Talk about what constitutes sexual abuse and when abuse is different from sexual exploration. Be sure to mention sexual exploration of oneself is normal and natural. Talk about sexuality itself, including LGBTQ[2] concerns.

If you are uncomfortable discussing sex with a victim of commercial sexual exploitation, then refer the child to a different therapist. An act of prostitution (forced or otherwise) involves a sexual act. If a child is involved with prostitution (forced or otherwise), then he or she is involved with sexual acts. This child deserves to have an understanding of what sex is, what it means, and what it doesn't mean. Society is saturated with messages about sex and sexuality, yet few people are having straightforward discussions with children about what all these messages mean.

Addressing the topic of prior sexual abuse/activity and healthy relationships/sexuality should be a long-term, not short-term, goal. It is unlikely these topics will be exhausted in immediate aftercare. This is why it's important for child victims to transition into intermediate/long-term services as soon as possible. Also, keep in mind that, despite their mature appearances and sexual histories, child victims of commercial sexual exploitation are still children. I was often treated by hospital staff as being more mature than my age, which reinforced my ideations of being an adult and capable of making adult decisions. One of my most favorite moments at Hampton Hospital was being chased by the nurses as another patient and I threw wet toilet paper on each other's bathroom ceiling. Breaking the rules was part of feeling like a child. I personally never felt any stigmatization from my peers in the hospital. We were a small group, and we had a strong camaraderie. Although we would never have admitted to it at the time, we all wanted and needed structure and discipline. Having the space and opportunity to just be a kid was as important as therapy.

I am often asked if immediate aftercare programs for child victims of commercial sexual exploitation should be "closed" or locked down, meaning the patients cannot leave. And I have to stress that every child is different and that every child's path that led to commercial sexual exploitation was also different. Some children require the freedom to leave in order to trust the people attempting to help them; others are a danger to themselves and require a closed setting in order to keep them safe from the streets. I actually needed a locked-down environment because I was a runner. I was a runner because I lacked the ability to deal with my emotions. I *needed* to be running or doing something dangerous in order to escape my emotions.

When my family moved five miles away from Crystal's house in eighth grade, it caused a chain reaction of issues for me—deepening depression, detachment, and increased impulsive behavior. My hitchhiking was a manifestation of these underlying issues, and I did it for the sake of experiencing danger and recklessness, a high I can compare only to non-superficial cutting. The act of climbing into a stranger's car can cause the brain to enter into a fight-or-flight response, which leaves little mental space for sadness. I didn't hitchhike to get caught or to gain attention; I did it to cope with my degrading mental health. I needed the dangerous activity to enable my walking into middle school every morning.

Running away was another form of repressing emotions. By middle school my running away was sporadic and frantic; it was a natural reaction to anything negative like arguing with my parents or being left out of Crystal's plans. I often found myself running alongside a dark street with trees shaking against a black sky. In her memoir, *Runaway Girl,* Carissa Phelps described skipping school, slipping in and out of friends' houses to sleep, and searching for food while on the streets.[3] Like Carissa Phelps, I felt a surge of adrenaline and freedom when I ran. However, once the adrenaline faded, I felt unsafe on the streets, and I returned home.

Whether in a closed or open facility, though, I think that all victims of commercial sexual exploitation should eventually transition into an open facility. Also, whether closed or open, all programs for victims should have a security system in place to keep outsiders from getting in. I have heard stories of traffickers boldly knocking on the front doors of facilities in search of their victims. One youth program in Florida, for example, was forced to install a security system and hire security guards after traffickers attempted to enter their premises in search of two girls.

Despite my constant plans to run away from Hampton Hospital, in the end I was afraid to leave; Hampton was a break from reality. I felt safe, and I was afraid of reentering society. I wanted to stay with the friends I had made there and I was just beginning to trust the psychiatrist. (See Appendix H: Discharge Summary #1 for my final assessments.) Also, just as I was beginning to feel like a kid again, the guy from the adult ward (with whom I had flirted) managed to sneak his information to me through another patient. After he and I were both released from the hospital, I met this guy at his house. It resulted in a sexual encounter that, of course, left me feeling empty. When I never heard from him again, I became angry and depressed.

My suicidal ideations changed from being implosive to explosive. I swore I would never attempt suicide again; I believed suicide would confirm that the world had won its war against me. I almost consciously made a decision to live as recklessly as possible until I met with death; I imagined I was like the Jim Morrison portrayed in Oliver Stone's biopic *The Doors.* I was determined to go down fighting; I actually envisioned some sort of dramatic fireworks ending. I decided to care about no one but myself, and to care about nothing except getting what I wanted in the present moment. I also viewed anyone who desired sex as inferior; I saw it as a weakness and a vantage point. I despised anyone and everyone who wanted sex from me, paid or unpaid.

How long is aftercare required before returning home? I don't know. But for me, twenty days was not enough. Seven days after my release from the hospital, I returned to Atlantic City with the intention to make money for new clothes. For those who are shocked by this news, my only explanation is this: without long-term specialized counseling, I wasn't "fixed." I wasn't "rescued." I still believed I was a sexual object and that money and material things equaled personal value and achievement. Following my suicide attempt, I should have been stabilized in the hospital and then transferred into a residential program *at least* until school started. Then, I may have succeeded with proper outreach services and a small school setting.

Also, when I returned to Atlantic City in August 1992, I managed to take a friend with me. I was still convinced that prostitution made sense as a profession, and my friend, who had been raised in the same community as me with the same outside influences, saw my point. I placed this friend in direct danger without realizing it. I thought I was exposing her to a great idea. Although in no way did I attempt to control or exploit this person, I was the reason she became a victim of commercial sexual exploitation. I instructed her on what to do and how to do it just as Nicki did with me. This is another reason I stress the need for immediate and long-term residential aftercare for victims. I was a danger not only to myself but to other children as well.

My friend and I were both arrested that night. The arresting officer was a different man than the officer who arrested me a month earlier, and he treated us differently. He took the handcuffs off of us, and he offered us popcorn as we waited for our parents to arrive. My friend and I swung in our chairs and tossed the popcorn at each other. We acted like unruly kids because that's exactly what we were. The officer scolded us and told us not to throw food. My friend and I both pouted, but this man's admonishment created a sense of structure. He was the adult, and we were the kids. He didn't treat us like adults, and he didn't treat us like criminals. Although I crossed my arms in anger, I felt safe within this dynamic. I needed boundaries. Unfortunately, I never saw this officer again.

HOSPITALIZATION #2

Memories after my second arrest are as clouded as they were after the first. I was immediately taken to a hospital to be seen by a mental health professional (see Appendix I: PESS #2). My exhaustion, anger, and depression are so apparent in this interview that I don't understand why I was forced to sit through it. Was a PESS evaluation really necessary to determine I was in some sort of crisis? I was interviewed from 7:30 a.m. until 12:15 p.m.; I had not slept, showered, or even changed out of the clothes I wore to Atlantic City the night before. The lonely hospital room that I described after my first arrest may have actually been a part of this arrest—I can't remember.

In this interview, I wanted something: I wanted to return to Hampton Hospital, or to go somewhere similar. I didn't necessarily want to return to Hampton for therapy, though; I wanted to return in order to be back with the friends I had made and to get attention. (When I say I wanted attention, I don't mean I wanted sympathy: I mean I literally wanted an active schedule with people talking to me.) I needed constant attention, and negative attention was the only thing working for me at the time. Knowing I would again be grounded, I didn't want to go home. Walking into my bedroom was like entering a torture chamber. Being alone was desperately difficult for me. I truly wanted help; I just didn't understand *what* was wrong with me and I didn't know how to ask for help.

Telling this to the therapist was not an option, though, because I didn't understand any of this at the time. Plus, my anger prevented me from offering genuine answers. I was sleep-deprived, hungry, and resentful. As a result, I continued to hide facts about my history that made me uncomfortable (i.e., prior sexual abuse); and I stretched the truth on other questions about prior history. After my first stay in Hampton Hospital, I knew what piqued these doctors' interests: potential abuse in the home, alcohol or drug abuse, and suicide attempts. Therefore, I elaborated and/or embellished in these areas.

For example, under "Substance Abuse" on my PESS #2 form, the doctor notes that I reported "alcohol use since age 12 ranging from 1 beer to half bottle Jack Daniels [*sic*]." I did drink a beer at age twelve, but this was experimentation, not addiction. I also snuck liquor from my parents' liquor cabinet at ages twelve, thirteen, and fourteen, but I never drank half a bottle of anything. Yes, when I drank liquor I sometimes did it to numb my emotions, but the more important question was *why* I needed to numb these emotions. What caused these emotions? (And, yes, I needed to learn that substance abuse was no way to deal with one's issues.)

Another exaggeration can be found under "Mood/Affect." The doctor notes that I reported "increased sleep—falling asleep in day [*sic*] since Hampton admission." During my first visit to Hampton Hospital, I learned that substance abuse and depression were both reasons to be committed, and so I alluded to issues in these areas in hopes of being re-admitted back there. I also intentionally mentioned a past argument between my father and me and painted the worst picture possible of my parents' drinking habits. I did this because I was angry with them. I was angry because I believed they had prioritized drinking over me, and because they had failed to validate and acknowledge my complaints about my cousin. In retrospect, I believe my parents truly did not realize the extent of my cousin's abuse and/or the effect it had on me. Had I been in a program with staff trained to work with victims of commercial sexual exploitation, I believe these root issues could have been exposed and addressed without so much grief between my parents and me. I'd like to also point out that parents of victims need equal support and understanding from aftercare staff if they are to be allies in the process of healing.

In the end, I was sent home. Sixteen days later, I called Hampton Hospital threatening to commit suicide and was again placed into treatment. My second stay at Hampton Hospital was different than the first. The juvenile ward was overcrowded, and some of the patients were much older and more aggressive than me. I was not comfortable or happy there, and I just didn't know what to do or where to go. In my discharge summary (See Appendix J: Dischage Summary #2 for final assessments), I was described as evasive, difficult, and manipulative; these descriptions were very true. At the time I wasn't interested in being honest—I was only interested in getting what I wanted. And, the fact was I had no idea what I wanted.

BORDERLINE PERSONALITY DISORDER AND PTSD

While under the care of Hampton Hospital staff, I was diagnosed with traits for Borderline Personality Disorder (BPD). This is *not* the case for every victim of commercial sexual exploitation, but I feel I must address this in my personal case analysis. Not only was I diagnosed with BPD traits, but I was diagnosed upon entry into my first in-patient hospital stay. I am speaking directly to mental health professionals and academics when I say I *wish* someone had told me this. I requested these files nearly twenty years after my victimization and hospitalization, and I had no idea of this diagnosis in 1992. Why is that? I have since learned that medical professionals do not want to stigmatize a child with the label of BPD.

But here's my problem with that. By age fourteen, I was stigmatized as a "slut," a "teen prostitute," and a "problem child." When children are diagnosed with having traits of BPD, aren't they typically in some sort of crisis that would warrant a psychological examination in the first place, thereby potentially indicating some level of stigmatization anyway? I was kept in the dark from my diagnosis, and this, I believe, was a detrimental mistake. In his book, *Borderline Personality Disorder Demystified,* Robert O. Friedel, M.D., lists the following diagnostic criteria for BPD, according to the *Diagnostic and Statistical Manual of Mental Disorders.* "In order to be diagnosed with borderline disorder," says Dr. Friedel, "you must experience and demonstrate a minimum of five of the nine symptoms . . .":

1. Frantic efforts to avoid real or imagined abandonment.
2. A pattern of unstable and intense interpersonal relationships characterized by alternating between extremes of idealization and devaluation.
3. Identity disturbance: markedly and persistently unstable self-image or sense of self.
4. Impulsivity in at least two areas that are potentially self-damaging (e.g., spending, sex, substance abuse, reckless driving, binge eating).
5. Recurrent suicidal behavior, gestures, threats, or self-mutilating behavior.
6. Affective instability due to a marked reactivity of mood (e.g., intense episodic dysphoria, irritability, or anxiety usually lasting a few hours and only rarely more than a few days).
7. Chronic feelings of emptiness.
8. Inappropriate, intense anger or difficulty controlling anger (e.g., frequent displays of temper, constant anger, recurrent physical fights).
9. Transient, stress-related paranoid ideation or severe dissociative symptoms.[4]

I was exhibiting and/or experiencing several of these traits even before hospitalization, including: frantic efforts to avoid real or imagined abandonment, identity disturbance, impulsivity, suicidal behavior or self-mutilation, chronic feelings of emptiness, and inappropriate and intense anger. If these are the traits for BPD, then why wasn't anyone working with me on these specific symptoms? Those feelings of emptiness that I experienced in middle school were like a physical part of me. I didn't question their presence; in fact, I believed that everyone had these feelings. I just figured that I was the only one struggling to cope with them.

If a medical professional *described* to me the traits of BPD and told me these feelings were treatable, I think the remainder of my adolescence would have been different. I believe teenagers should be allowed an active role in their treatments and diagnoses. If someone had discussed BPD with me in 1992, I believe I would have been not only open to treatment, but also desperate for it to begin. But, I have no memories of anyone talking to me about feelings of emptiness or fears of abandonment. I realize treatment was limited in 1992, but there are viable therapies available for BPD today. I also understand that some therapists prefer to focus on the symptoms of mental health disorders as opposed to labeling a person with a disorder, and I can see this point. And, I agree so long as the symptoms are acknowledged, explained, and addressed.

Unlike BPD, post-traumatic stress disorder (PTSD) is commonly recognized as being experienced by victims of commercial sexual exploitation, especially sex trafficking. The trauma that is causing symptoms of PTSD may have been experienced by that victim before, during, and/or after the commercial sexual exploitation. A connection between symptoms of BPD and symptoms of PTSD is widely recognized by therapists today; many even argue that some diagnoses of BPD are inaccurate. They say that in some cases symptoms of BPD are actually symptoms of PTSD, especially in victims of commercial sexual exploitation. And, I can see the relation. Those bad feelings I associated with my cousin were intermittent in intermediate school and overwhelming in middle school. I believe they led to my intense anger, impulsivity, and attachment to Crystal. By the time I was re-admitted to Hampton Hospital, those feelings had snowballed as a result of what I experienced during and after Atlantic City. Therefore, I encourage mental health professionals working with victims of commercial sexual exploitation to address PTSD and symptoms of PTSD, as well as any other symptoms for mental health concerns, throughout a child's intermediate and long-term aftercare.[5] I also encourage therapists who are working with children they deem to have traits of BPD to consider that they may instead be suffering from symptoms of PTSD.

12

INTERMEDIATE AND LONG-TERM AFTERCARE

FOR THOSE PROFESSIONALS WORKING WITH CHILD victims of commercial sexual exploitation in an immediate aftercare program, it is important to determine a plan for intermediate and/or long-term aftercare for each child (if not available within your program). Commercially sexually exploited victims (especially and specifically those who are labeled "willing victims") require intermediate and/or long-term care in order to successfully work with a therapist or case manager to understand and overcome commercial sexual exploitation. An intermediate and/or long-term care program should offer a child consistency, safety, and structure while undergoing therapy. A victim of commercial sexual exploitation likely endured years of abuse and neglect or exploitation before the commercial sexual exploitation. It may take months or years to reverse these effects, so try to be patient if the child is uncooperative while in immediate aftercare.

RESIDENTIAL TREATMENT VS. OUTREACH SERVICES

Again, every child victim of commercial sexual exploitation is unique and placement should be considered on an individual basis. Returning home may not be a viable option for many victims; therefore, an in-house program or residential treatment may be best. For children with supportive home environments, returning home may be a solution if, and only if, there are appropriate outreach services available in the child's community. Outreach services that are led by or employ healthy, empowered survivors of commercial sexual exploitation are ideal, if available.[1]

The Gray Haven (TGH) in Richmond, Virginia, is an example of a community-based organization that offers comprehensive case management specific for victims of human trafficking and commercial sexual exploitation. TGH collaborates with other community programs in order to connect a child victim of commercial sexual exploitation with all available and appropriate services. TGH also works closely with law enforcement to offer crisis response when a victim is identified through law enforcement raids and other operations.[2] Other community programs serve a variety of populations with services or programs that are specific to or inclusive of victims of commercial sexual exploitation. There are also therapists across the country who can offer commercial sexual exploitation–specific counseling and/or case management to victims on an outpatient basis. See Appendix B: Resources for Law Enforcement and Other First Responders.

If a child or family chooses outreach services over residential treatment, then I recommend the following while the child is receiving immediate aftercare services. First, be sure to choose outpatient services that offer family therapy. Second, teach the child various coping skills while in your care; these could include meditation, anger management, and breathing exercises. Victims of commercial sexual exploitation who are returning home after immediate aftercare are often returning to the situations from which they were originally trying to escape. Third, be sure the child has his or her own copy of the outreach services available in his or her community.

What's unique about child victims of commercial sexual exploitation is that they are often very motivated to help themselves. While some child victims of abuse see no way out of their situations, victims of commercial sexual exploitation often attempt to help themselves by running away, or otherwise seeking ways toward a better life. Equip these victims with the proper tools needed to seek effective help. Include on this list *any* youth-based organizations in their areas (e.g., Big Brothers Big Sisters and Girls and Boys Club) and *any* local and national hotline numbers for children, including those specific for commercial sexual exploitation. See Appendix A: Resources for Parents and Victims for a starting list.

Upon release, I strongly suggest following up with the child and the child's family either by phone or in-house visits. A model similar to the High Risk Victims and Trafficking (HRVT) model in Dallas, Texas, could be beneficial for children with limited resources for outreach services. The HRVT model, which was discussed in chapter 10, ensures that a detective will follow up with a child on a regular basis. I was placed on house arrest for drug possession charges a few years after Atlantic City. A detective visited me at school on a regular (albeit short-term) basis to make sure I was showing up to class while awaiting my court date. Although these visits were short, I liked knowing that someone was checking on me. Something similar could have been useful for me in 1992.

ONGOING THERAPY

Child victims of commercial sexual exploitation require consistent therapy and/or case management over time. Discussing the dynamics of control and manipulation in sex trafficking cases should be a priority; however, convincing a victim that he or she is, in fact, a victim should *not* trump the attention paid to experiences *prior* to trafficking. Because of prior experiences, prostitution honestly made so much sense to me that I was actually confused by everyone's attempts to dissuade me from it.

I felt like society *encouraged* prostitution and that those discouraging it were hypocrites. Before I could grasp that I was a victim, I needed to first understand my rights as a human being and a young female. Then, I needed some perspectives on love, dating, and sex outside of what popular culture was telling me. I also needed education on how media messages can influence people and an understanding of who was really behind these messages, especially advertising. I needed help in developing a sense of critical thinking about the media and morals.

Please note that although I use the term "victim," it is important for therapists to refer to child patients of commercial sexual exploitation as *survivors.* Because I was unable to see that I was victimized, I was unable to see myself as a victim. I saw myself as an adult making decisions to survive. I believe it's good to acknowledge that a child was *surviving* his or her circumstances. The choice to run away was a choice of survival. The choice to comply with prostitution was a choice to survive. If you project victimization onto the child, it may build a wall between you and your patient. Make it clear that you believe the child was victimized and you intend to revisit the topic. Allow the child time to make the connections for him or herself over continued therapy.

First, a child must understand what it means to be in a position of vulnerability. If a child you are working with was potentially abused, exploited, and/or assaulted before being commercially sexually exploited, then he or she must first understand the dynamics of that victimization in order to grasp the dynamics of further victimization. This process may require a deep reach into the child's history; commercial sexual exploitation is often the end result of a long list of traumatic and exploitative experiences (see chapter 2).

For me, it was necessary to first understand that I was sexually exploited by older boys and men in my community before I could grasp the idea that I was exploited by the man who trafficked me. Further, I couldn't understand that I was exploited by older boys and men until I understood what put me in a place of potential exploitation. This included a lack of guidance and supervision, confusion about personal boundaries due to early sexual abuse, lack of an assertive personality, influence from negative messages in the media, and a natural vulnerability at ages eleven, twelve, and thirteen. Other victims may need to grasp the vulnerability associated with growing up in poverty, or losing a mother or father, or having parents already involved in commercial sex, among other predisposing factors (see chapter 1).

My therapists asked me about "dating" and "sexual activity" in PESS evaluations #1 and #2. In my mind, the only person I ever really "dated" was an eleven-year-old boy in sixth grade. I saw this boy on the weekends at the skating rink because he lived in a different town. We "couple-skated" to songs like "Kokomo" by The Beach Boys and "Is This Love" by Whitesnake. I did not associate "dating" with being "used" or allowing someone to "use" me. Possibly, the following questions would have been more useful in sparking a dialogue about dating and/or sexual activity:

Have you ever been "used" by a guy for sex?
Have you ever had a "one night stand"?
Have you ever "hooked up" with a guy?
Were you ever "touched" or "used" by someone but felt like you had to keep it a secret?
Has anyone ever forced a hickey or a kiss?
Have you ever felt bad after making out or having sex?

Remember, therapy regarding prior sexual activity is a marathon, not a sprint. This topic is usually very personal, complicated, and uncomfortable for a victim of commercial sexual exploitation. If the child is unwilling to share this information, I recommend using the journal technique discussed in the last chapter. It's also important to remember that prior sexual exploitation is not a historical component to every case of commercial sexual exploitation of a child. Consider Katrina Owens's story from chapter 1. A relationship with her father was what Katrina was missing; and after her parents' divorce, a trafficker was able to exploit this vulnerability. Therefore, it is important to explore all the elements of a child's past and not to force any assumption.

I recently spoke at a conference near Boston where I gave a presentation on predisposing factors, including negative messages in the media, and their connections to my frame of mind before, during, and after Atlantic City. There I also met Stephen R. Gaddis, PhD, LMFT.[3] Dr. Gaddis is Co-Director for the Narrative Therapy Program at The Salem Center for Therapy Training & Research in Salem, Massachusetts. Dr. Gaddis and his colleague, Zoe Kessler, MSW, gave a joint presentation on their program later that day. Narrative Therapy helps a person connect outside influences and events to that person's feelings, actions, or inactions. It also helps a person identify different events in his or her life and to build a new storyline outside of trauma and victimization. I highly recommend this form of therapy to professionals working with victims of commercial sexual exploitation.[4]

THE TURNING POINT

What made you finally stop running away?
What made you stop returning to Atlantic City?
What was the turning point?

These are common questions most often posed to me by professionals working with victims. Unfortunately, there was no immediate turning point at which I realized I was worth more than prostitution. Instead, I had a moment at which my greatest fears were realized all at once. A particular friend gained knowledge of what had happened over the summer, and she spread rumors about me. I was called a *hooker* and ostracized by my friends. I became a target to bullies, and I lost my friendship with Crystal. What's funny is that I actually felt a sense of relief once this happened. Sometimes the greatest sense of freedom can come from having nothing left to fear.

In an attempt to "start over," I agreed to live with an aunt and uncle in Florence, New Jersey. My aunt sincerely wanted to help me, and she set out to keep me busy with cooking lessons. She gave me a recipe holder and the first dish we made together was macaroni and cheese from scratch. Keeping me busy in this way was an excellent idea; however, without counseling services, it wasn't enough. I watched my aunt boil noodles and mix melted cheese, and the emptiness bubbled up inside me. I tried to do well in school, but without Crystal, I was painfully shy and afraid of bullying. I once witnessed a boy get beat up in the hallway of my new school. Two boys kicked in the other boy's guts; and when the bell rang, they all dispersed. Even the beat-up boy limped away from the scene. I clutched my books to my chest and continued to class.

Only two months after walking the streets of Atlantic City I found myself in this strange and hostile high school. Located near Trenton, New Jersey, the students of Florence High School were much more diverse and urban than those at Pinelands Regional Middle and High School. Drugs and violence were much more apparent there than at home. When I was in Hampton Hospital, one of my peers, T.C., was a boy addicted to crack cocaine. T.C. was usually angry and withdrawn. Once, I asked him what it was like to smoke crack, and his eyes lit up.

"It's beautiful," he said. "Everything is bright and colorful, and all your worries just slip away."

I wanted this; I wanted my worries to slip away. I met a boy at Florence High School whose older brother sold drugs out of their house. The following Saturday morning, I convinced my aunt that I left a homework assignment at this boy's house. I climbed into my aunt's Mary Kay van, and we drove toward the city. My aunt turned her large van down a narrow street and looked nervous.

"Are you sure this is the right address?" she asked.

"I'm sure," I said. "Just wait here."

Inside the boy's house, there were toddlers in diapers watching cartoons and teenagers sleeping on the floor.

"What are you doing here?" the boy from school asked me, obviously sleepy from Friday night's activities.

"You said I could come here today," I said, holding out money.

The boy looked astonished that I was there on a Saturday morning asking for crack cocaine. We both looked at my aunt's van through the curtains of the front window.

"I'll be right back," the boy said.

He returned with a baggie full of tiny vials.

"What do I do with it?" I asked.

"You smoke it," he said.

He gave me some homework paper, and I returned to my aunt.

"Got it," I said.

That afternoon, after my aunt left the house to go grocery shopping, I opened the bag and inspected the vials. There were tiny rocks of white powder in each of the vials. One by one, I emptied the vials and tried to smoke the contents by stuffing the powdered rocks into the ends of cigarettes. I lit each cigarette and smoked, waiting for the feeling T.C. described—but nothing happened. After I had wasted all the vials, I threw everything into a ceramic bowl that I had made in Hampton Hospital, and I hid the evidence in the drop-tile ceiling of my aunt's spare bedroom. I was disappointed. To this day, I don't know if the boy sold me fake drugs, or if the lack of effect was based solely on the fact that I had no idea what I was doing. In any case, I consider myself lucky.

Later, I met another boy my age at school. This boy had just been released from juvenile detention. He lived with his father but had spent time in foster care. The boy wasn't mean or angry; he seemed empty like me. He asked to be my boyfriend, and he never pressed for more than hugging and kissing. This lasted for only a few days. We were spotted smoking pot outside of the school, and the police were called. The boy was going to be taken away to detention again, and we clung to each other in the principal's office. We cried not out of love, but out of desperation. We were two lost kids who found meaning in being together. When he was taken away by police, I bolted out of the room. A police officer chased me through the halls of Florence High School. Students pressed their faces against the windows of their classroom doors as I ran past. This is what a child in extreme crisis looks like: dramatic, erratic, and lacking any concept of consequences or foresight. I lunged toward a set of windows that opened to the outside, and the officer tackled me to the floor. I was led back to the principal's office. My aunt and uncle discovered the bowl of crack vials in my ceiling, and I was sent back home to my parents.

Two things happened that finally calmed me down. First, a counselor at my original high school recognized that I could not handle being in a large school. I was offered the opportunity to attend a special school for kids with drug and alcohol addiction issues. Although I wasn't addicted to drugs or alcohol, I was happy for the alternative to high school. And so, I was driven daily to Schaeffer Treatment Center in Toms River, New Jersey, in a short, yellow bus or taxi. This was where I spent the rest of ninth grade. Teachers at my high school sent assignments to the part-time teacher at Schaeffer; and I spent half my day in substance abuse counseling and the other half in school. The classroom was small, and I could finally concentrate on my schoolwork without worrying about gossip or fist fights in the hallway. My grades changed from D's and F's in eighth grade to all A's and B's in ninth grade. Schaeffer Treatment Center could have been my turning point had the counselors been trained to work with victims of commercial sexual exploitation. In fact, after a few months of group therapy on addiction issues, I opened up and briefly disclosed to the group my experience in Atlantic City. However, everyone, including the counselor, was visibly uncomfortable; so I never brought it up again.

The second thing to calm me down was that I began dating an older guy. This relationship replaced counseling for me. Despite the rumors about my being an "ex-hooker," which were spread by some of Crystal's friends, this guy accepted and loved me. He brought meaning to my life, and I finally wanted to live again. I finally felt accepted, worthy, and happy. But, do you see the problem with this? I never learned to want to live for myself. I never learned to accept myself, to love myself, or to feel worthy by myself. Naturally, my parents encouraged the relationship with this guy because I was finally acting happy again. But this relationship was destined to fail. I was only fourteen years old.

Within months, I wanted to stop dating this guy, but the idea of being alone was desperately scary. My depression returned and I again became a statistic at age fifteen: I got pregnant in an attempt to gain unconditional love both from my boyfriend and from a baby. The boyfriend broke up with me, and I found myself very sick and very alone. Without having anyone to support me otherwise I made the painful and difficult decision to terminate the pregnancy. By age sixteen, I began drinking and using drugs. By age seventeen, I discovered a drug called PCP (i.e., phencyclidine), otherwise known as "angel dust." Throughout my teens and early adulthood, I would oscillate between bad relationships and drugs. I would know the depths of domestic violence and addiction over and over again, each time worse than the last. The turning point for any child victim of commercial sexual exploitation should not be a boyfriend or girlfriend, or drugs or alcohol; it should be proper treatment.

AFTERCARE PROGRAMS

Aftercare programs should offer services similar to prevention programs; and in some communities, perhaps prevention and aftercare services could go hand-in-hand. For example, My Life My Choice (MLMC) offers a prevention curriculum for victims (to prevent re-victimization) and to at-risk youth. When considering prevention and/or aftercare services for your program, think of chapter 1. Start by asking yourself what predisposing factors played a role in prior CSEC cases within your community. Then, as you encounter each new case of CSEC, ask yourself what predisposing factors played a role in this particular child's path into commercial sexual exploitation.

Victims will vary in their aftercare needs; therefore, aftercare services should be as diverse as the predisposing factors discussed in chapter 1. For example, a twelve-year-old girl lured out of foster care by a pimp trafficker who promised romance may have different needs than a seventeen-year-old mother who was blackmailed into submission by a violent gang trafficker. Likewise, an eleven-year-old boy sold for sex by a family member for drugs may have different needs than a fifteen-year-old transgender boy lured into pornography by a man promising friendship and romance. All of these differences must be considered when weighing the options for residential treatment vs. outpatient services, closed vs. open facilities, and CSEC-specific programs vs. youth-focused programs that include services for victims of commercial sexual exploitation, and so on.

Had I been offered intermediate aftercare following Atlantic City, I believe treatment could have been successful whether it was residential treatment or outreach services. The knowledge of CSEC, especially pimp-controlled sex trafficking, and an understanding of the mindset of "willing victims" within that program (or by the therapist/case manager) is what would have determined my success. First and foremost, I would have needed consistency, safety, and structure. By consistency, I mean I would have needed to remain in the same program(s) with the same staff, therapist(s), and/or case manager(s) throughout high school. By safety, I mean I would have needed small-group settings in both treatment and in school for at least the first year if not longer. By structure, I mean I would have needed goals, guidance, and planned activities.

For those working in intermediate and/or long-term aftercare programs (whether they are residential or outreach services), I highly recommend working in small-group settings. Victims of commercial sexual exploitation have often fallen through cracks in the system; they need attention and accountability from adults. I also recommend connecting kids in your program with other reputable programs in the community. Any and every youth-focused program may be a potential partner. Established programs like Big Brothers Big Sisters (BBBS) and the Boys and Girls Club may offer mentorship opportunities for at-risk youth. Other organizations may offer services ranging from athletic programs for home-schooled youth, parenting skills for teen parents, and food pantries for children from low-income families. The following are additional services I recommend to include in your prevention or aftercare program; these recommendations are based on my experience as a fourteen-year-old female victim of commercial sexual exploitation, specifically pimp-controlled sex trafficking.

Exposure to Survivors

First and foremost, I recommend exposing victims to healthy and empowered survivors. One way to do this is via a Survivor Mentor model like the one created by My Life My Choice (MLMC). Another way to do this is by instituting a ten-week Exploitation Prevention Curriculum also designed by MLMC. This curriculum is relevant for any girl between the ages of twelve and eighteen; however, it was designed specifically for at-risk girls and girls who have survived commercial sexual exploitation. MLMC's ten-session curriculum is designed to change girls' perceptions of the commercial sex industry, as well as build self-esteem and personal empowerment. It includes interactive activities and journaling, and it is infused with authentic testimonies from survivors. The MLMC model pairs a licensed clinician or clinically trained service provider with a trained survivor of exploitation.

For aftercare programs unable to connect with empowered survivors, I recommend sharing this book with victims. Other books written by survivors include *Runaway Girl* by Carissa Phelps, *Girls Like Us* by Rachel Lloyd, and *The Slave Across the Street* by Theresa Flores. I recommend reading each one in order to determine which, if any, might be best for each client. For those aftercare programs that specialize in CSEC, please reach out to GEMS in New York City for color posters of survivors of commercial sexual exploitation. These posters portray survivors in empowered positions today, including Rebecca Bender, author of *Roadmap to Redemption;* Shamere McKenzie, motivational speaker; Marlene Carson, Founder of Rahab's Hideaway; Nola Brantley, Co-Founder and Executive Director of MISSSEY;[5] Stacy Jewell Lewis, playwright, director, and performer; Sheila White, Survivor Leadership Coordinator with GEMS; Kathleen Mitchell, Founder of DIGNITY House;[6] and Sherry Dooley, artist.

An Understanding for Healthy Relationships

As mentioned in chapter 11, therapists or case workers should include discussions or workshops on what constitutes healthy relationships with family members, friends, and boyfriends or girlfriends. Discussions of romantic or dating relationships should include a discussion of healthy sexual activity; however, it should be stressed that sex does not define a dating relationship. Learning about healthy boundaries and one's personal rights is the first step to gaining self-confidence and learning self-assertion. LGBTQ concerns should be discussed as well. Consider bringing in speakers and screening documentaries that will address these topics.

Planned Activities

Some of the best therapy I had at Hampton Hospital was going on planned outings with peers, including an afternoon spent playing miniature golf. Planning activities that allow and encourage kids to just be kids can be more therapeutic than any session of counseling. Planned activities can include the following:

- Fun group activities (e.g., going to a baseball game, bowling, roller skating)
- Activities that explore different interests (e.g., ballet performance, painting workshop, cultural festival)
- Activities that encourage stress management (e.g., exercise, yoga, meditation)
- Activities that develop skills for conflict resolution (e.g., self-defense classes, assertiveness workshops, anger management)
- Activities that encourage nutrition and healthy living (e.g., hiking, Zumba class, cooking class)
- Activities that encourage team-building skills (e.g., whitewater rafting, treasure-hunts, outdoor obstacle courses)

Education and Social Awareness

I also recommend exposing children to local, national, and global issues and concerns. Remember, victims of commercial sexual exploitation have often been influenced by pitfalls in their communities and by negative messages in the media, or greater society (see chapters 3-6). Get the kids thinking about their environment and the ways in which national and global issues affect them and their communities. One way this can be done is by incorporating educational workshops or documentary nights into planned activities. Research what documentaries are kid- or teen-friendly and include topics that may be relevant to the population with whom you work. Documentaries available today that would have greatly impacted me before or after Atlantic City include Nicole Clark's *Cover Girl Culture;* Sut Jhally's *Dreamworlds 3: Desire, Sex & Power in Music Video;* Jean Kilbourne's *Killing Us Softly 4: Advertising's Image of Women;* and Adriana Barbaro and Jeremy Earp's *Consuming Kids: The Commercialization of Childhood.* If the kids' interests are piqued by a particular topic, find ways to continue their education on that topic or to get them more involved in the issue.

Community Involvement

Another way to get kids thinking about bigger issues is by volunteering in the community. Volunteering can help a child relieve stress and explore different interests, whether it's walking dogs at a local animal shelter, serving food at a soup kitchen, or spending time with senior citizens at a nursing home. Help kids to see the world from someone else's perspective. Help them understand how fortunate they are by helping those less fortunate.

Also, discover role models in your communities. Victims of commercial sexual exploitation may be overly influenced by negative role models in the media. Research young adults with interesting positions in your community and invite them to speak to your kids. Or, better yet, take your kids on a field trip to see them in action. One way to promote these role models and to give back to the community would be to have the kids in your program create posters of the local role models to distribute at local schools.

I also encourage you to reach out to local businesses in the community for potential partnerships. Some businesses (e.g., yoga studios, fitness gyms, performing arts) may offer discounted tickets to children in your program. Other businesses may be willing to donate financial scholarships toward events or programs, or they may provide products for events or auctions (e.g., food, gift certificates, business space). I have reached out to businesses within my own community for various events, resulting in donations ranging from free pizza to gift packages and gift certificates. It doesn't hurt to ask; the worst they can say is no. But I think you will be surprised by how many businesses choose to support programs within their communities.

Life Skills and Job Training

Life skills workshops and job training skills are always useful. Life skills workshops can include anything and everything from understanding nutrition labels to reading bus schedules. Job training skills can include anything from part-time or full-time job-seeking assistance to resume-writing tips. Ideal workshops and job skills will vary according to the ages and populations with whom you are working. For example, after Atlantic City, I would have benefitted from a training program for babysitters (e.g., Red Cross certification). I babysat for kids in my neighborhood and sometimes encountered situations outside of my teen expertise. However, teens facing bigger obstacles may have different and more immediate needs. In her memoir, *Girls Like Us,* Rachel Lloyd describes the early process of offering outreach services to victims in New York City and the importance of knowing what social services are available:

> The first girl that I really work with one-on-one is Melissa, a strikingly beautiful seventeen-year-old who towers over me even in her sneakers. Melissa is an angry young woman who is often frustrated by my lack of knowledge about the welfare system, the housing system, the subway system, and anything else even remotely useful. I'm woefully naïve in thinking that I just need to be supportive and caring and offer encouraging platitudes, which Melissa often throws back in my face as she struggles to leave her one-year-old daughter's father, who has also been her pimp since she was fourteen.[7]

13

PREVENTION AND ADVOCACY

IN JUNE 2013, I JOINED FORCES WITH A SOUTH JERSEY advocacy organization called the HEAAT[1] Foundation to speak to students attending the middle school from which I graduated in 1992. After I shared my story of child sex trafficking, I met with a group of at-risk girls; and one of them asked me: *Why am I just now hearing about this?* Too many children and teens across the country, as well as their parents, have never heard about child sex trafficking in the United States, and this must change. Educating youth, as well as parents and other community members, is an important step to combating this crime.

Human trafficking is a global issue and should be incorporated into every school social studies group or similar class, with discussions on both labor and sex trafficking as well other forms of human trafficking covered under the United Nations (e.g., organ trafficking). Because these crimes are also happening to children in the United States, the tactics of child sex traffickers should be discussed as early as fourth, fifth, or sixth grade; but no later than middle school (i.e., seventh or eighth grade).

It must be made clear to students that sex traffickers do not always look like stereotypical predators. At age fourteen, I imagined rapists and serial killers hung around dark alleys and that pedophiles were old, creepy men with pockets full of candy. My trafficker did not look scary to me; he looked to be in his early twenties and was dressed in trendy clothes. Teens and parents alike must be made aware that traffickers look for young victims online, in malls, at bus stops, and any other place a teen may be without adult supervision. (See Appendix C: 10 Tips for Teens for Protection Against Traffickers.)

As a survivor of pimp-controlled sex trafficking, I offer tips to parents in Appendix D. As a survivor of gang-controlled trafficking while living at home, Theresa Flores offers the following warning signs to parents in a 2010 Mission Network News article: a drop in grades; unexplained school absences; frequent bouts of sickness, especially urinary tract infections or bladder infections; and acquiring new clothes, jewelry, and other expensive items.[2] Flores also recommends that parents stay involved in teens' lives and continue to check on their whereabouts. Additional tips from Flores can be found in her memoir, *The Slave Across the Street.*

Community members in general must be made aware of human trafficking and commercial sexual exploitation of children (CSEC). Well-informed organizations that are spreading awareness about CSEC to parent organizations, churches, and other populations in the community are important. One way to raise awareness about CSEC, including child sex trafficking, in communities is to screen the movie *Very Young Girls* (2007), an exposé of the commercial sexual exploitation of girls in New York City. Other films include *Sex + Money* (2011), ECPAT-USA's[3] *What I Have Been Through Is Not Who I Am* (2011), and *Nefarious* (2011). Runaway Girl, FPC (a California-based flexible purpose corporation), offers a one-day workshop designed to train all community members on action steps to prevent and recognize CSEC. Titled "CPR: Community Protocol for Response," this training aims to cover the basics (or ABCs) of commercial sexual exploitation of children: Awareness, Belief, and Capacity. Runaway Girl, FPC, was created by author, attorney, and child sex trafficking survivor Carissa Phelps; the company makes efforts to include local survivors in order to provide the most relevant, victim-centered information to community stakeholders.

Become an advocate for child victims of commercial sexual exploitation. Talk to friends and family about the realities behind "child prostitution." Advocate for law enforcement to use appropriate language in police reports and press releases. Hold community members accountable, including reporters, when they refer to child victims in derogatory ways, or when they project blame onto the children for their circumstances. Many times news reporters will refer to perpetrators as men or women or *alleged* pimps, while children are often unequivocally called *child prostitutes,* or worse, in the article. If a child is recovered from commercial sexual exploitation, stand up for that child's rights. If his or her photo is shown in the article, then demand that the photo be removed.

One fourteen-year-old child was recovered in Richmond, Virginia, in 2011 and her photo was posted online with a news article that covered the story. Although the photo was eventually removed, it was still visible on Facebook. Reporters must treat child victims of commercial sexual exploitation the same as all child victims of sexual abuse. Another example comes from a 2009 *Wired* article in which author Kevin Poulsen writes the following below a large, half-nude photo of a sixteen-year-old victim (which is still visible on the site today, four years later):

> She was a 16-year-old California girl looking for trouble on MySpace; he was a 22-year-old self-described pimp who liked the revealing photos she posted to her profile. Three weeks after they met on the social networking site, they were arrested together in real life outside a cheap motel in Sacramento, 50 miles from her home. She was turning tricks. On her arm, a fresh tattoo showed bundles of cash and her new acquaintance's street moniker in 72-point cursive.[4]

Law enforcement officials are often at a loss with what to do when faced with a child victim in the middle of the night while on patrol. Advocate for your local law enforcement and other first responders to develop a victim-centered response when working with child victims of commercial sexual exploitation. The U.S. Department of Justice's AMBER Alert Initiative has pioneered a training program for law enforcement and other partners that offers a multidisciplinary team approach involving prosecutors and service providers. Their goal is to address not only the recovery of the victim but also his or her long-term well-being. Their focus is for law enforcement to play a major role in the rescue and stabilization of the victim with the understanding that support services must be in place.

When it comes to creating a *prevention* curriculum for intermediate, middle, or high school students, however, I believe the focus should be to prevent all forms of CSEC, not just child sex trafficking. The program should either begin or end with a discussion about CSEC, including child sex trafficking as a form of human trafficking across the world. Then, a bulk of the curriculum should focus on media literacy (including a deconstruction of advertising messages and negative messages in the media), healthy relationships, healthy role models, mental health education and resources, coping skills, volunteer projects, education about social issues in the community and abroad, and education about community resources, among other ideas.

CSEC *prevention* must go deeper than just exposing the presence and dynamics of child sex trafficking in the United States. To prevent CSEC, children must be made aware of their own vulnerabilities and be given strategies to cope. Any and all professionals working with *at-risk* girls should *require* a CSEC-prevention curriculum; one example model is the ten-week program from My Life My Choice (see FightingExploitation.org).

After speaking, I am often asked by audience members what they can do to prevent CSEC, and my #1 answer is: *Support services in your community!* Victims of commercial sexual exploitation, including child sex trafficking, are kids who have often fallen through cracks within the system. And, victims of commercial sexual exploitation are often raised by families struggling with a myriad of personal and social issues, including poverty, domestic violence, addiction, and mental illness. Supporting *any* organization that provides services to vulnerable children *and their families* will help to combat CSEC. Such services include:

- Programs that prevent the abuse and neglect of children; and programs that support abused and neglected children.
- Programs that prevent poverty; and programs that support children and families living in poverty.
- Programs that support children living in foster care and children living without one or both parents.
- Programs that prevent children from dropping out of school; and services that support children who are struggling in school.
- Programs that prevent bullying; and services that support children affected by bullying.
- Programs that prevent children from running away; and services that support runaway children.
- Programs that provide mental health care services to children and their families.
- Programs that provide services to those working in the commercial sex industry.
- Programs that provide services to LGBTQ youth.

- Programs that provide services to children and adults struggling with substance abuse or addiction.

Breaking Free is an organization in Minnesota that provides services to girls and women "involved in systems of abuse and exploitation/sex trafficking." They recognize that sex trafficking is "a cyclical system of poverty, drug addiction, rape, abuse of power, and degradation." A representative from Breaking Free writes, "This cycle will continue to be passed down from one generation to the next unless intervention occurs and women have the resources and opportunities to build a new life for themselves and their children."[5] Education and opportunities must be made available to both child and adult victims of commercial sexual exploitation. There should be no line drawn between who deserves services.

Without proper services, child victims of commercial sexual exploitation cross into adulthood and are further blamed by society for their circumstances. Once a "willing victim" crosses over the age of eighteen; he or she is often labeled a criminal. I have met victims across the country between the ages of 18 and 25 who appear to be teenagers, some with developmental disabilities. I have also met women over the age of 25 who have been so tortured in "the life" that they often live in fear, pain, poverty, and loneliness. Many adult victims have lost their lives without effective intervention. Beth Jacobs, Founder of Willow Way, commented on the public perceptions of adults in prostitution:

> People often feel like [adult survivors of commercial sexual exploitation] have made a choice, so they are not worthy. It all seems to land on this magical age of 18. Like on this day, all of a sudden someone mails us this information about choices. It seems if you are trafficked at 16, people want to help, but when you grow older, even though your experience has not changed, we are relabeled to be grown-ups making an educated . . . "career" choice. I have a hard time reinforcing this thought pattern. It seems to be a way for blame to be put back on us, as well as reinforcing the "oldest profession theory." I hope we can educate people on this topic. . . . Personally I missed the information fairy when I turned 18; she must have forgotten where I was.[6]

You can support services in your community in a variety of ways: you can donate your time, money, skills, and/or gifts in kind. For example, are you a photographer? Then offer your skills to create fundraising or education materials for a local domestic violence shelter. Are you a web designer? Help a nonprofit by updating their website. Are you an accountant? Volunteer as a bookkeeper for a nonprofit business. Do you own a restaurant? Donate catering services to a fundraising or advocacy event. Be creative with your volunteer efforts; use your time, talents, and resources to benefit your community. Keep in mind that, at the core of your philanthropic efforts (i.e., donations, volunteerism, or advocacy); there should be a community service benefiting. If community services are lacking/needed, then awareness should draw attention to that.

Nonprofit and nongovernmental organizations are always in need of monetary donations. As a financial supporter of local services, especially youth-based organizations, you empower the children in your community to realize their full potential. With that being said, investigate those organizations you wish to support; and choose which organization(s) will benefit the most from your money. CharityWatch offers ten tips for "giving wisely," the first of which is to "know your charity," recommending that you request detailed information including a list of the board of directors, financial statements, and a mission statement.[7] Take your time in reading the mission statement. If the organization's mission is unclear to you, then it's likely unclear to the organization. While it may change over time, the mission statement must have a clear baseline. Without this, neither you nor the organization can understand its goals or boundaries.

In the nonprofit world of anti-trafficking, an organization's goals may be geared toward raising awareness, implementing methods of prevention, advocating for stronger laws, providing services to victims or victims' families, or any combination of these and more. All of these agendas are important, but you should pick and choose which agenda is compatible with your interests and the needs of your community. If you want to support an organization that offers services to victims, be sure you aren't donating to a nonprofit that concentrates its funding toward raising awareness, and vice versa. There needs to be a balance between awareness and supported services.

Ask questions in order to ensure that the organization has a viable plan in place to achieve its goals. For example, if the organization is currently providing services to victims, then inquire about the services. How many children or adults is the organization currently serving? What services are provided, and how are they provided? Is it a group home or do they manage case work involving service providers within the community? Who are the service providers? An honest organization will be transparent and will welcome an open discourse on its inner workings, except when it compromises the safety of its clients.

If the organization is raising money in order to provide future services, then ask for a timeline. Without goals, the organization may be disorganized. If the organization is implementing methods of prevention within the community, then ask for details. With whom are they working? Ask to participate in one of their programs or to visit their facilities. Heed the advice from CharityWatch: *know your charity.* Be wary of organizations that evoke emotion via documentaries, films, picture images of abuse, or survivor accounts of trauma, and then ask for your money.

Set aside your emotions and ask questions. As in all causes, there are those organizations that are making huge changes in their communities, and there are those looking to exploit a cause and a donor's generosity. There are also those organizations led by passionate but misdirected advocates who unintentionally spend donations on fruitless efforts. Your community service to the latter organization could be guidance and supervision as a member of the board. Reach out to others in the community for reviews on the organization(s) you wish to support. If you are proactive in vetting your local organizations, then you will strengthen your community's response to children and families in need. Otherwise, you risk loss of your time and money. For more tips on giving wisely, see CharityWatch and Charity Navigator.

There are two community services I'd like to highlight in the prevention of CSEC: mentoring and mental health services. Organizations that offer mentoring services are especially important in the prevention of CSEC. Child predators, including child sex traffickers, will target those youth who lack the support and guidance needed to overcome and avoid the many challenges associated with adolescence. Mentors can help children build self-confidence and coping skills; and they can expose children to different interests and ideas.

Little Egg Harbor Township, located in southern New Jersey, is broken down into several smaller communities, including Mystic Islands. Crystal and I lived less than a mile from Mystic, and we often walked there and hung out in the streets with friends. I often saw kids roaming the streets on foot or by bike; many got into trouble with fist fights and vandalism. For those students who lacked the confidence or interest to get involved with sports or other after-school activities, there was little for us to do. Those of us who were too young to drive and were generally unsupervised, we often hung out in parking lots or visited the Tuckerton Skateway on weekend nights. Mentorship organizations like Big

Brothers Big Sisters (BBBS) are vital for those kids lacking in guidance from or interaction with positive role models. Such an organization would have been very beneficial to me, and I believe a BBBS is a necessity to all communities.

Little Egg Harbor is a community that lies between the Little Egg Harbor Bay, the Pine Barrens, and the beaches of Long Beach Island. The actual list of things that had been available to us to do in Little Egg Harbor and the surrounding areas was endless: fishing, clamming, crabbing, decoy carving, bird watching, shell collecting, drawing and painting landscapes, photography, boating, sailing, canoeing, kayaking, hunting, trapping, taxidermy, surfing, lifeguarding and other summer beach jobs, volunteering in forestry or maritime industries, hiking, outdoor running, and swimming. Most communities have a local culture with local recreational resources; however, it takes interested and available adults to engage with children and expose them to these activities. Every community, no matter how big or small, must make an attempt to connect with its youngest citizens. If we don't look out for those kids who are most at risk in our communities, then who will?[8]

Along with mentoring services, mental health education and services are vital to every community member, but especially to those who are unable to access services on their own. Access to mental healthcare services must be made available to children in public schools; and comprehensive education about mental illness must be made available to students, parents, teachers, and school counselors. The lack of appropriate mental healthcare available to me during my school-age years proved to be detrimental. After I inadvertently reported the sexual abuse/exploitation by my cousin in elementary school, my case was handled poorly. I clammed up and told the social workers that I had lied about the abuse. Any child who reports abuse, regardless of whether he or she recants the statement, should receive extra attention or counseling in school. Even if the child actually did lie about the abuse, I believe that indicates that *something* is wrong. It could be something as simple as the child needing more attention.

For me, the first signs of depression, anger, and anxiety appeared in late elementary school. Although I was seen by a professional counselor in sixth grade, the counseling sessions were unsuccessful. The first problem was that the counselor was a man. As a preteen and as a survivor of sexual abuse, I was *not* comfortable talking to a man. Second, the counselor had a significant speech impediment and stuttered when he spoke. As an awkward and self-conscious preteen, I was barely comfortable with my own disadvantages. I was embarrassed and completely distracted by the man's difficulty in speaking to me. It was impossible for me to connect with this person, and so I never returned.

Failure to connect with the first therapist one meets with is not uncommon. It may take several attempts before a patient, especially a child patient, finds a compatible counselor. I should have been taken to a different office, but my mental healthcare ended there. By intermediate and middle school, I was exhibiting full-blown rage, which was directed both internally and externally. My behavior was above and beyond the angst experienced by a typical teenager, but neither I nor my family had the education to understand or recognize this.

I needed help. Real, professional help.

Unfortunately, the only person who recognized this and invested personal time responding to my distress was a sex trafficker. As I've discussed, traffickers target girls and boys who are vulnerable, and vulnerability manifests in many ways, including untreated symptoms of mental health issues. While some of my teachers and counselors recognized that I was struggling, their ability to help me was limited. I remember my eighth grade middle school counselor, Ms. Somma, sitting next to me after I had experienced another meltdown. I knew she wanted to help me, but I also knew she didn't know how. I remember wanting to ask for help but having no idea what was wrong.

Many have argued with me on this topic; they say parents, not the schools, should be responsible for the mental health of children. But, this is exactly the problem. Many (if not most) child victims of commercial sexual exploitation are raised in environments in which their needs are not being met at home. Without mental health treatment or support, these children will struggle in school, as I did. My grades dropped from all A's and B's in elementary school down to D's and F's in middle school. The one professional population to whom children have open access is their school teachers and counselors. If their needs can be met by them, then perhaps they will overcome their issues and succeed in school, thereby helping to prevent CSEC.

I believe many teachers and school counselors *want* to help students struggling and/or suffering from symptoms of mental illness, but they lack training and access to resources. My teachers and school counselors were the *only* adult professionals looking to help me, and the only adult professionals whom I could access *on my own.* I met with teachers and counselors before and after Atlantic City. Had I received education and awareness regarding mental health, perhaps I would have then known how to *ask* for help. New Jersey is one state attempting to provide resources to students through their School-Based Youth

Services Program (SBYSP). The mission of SBYSP is "to help young people navigate their adolescent years, finish their education, obtain skills leading to employment or continuing education, and graduate healthy and drug free."[9] It was an SBYSP counselor, Carol, who helped to place me in the Schaeffer Treatment Center after Atlantic City. Although Schaeffer was not the best treatment for a child victim of commercial sexual exploitation, it was the only local program that could offer counseling and a small school class setting. I recommend programs like SBYSP for every school in the United States; I recommend these programs provide education to students about mental health issues and resources for mental health services. But these programs also need to receive training on CSEC prevention, identification, and care, and they also must have working relationships with other programs in the community that offer services to youth. Remember, the availability and success of resources in the community are dependent on support from community members. Appendices E and F offer some CSEC prevention tips for elementary and middle school teachers and counselors.

The protection of children from abuse is also the responsibility of all community members. If you suspect child abuse or neglect, report it to your state's Child Protective Services agency; or report it to Childhelp. Childhelp is a national organization whose mission is "to meet the physical, emotional, educational, and spiritual needs of abused, neglected and at-risk children." Their efforts are focused on "advocacy, prevention, treatment, and community outreach."[10] If you suspect sexual exploitation of a child, make a CyberTipline report to the National Center for Missing and Exploited Children (NCMEC). The CyberTipline serves as a clearinghouse for tips and leads about potential child sexual exploitation. Reports to the CyberTipline assist law enforcement and prosecutors in their detection, investigation, and prosecution of child sexual exploitation crimes. According to NCMEC, more than 1.9 million reports of suspected child sexual exploitation have been made to the CyberTipline between 1998 and June 2013.[11]

Remember, no community is immune to the sexual exploitation of children. Minh Dang, former Executive Director of Don't Sell Bodies, explains that growing up within an insular Vietnamese-American community was a contributing factor to her ongoing sexual abuse and family-controlled trafficking. "Ethnic enclaves are important sources of support for many people," Minh wrote in a personal e-mail, "[but I think warning signs were missed in my case because] it was easy for people to [assume] 'oh, those are just strict immigrant parents who don't let their kid go out and play.'"[12] If you suspect any of the following online or offline, call 1-800-The-Lost (1-800-843-5678) or fill out a report online at www.missingkids.com/cybertipline:

- Possession, manufacturing, and distribution of child pornography
- Online enticement of children for sexual acts
- "Child sex trafficking"/CSEC
- Sex tourism involving children
- Child sexual molestation
- Unsolicited obscene material sent to a child
- Misleading domain name with the intent to deceive a minor into viewing harmful material
- Misleading words or digital images on the Internet with the intent to deceive a minor into viewing harmful material

If you suspect child sex trafficking activity, or any type of human trafficking crime, contact the National Human Trafficking Resource Center (NHTRC) hotline at 1–888–373–7888; or send a text message to BeFree (233733); or report a tip online at www.PolarisProject.org. Hotline Call Specialists are available 24 hours a day, 7 days a week, 365 days a year to take reports from anywhere in the country related to potential trafficking victims, suspicious behaviors, and/or locations where trafficking is suspected to occur. All reports are confidential, and interpreters are available.

If effective services are lacking in your community, then it may be your calling to advocate for laws that will aid in the prevention of child exploitation, including CSEC, and in the protection of victims. This can include laws that will:

- bolster or create preventative community services, including mental health services;
- require mental health education and awareness in schools;
- require education and awareness about CSEC, including child sex trafficking, in schools and in the community;
- require parents and foster care services to report missing children to law enforcement and/or NCMEC;
- require education about healthy relationships in schools and other youth programs;

- require media literacy programs in schools and other youth programs;
- discontinue advertising to children;
- require training in CSEC for law enforcement, mental health professionals, and other first responders;
- and require services and protocols to be implemented for a victim-centered response to cases of CSEC.

Polaris Project works with advocates and legislators across the country in efforts to improve laws related to human trafficking in America, including mandates for victim services. One such bill pioneered by Polaris Project in Virginia in 2012 required that human trafficking awareness and training materials be made available to local schools. This bill was sponsored by Senator Adam Ebbin and Delegate Vivian E. Watts. On January 16, 2012, I testified in Richmond, Virginia, before the General Assembly Education Committee in support of the bill. It passed and was signed into law by Governor Bob McDonnell. My hope is for these materials to include ideas for prevention, including media literacy.

One way to promote media literacy is to create or support education and awareness campaigns within your community and schools that expose children's advertising. The Media Education Foundation (MEF) offers a documentary called *Consuming Kids* by Adriana Barbaro and Jeremy Earp; this documentary is an effective tool to inform and raise awareness about children's advertising. It exposes many tactics including use of the "cool factor" to promote designer brands. The MEF offers a discussion guide with which teachers can engage students after watching the film. In her book *Consuming Kids,* Susan Linn offers solid advice to parents and professionals working with children about how to avoid and handle children's advertising. Linn also offers additional ways for community members, policy makers, and others to advocate against children's advertising.

Become aware of the advertising around you, and consider how these consumer messages are affecting you and your family's purchasing habits and personal values. Be mindful of which companies advertise to children, especially those that advertise designer brands to children. Refuse to purchase products from companies that advertise using unhealthy images or messages, especially when these ads are directed at children. Bring attention to these advertisements, and write to the companies. If a television show or movie acts as a vehicle for children's advertising, then refuse to watch it, bring attention to it, and demand a change. Our collective consumer decisions will be the driving force to change children's advertising and to influence what messages are seen and heard in other advertising.

Become aware of what messages and values are being projected in the media, including in advertisements, music videos, music lyrics, movies, and television. Refuse to consume products from companies that promote the objectification and/or sexual objectification of women, or other forms of violence against women; and refuse to promote or support celebrities who project negative values or behavior, especially to teens. We consumers have the power to influence what messages are in the media; our voices and our dollars do make an impact.

In chapter 6, I presented examples of music lyrics that promote violence against women. One of those examples was a lyric from the song, U.O.E.N.O, in which rapper Rick Ross, who was also a spokesperson for Reebok, describes an act of date rape. "On April 4, scores of protesters with the women's activist group UltraViolet picketed outside a Reebok store in Manhattan," writes CNN reporter Lawrence Crook III, "and [they] delivered a petition demanding the sportswear manufacturer break with Ross." Days later, rapper Rick Ross was dropped as a spokesperson for Reebok.[13] Whether you choose to spend your money elsewhere or picket on the streets, you have the power to hold artists and businesses accountable for their decisions.

All community members, but especially teens and preteens, must be educated about negative messages in the media. For those teachers or counselors (or anyone else working with children) who are interested in providing this education, the MEF offers excellent documentaries along with discussion guides. Documentaries I recommend include *Dreamworlds 3, Killing Us Softly 4, Flirting with Danger,* and *What a Girl Wants.* Documentaries are available for preview on their website at www.mediaed.org; choose one that best fits your grade level and goals. Documentaries are added on a regular basis, so check back often.

Another documentary that raises awareness about negative messages in the media and their effects on girls' self-image and self-esteem is *Cover Girl Culture* by Nicole Clark. As a former Elite fashion model, Nicole gained valuable insight into the inner workings of the fashion industry. Through exclusive interviews with the editors of *Teen Vogue* and *Elle* magazines, the film takes a hard look at what messages are being conveyed to young people in our celebrity-centered culture. *Cover Girl Culture* also includes a curriculum for teachers and other caregivers to explore this topic more deeply with students. For more information, visit www.CoverGirlCulture.com.

Creating and supporting campaigns that promote healthy messages to teens is another way to negate negative messages in the media. For example, the Parents Television Council (PTC) has an awareness campaign called "4 Every Girl" which "strives to create a media environment where girls feel valued and are defined by healthy images of themselves."[14] Find and support role models and other organizations that promote positive images, messages, and values to children. Also, create opportunities for young local role models to connect with children and teens. Connecting with young, diverse, and local role models will counteract the ideal images of success seen in the media.

EPILOGUE

MY JOURNEY FROM VICTIM TO SURVIVOR BEGAN WITH acceptance, personal responsibility, and determination. My parents had had another late argument sometime after Atlantic City. I listened from my room as my mother stormed into her bedroom. There was the usual long silence as I imagined my father balking in the living room, but then I heard a loud noise from the kitchen. Silence followed. I usually stayed in my room when these arguments occurred; not out of fear but out of contempt. I hated my parents' drinking and arguing, and I refused to get involved. But this night was different; something led me to the kitchen to investigate the noise.

I peeked around the corner to see my father sitting on the floor with an explosion of Hershey's chocolates around him. He sat like a child with his feet sprawled in front of him, unwrapping the chocolates and eating them one by one. It occurred to me that my parents' drinking and arguing was not intentional on their parts. It was something out of their control. I sat on the floor next to my father, and we ate chocolates together, peeling at the wrapping and smiling at each other. I eventually let go of my anger about their drinking; and I tried to accept my parents for who they were and where they were at. They were human; they both had shortcomings, and they were both struggling in their own ways. But they both loved me the best that they could.

I forgave them for the nights I was left at my cousin's house because I knew they would have never left me there had they known what was really going on. My parents loved me; they just loved me to the best of *their ability during that trying time.* My mom tried her best to make up for those earlier years and she tried her best to help me in high school. It was difficult to write about my parents' shortcomings in this book because I don't want to hurt them, and we still have never really talked about those days. I love them, and I'm sorry that we all missed out on better times together. I write about these events now not to embarrass my family but to help professionals working with today's victims of commercial sexual exploitation.

Without appropriate counseling, depression led me to substance abuse in high school. What began as as recreational use of PCP (i.e., phencyclidine) led to addiction and incarceration in juvenile jail. As I faced adulthood, high school graduation, and criminal charges for possession and intent to distribute street drugs, I made a decision: I wanted a better life. I realized that nobody was going to swoop in and "save" me—I had to save myself. I had to *want* it for myself. I'm speaking to both victims and those who work with victims of commercial sexual exploitation when I say that, regardless of how many services are available, in the end, it is up to the victim *to want* and *to accept* help.

In a 2012 AMBER Alert video, Keisha Head talked about her determination to move forward. "Every decision I make from now on is up to me," Keisha said. "I cannot blame my molesters, my pimp, my aunt, all these people who I had allowed to form my future. I knew that I had to take control of that, and that's what I did; and I never looked back."[1] Today, Keisha is a wife, a mother, a professional speaker, and a powerful advocate for victims in Atlanta, Georgia, and beyond.

Like Keisha, I stopped allowing the past to hold me back, and I took control over my future. Who was to blame was no longer my concern; it was *how* am I going to overcome? I enrolled in community college after high school and applied for student loans to cover tuition fees. My Aunt Ruth and Uncle Dennis (relatives I did not see often in childhood) paid for my college books each semester, and my parents continued to support me at home. Having the ability to attend college without worries over rent or food was a blessing even greater than I realized at the time. Despite having this support, however, attending college was not easy. Having had my license suspended for the drug charges, I depended on public transportation to get to school and back.

I walked to Main Street every day and waited for the New Jersey Transit bus often in heavy rain, sleet, and snow. It took two public buses to travel the hour-long trip to Ocean County Community College. Without Crystal's friendship and the influence of drugs, I was painfully shy. I ate homemade ham sandwiches in a bathroom stall at school, and I stared out the window of the bus back and forth to school, alone and lonely. Nobody says the process of overcoming is easy. Choosing to move forward can be a difficult process. It takes hard work and determination. I had to take it one day at a time. And, I had to force myself to hold my head up high until it felt normal to stand upright. I had to consciously force myself to look people straight in the eye until I no longer feared being seen.

I applied and was accepted to the Richard Stockton College of New Jersey. My parents gave me their car to go to school and back; and I cannot thank my parents enough for their love and support during this time. Although we never really talked about the past, my years in college were a healing period between my parents and me. I loved being at home with them. My mother became my ally again. My personal story before and after Atlantic City follows a dark path in my family's history. But I want to point out the many wonderful things about my parents from childhood.

My favorite memories of my mom are when she scrambled eggs with ketchup for me in the morning, and when she laundered my sheets and made my bed at night. She allowed me to eat cereal in my room while playing video games, no matter how many times I spilled the milk. And she never forced me to eat food that grossed me out. My mother stood up for me even when I was wrong, and she played Nintendo with me on the floor of my bedroom when I had no friends in the neighborhood. My mom tried to make up for the lack of guidance and supervision before Atlantic City, and she was forced to make some difficult decisions for me in high school. Although, at the time, I was angry with her for some of these decisions, I am so grateful today. I feel lucky to have my mom by my side as a friend and confidante.

My father was my caretaker whenever I was sick, and he was my cheerleader whenever I was unsure. On some arbitrary day in elementary school, my father took the training wheels off my bicycle. Despite my adamant protests, he sent me down the driveway toward the road. I pumped the pedals in disbelief, but my dad knew all along that I could ride my bike on my own. My dad and I shared cartons of rice pudding and pounds of cheesecake together in high school, and he supported me in everything I did and everything I wanted to do. When I wanted to travel across the country, he pasted a giant map onto a giant piece of cardboard; and then he gave me a pile of pushpins. My dad and I were buddies before Atlantic City, and we became buddies again. I love both of my parents, and I'm glad I had them then and now.

After two years at Stockton College, I graduated in 2000 with a 3.6 GPA in Biology, with a minor in Writing. My first job out of college was a scientific writing job in Philadelphia, and I felt like I was on top of the world. There was only one problem: *I used to be a prostitute.* At least, this was what I thought to myself every time my coworkers got to talking about life in middle school, high school, and college. My whole life had been defined by Atlantic City. Without understanding the dynamics of commercial sexual exploitation, especially child sex trafficking, I still thought that I had *chosen* to be a prostitute.

I harbored this dark secret from my past, and as a result, drug use returned and bad relationships followed me through my twenties. I lacked the self-esteem and self-confidence to know that I deserved better. I fled to different states as I tried to start my life over, each time falling into the same patterns. In February 2006, I moved to Richmond, Virginia. Although it was a long process, I again worked toward making changes. I met my husband, Ben, who taught me that love is about respect, trust, encouragement, and accountability. We have helped each other move forward together, as we each move toward our own personal goals. (Ben completed his certification to become a yoga teacher while I wrote this book.)

I joined a boot camp exercise group for women a couple years after relocating to Richmond. Exercise, especially running, was never anything I *ever* saw myself doing. It was difficult at first, but each week I felt myself getting physically, mentally, and emotionally stronger. The support and encouragement from my boot camp buddies Bethany, Anna, and Wendy helped me to achieve a personal state of empowerment that I had never known. Exercise helped me to overcome smoking and binge drinking. I also discovered yoga and the teachings of Eckhart Tolle, which bolstered my coping skills and personal empowerment. I highly recommend yoga, meditation, and Tolle's books, including *The Power of Now,* to anyone and everyone, but especially to survivors of commercial sexual exploitation and other trauma.

AS I EMBRACED MY NEW SENSE OF SELF, SOMETHING unexpected happened in 2009. One night I came across a documentary about human trafficking in India. The program featured many women and girls who were tricked, sold, or otherwise forced to work in brothels. I was completely taken in by the stories of these women—some of them seemed so similar to my own. I initially dismissed the idea that I might be *like* these women, believing that human trafficking only happened overseas. After the program ended, I searched the Internet and found the organization, Children of the Night (COTN) in Los Angeles. "*Rescuing America's Children from Prostitution,*" the website says.[2] I stared at my computer screen. Nearly twenty years later, I learned not only that my story was not unique but that it also was repeating itself regularly in cities across America. I thought I was the only person in the world who experienced this, *this* being a victimization I then understood to fall under the scope of "human trafficking."

I called the hotline for COTN in search of an organization close to Richmond. I was connected with several other organizations until I reached Courtney's House in Washington, D.C. I met the Founder, Tina Frundt, who is also a survivor of child sex trafficking. Meeting another survivor was life-changing. Literally, for nearly twenty years, I believed I was the only person to whom this happened. I was immediately embraced by survivors and advocates from Courtney's House and Shared Hope International. Their unconditional friendship, love, and support was the platform from which my true healing from Atlantic City was launched. I have since connected with survivors and advocates across the country who continue to teach, support, and inspire me every day.

After hearing the stories of other survivors, I realized that I had been a victim, that I did not "choose" to become a prostitute. Documentaries like *Dreamworlds 3* and *Consuming Kids,* among others, also helped to make the connections in my victimization. Hearing the stories from victims, from young survivors, however, was heartbreaking. I heard girls question their status as a victim because they "chose" to run away; I heard other girls claim their biggest difficulty in moving forward was the "easy money" from commercial sex. These sentiments were so similar to those held by my fourteen-year-old self. Hearing these stories, the stories of children, is what inspired me to start speaking out.

Today, I pull this secret from my past and share it because I am no longer ashamed. I was not at fault, and neither are the girls and boys I meet today. I was a child, exploited and manipulated, but it took many years of growing up for me to understand my vulnerability at age fourteen. It is for this reason I am most passionate about speaking to law enforcement, therapists, and others who work with victims of commercial sexual exploitation. It takes *time* for a teen to mature enough to see his or her limitations; therefore, it's imperative that the adults who work with such children are informed. I share my story with professionals and the public alike in order to shed light on those whom the media often call *child prostitutes.* These *prostitutes* are children, and they have been raised in the world that *we* have created for them. An oversexualized, consumer-driven society will create oversexualized, consumer-driven children who are vulnerable to the likes of sex traffickers.

The last message I have is for those professionals working with victims of commercial sexual exploitation: To all the officers, social workers, therapists, and other advocates who face frustration when working with this population, I promise you that every bit of work you do is effective. You may not see it right away, but your actions will stick with victims for a lifetime. For me, it took many years of nudging from my parents, teachers, and other family members before I finally snapped out of my tunnel vision. I hope the success of my story and many others will inspire you to keep moving forward with victims. Barbara Amaya, Greg Bucceroni, Neet Childs, Minh Dang, Tina Frundt, Stacy Lundgren, T Ortiz, Katrina Owens, Carissa Phelps, Jes Richardson, and Savannah Sanders are only a few of the many survivors of commercial sexual exploitation of children in our country who are success stories today.

APPENDIX A

RESOURCES FOR PARENTS AND VICTIMS

VICTIMS/SURVIVORS

- National Human Trafficking Resource Center (NHTRC): 1-888-373-7888
- National Center for Missing & Exploited Children (NCMEC): 1-800-THE LOST® (1-800-843-5678)
- Children of the Night (COTN): 1-800-551-1300
- Courtney's House (Support Hotline for Survivors, By Survivors): 1-888-261-3665
- Boys Town (for girls and boys feeling depressed or struggling): 1-800-448-3000
- The National Suicide Prevention Lifeline: 1-800-273-TALK (8255)
- RAINN (for victims of rape or other sexual abuse): 1-800-656-HOPE (4673)
- National Domestic Violence (for victims of physical or emotional abuse): 1-800-799-SAFE (7233)
- National Runaway Switchboard (for kids who have or want to run away): 1-800-RUNAWAY (786-2929)

PARENTS OF VICTIMS

The National Center for Missing & Exploited Children (NCMEC) will assist in any missing-child case at the request of law enforcement or the child's legal guardian. If your child is missing or has been exploited, call NCMEC's Family Advocacy Division. This division employs master's-level-trained mental health and child welfare professionals who work together to proactively help families, law enforcement, social service agencies, and mental health services by providing a support network for child victims and their families. While NCMEC provides crisis and mental health support via telephone, families often require immediate and in-person intervention. The Family Advocacy Outreach Network (FAON) connects families of missing and sexually exploited children with resources in their communities. FAON recruits professionals experienced in crisis management who are willing to provide therapeutic services for families on a pro bono basis or sliding fee scale. FAON professionals provide ongoing crisis management and therapy to strengthen families as they work through trauma. To reach NCMEC's Family Advocacy Division, please call 1-800-THE-LOST (1-800-843-5678) or e-mail family-advocacy@ncmec.org.

Another NCMEC program offered to families is Team Hope (Help Offering Parents Empowerment). Team Hope offers peer support for families with missing or sexually exploited children. NCMEC matches families with experienced and trained volunteers who provide them with support, friendship, coping skills, and compassion. Team HOPE volunteers are mothers, fathers, siblings, and extended family members who have had, or still have, a child who is missing or has been sexually exploited. Team Hope volunteers turn their personal tragedies into vital lifelines of support for other families; they are passionate about extending their hearts, time, experience, knowledge, and wisdom to those who have a missing or exploited child. For more information, call 1-866-305-HOPE (4673).

For additional resources, contact the National Human Trafficking Resource Center (NHTRC) hotline at 1-888-373-7888.

APPENDIX B

RESOURCES FOR LAW ENFORCEMENT AND OTHER FIRST RESPONDERS

TRAINING FOR ALL LEVELS OF LAW ENFORCEMENT AND FIRST RESPONDERS

Traffickers often tell their victims that, if they turn to the police, they will be arrested and ridiculed. Unfortunately, this is sometimes true. The initial exchange between a child victim of commercial sexual exploitation and an officer sets the tone for all subsequent interactions between that child and other law enforcement, victim advocates, social service providers, and clinicians. If law enforcement officers or other responders do not offer compassion or sympathy, a child may come to view anyone involved in his or her case with contempt and distrust, thereby compromising the child's openness toward aftercare services. By the time I was recognized by law enforcement as being a victim, not a criminal, I had mentally and emotionally shut down. Child victims *need* law enforcement to be on their sides, especially those victims who present as uncooperative toward officers or other first responders. When encountering such victims, officers must respond with discipline and constructive action, not prejudice or discrimination.

Education and training for *all* levels of law enforcement are the only ways to prevent any initial mistreatment of a child victim. Such training should include the perspective of a survivor, especially one who was deemed a "willing victim" (see chapter 2). Ideally, this training would include perspectives from several survivors of various situations of child sex trafficking and other forms of commercial sexual exploitation. Through survivor testimony, law enforcement officers can gain insight into the potential mindset of victims. The U.S. Department of Justice's (DOJ) AMBER Alert Initiative has pioneered a training program for law enforcement and other partners that offers a multidisciplinary team approach involving prosecutors and service providers and offers testimony from survivor speakers, including myself, when available.

DEVELOP A PROTOCOL FOR CASES OF COMMERCIAL SEXUAL EXPLOITATION OF CHILDREN (CSEC)

The goal of AMBER Alert's program is to address not only the recovery of the victim but also his or her long-term well-being. The AMBER Alert team urges prosecutors to work aggressively with law enforcement at targeting traffickers and criminal organizations promoting or engaging in human trafficking, as well as addressing the demand side. Sergeant Byron Fassett, Detective Cathy De La Paz, San Diego Deputy District Attorney Gretchen Means, Jim Walters (Southern Methodist University), and Sergeant Holly Joshi with the Oakland Police Department are just a few of the exceptional trainers in this program. For more information, please contact askamber@fvtc.edu. I also recommend reaching out to the FBI's Innocence Lost Initiative for additional training and resources.

Develop a formal victim-centered protocol response for working with victims of child sex trafficking and other forms of commercial sexual exploitation, and ensure all officers and personnel are informed and trained on the policy. Included in the AMBER Alert Initiative's training program is an overview of the Dallas Police Department's High Risk Victim and Trafficking (HRVT) model mentioned in Chapter 10. If you are interested in learning about alternative models implemented in other counties and states, I recommend a few articles from the journal, *National Center for Prosecution of Child Abuse*.[1]

I'm often asked by law enforcement for advice on what to say to potential victims in order to gain their trust and cooperation. My best advice is to speak with sincerity and to know what options are available for victims. When working with an uncooperative victim, I encourage law enforcement and other first responders to put away their clipboards and *talk* to the child. Don't treat him or her like a criminal. Be professional and authoritative, but talk to him or her as you would with any child for whom you really cared. If a child won't talk to you, start small. Most teens' and preteens' thoughts and experiences revolve around music and celebrities, so start there. I believe I would have responded to questions about my favorite songs or bands. Then, I may have opened up about friends and reasons for running away.

CREATE A LIST OF OPTIONS

When creating a formal protocol, investigate and include potential services for victims and their families. Each case of commercial sexual exploitation that you encounter that involves a child will likely differ; so it's important to know what services are and are not available in your area. For example, some child victims may require drug and alcohol treatment, while others may not. Hotline operators at the National Center for Missing and Exploited Children (NMCEC) and at the National Human Trafficking Resource Center (NHTRC) can help with locating resources in your area. I also recommend visiting the facilities of these programs, especially local programs. Meet with those in charge of each program, and ask questions about their services. While such investigating may seem like the parents' responsibility, it is often the case that parents of victims are uninvolved for various reasons. If you care about keeping these kids off the streets, then ensure placement or enrollment in the best available program(s). You may be the only chance these kids have at getting on the right track.

It's important to provide a copy of this list not only to the child's parents (or legal guardian) but also to the child. Such children are often known to run away; should that happen again, they need to have an idea of what resources are available to them. One of the reasons child victims of commercial sexual exploitation run away is because they want to gain some control over their own lives. Providing a list of resources directly to them will enable them to seek assistance on their own, if needed. This empowers and equips them with the right tools to seek safe and effective resources. Otherwise, they are left only with the options they knew before being exploited. See Additional Resources at the end of this appendix, and see Appendix A for a list of national resources to offer victims and their families.

Without effective programs in place for child victims of commercial sexual exploitation, law enforcement may be forced to arrest a child victim for the sake of protection from further exploitation. This is why every state and commonwealth needs programs that are properly trained to work with such victims, including in-patient programs and out-patient services. Once these programs are in place, protocols must be created to allow for easy communication and collaboration between law enforcement and the programs. Until these resources are available in your area, please know that there *are* national programs available for placement of child victims of commercial sexual exploitation (e.g., Children of the Night in Los Angeles). However, not all programs are "locked-down." In other words, although most programs are secured to prevent outsiders from getting in, not all are secured to prevent victims from leaving. I realize this may be viewed as an obstacle for law enforcement officers who are working with victim witnesses; however, consider the best interests of the child. Don't incarcerate a child only to ensure cooperation.

I don't believe in placing a child victim in juvenile detention unless there are no other options. At fourteen, I was terrified of getting beat up in high school; this was one of the many reasons I wanted to run away in the first place. I cannot imagine how abandoned and scared I would have felt inside a juvenile detention facility after those 36 hours in Atlantic City. However, if I had been released back to the streets, I likely would have returned to Greg and Nicki. I know they were planning to take me to New York City the following day. Had that happened, there is no telling where I might be today.

IDENTIFYING VICTIMS

While on the street that first night in Atlantic City, I was warned about a group of undercover police officers. As you can guess after reading my story, I avoided this team of police. Had I met them that night, the night before Greg raped me, I would have likely lied about my age and been generally uncooperative. Commercially sexually exploited youth are a difficult population to identify. There are many reasons for a victim's lack of compliance or inability to self-identify; every survivor has a different story.

As was I, child victims of sex trafficking are often instructed to lie about their age, and they are sometimes even given fraudulent identification. Not only are child victims told by traffickers to distrust police, but they often come from backgrounds of abuse and neglect in which people in positions of authority have consistently let them down. Many kids feel safer and/or more "in control" on the streets than at home (as did I), so they are unlikely to cooperate with law enforcement. I realize this can be difficult and frustrating to officers, but try to keep in mind what these kids may have endured up until the moment you meet them.

After speaking, I am often asked what indicators about my situation might have tipped off law enforcement that I was a victim of child sex trafficking. At first I thought this question was odd. I answered with tips like: *I looked like a child on the street in the middle of the night wearing a red dress and high heels on a corner known for prostitution.* I realize now that it's not always this simple. Many children who are being commercially sexually exploited may be dressed in jeans and other street clothes, while others are often kept in motels as photos of them are posted on Internet sites. Also, many adult women involved in commercial sex look so young that they appear to be teenagers, while some teenagers appear to be over eighteen.

Because many child victims claim to be and can appear to be adults, it is necessary to consider *any* young adult involved in prostitution to potentially be under the age of eighteen and/or under the control of a trafficker. Regardless of the person's age or consent, he or she is likely in need of services. Have compassion and offer compassion; inform these individuals of local services. You have no idea what this person may have been through; your kindness or concern may be the first step toward his or her ability to trust in others and to seek help. Also, this person could be a future ally in reporting cases of minors, or adults who are working against their will. Another tip is to keep track of children reported missing in your area, especially reports of Endangered Runaways. The National Center for Missing and Exploited Children (NCMEC) will list by state all cases of missing children reported to NCMEC, including endangered runaways. See www.MissingKids.com.

Reactive Victim Identification

Polaris Project generated a list of reasons why many victims of domestic sex trafficking (children or adults) may not self-identify or seek help on their own. When investigating crimes and interviewing potential victims, they recommend looking for any of the following signs which may indicate sex trafficking.

- Captivity/Confinement—locked indoors, locked in rooms, locked in closets
- Frequent accompaniment/guarded—interactions are monitored or controlled by the [trafficker]
- Use and threat of violence—severe physical retaliation (beatings, rapes, sexual assault)
- Fear—of physical retaliation, of death, or of arrest
- Use and threat of reprisals against loved ones—against children or family members
- Shame—about the activities they have been forced to perform
- Self-blame—brainwashed by the [trafficker] to blame themselves
- Dependency—on the [trafficker] after years of control
- Debt bondage—may have a debt to the [trafficker] that they feel they need to pay off
- Loyalty to the [trafficker]—Stockholm syndrome, similarities to Battered Women's Syndrome
- Social barriers and unfamiliarity with surroundings—due to frequent movement
- No personal ID or documentation—which is often confiscated by the [trafficker]
- Distrust of law enforcement—brainwashed to fear law enforcement by the [trafficker] or learned distrust of law enforcement due to direct negative experiences
- Isolation—from others, from other support structures, from means of relief
- Misinformation and false promises—have been told lies or deceitful information
- Hopelessness/Resignation—feelings of no self-worth, disassociation, giving up, apathy
- Lack of knowledge of social systems—may not understand social service infrastructure or how and where to access help

Proactive Victim Identification

Be proactive in your search for child victims of commercial sexual exploitation. First, coordinate training sessions for those who may regularly work with child victims. This would include school teachers and school counselors, as well as personnel working at youth shelters, foster care programs, and other social services. The most important instructions for trainees would be to *report* missing or runaway youth, especially foster youth, to local law enforcement *and* to NCMEC. Andrea Powell, Co-Founder of FAIR Girls, also recommends training these groups to watch for the following signs of potential trafficking: a sudden withdrawal from friends or classmates; a drop in grades; unexplained absences, particularly on Thursdays or Fridays; falling asleep in class; a sudden shift in dress—particularly toward provocative or risqué clothing; a new, much older boyfriend, especially one who seems controlling; a growing occurrence of suddenly texting or wanting to step out of class to talk to someone; acquirement of expensive items like cell phones, designer clothes, beauty products; and discussions about going to bars, dance clubs, or traveling outside of the city.[2] Perhaps a combined number of warning signs would warrant further questioning of the child and/or further actions.

Also, warning signs may differ. For example, child victims of family-controlled trafficking may display warning signs similar to victims of early childhood sexual abuse, while victims of gang-controlled trafficking may show warning signs similar to victims of physical abuse or domestic violence. Those who work with youth, especially at-risk youth, must institute an awareness program and/or prevention curriculum (see chapters 12 and 13). Runaway Girl, FPC (a California-based flexible purpose corporation) offers a two-day training workshop intended for anyone in regular contact with youth who are at risk of commercial sexual exploitation. Runaway Girl, FPC was developed by Carissa Phelps, author, attorney, and survivor of child sex trafficking. Runaway Girl, FPC includes survivor trainers from across the country, including myself, when available. To learn more or to schedule a training, visit www.RunawayGirlTraining.com or contact Training@RunawayGirl.org.

Second, coordinate training sessions for those who are most likely to encounter youth who are actively being commercially sexually exploited. This would include those working in the transportation industry, including taxi drivers, bus drivers, and personnel working at train and bus stations, toll plazas, truck stops, and airports, among other transportation hubs. There may be local chapters for larger organizations already doing this work (e.g., Truckers Against Trafficking and Airline Ambassadors); connect with them to ensure an effective partnership. I offer the following warning signs for taxi drivers:

- Watch for victims of any kind of abuse or exploitation.
- Child victims of commercial sexual exploitation may appear to be confused, inexperienced, withdrawn, or afraid of their older (or generally more authoritative) companions. Be aware and report anything suspicious to police or to the NHTRC.
- Watch for minors or young adults who are dressed maturely/provocatively and traveling alone or with older companions, especially late at night or early morning, in unsafe areas or places known for prostitution, and/or if the minor appears to be lost or inexperienced with using taxis.
- If an adult is instructing a minor or young adult about sex or prostitution practices, including handing the child or teen prophylactics, report it immediately to the police or to the NHTRC.

- If a man or woman appears to be hiding a minor or young adult companion within the taxi (i.e., pushing the minor to the floor or below the level of the window), then report it.

Other populations likely to come into contact with child victims of commercial sexual exploitation are those working in the hospitality industry and medical fields. FBI Agent James Melia regularly trains and works with hospitality staff in his area as a way to proactively identify victims of sex trafficking. Agent Melia recommends looking for a combination of the following signs of potential trafficking:

- Guests insist on paying bills from a large amount of cash and insist on paying for the room one day at a time; or guests often use Green Dot or Vanilla prepaid Visa or MasterCard debit cards
- Guests excessively use taxis, have no personal transportation, and are often without luggage
- Excessive traffic in and out of the room; and excessive meetings in the lobby between men and the guests
- Excessive requests for towels; and requests that the room not be cleaned
- Discovery of the following items when rooms are cleaned: provocative clothes; large amounts of beauty products; sex toys; massage oils and lubricants; feminine products; Viagra pills; large quantities of new condoms, used condoms, and/or condom wrappers; computers; notebooks, ledgers, and other papers with names and addresses; and multiple cell phones[3]

When training and collaborating with motels and hotels, be sure to inform management about End Child Prostitution and Trafficking (ECPAT) USA. ECPAT-USA, has a partnership with the American Hotel and Lodging Association to offer online training to educate staff on commercial sexual exploitation of children (CSEC) and the signs of trafficking and to create protocols for action. Once internal training and procedures are established, businesses can sign the Tourism Child—Protection Code of Conduct; the Code is "an industry-driven, multi-stakeholder initiative" that offers travel and tourism businesses the tools to become wholly proactive in the fight against CSEC.[4]

In 2011, Hilton Worldwide signed the Code becoming the second U.S.-based multi-brand hospitality company to sign it. "As part of [our] commitment to the code, Hilton Worldwide developed an internal awareness and training program for its hotel employees to help them recognize the signs of child trafficking and take appropriate action," stated Jennifer Silberman, Vice President of Corporate Responsibility at Hilton, "The company is part of several anti-trafficking coalitions and supports [nongovernmental organizations] in their advocacy, awareness and survivor services programming." Whether big or small, all businesses in this industry can get involved.[5]

Medical staff may also come into contact with victims of commercial sexual exploitation. For training health professionals, consult the DVD, *Uncovering the Truth: Identifying Sexually Exploited Youth in a Health Setting,* co-produced by Global Health Promise, ECPAT-USA, and GEMS. The following indicators, which apply specifically to child victims of commercial sexual exploitation, have been compiled and are offered by the Girls Education & Mentoring Services (GEMS) of New York City:

- The age of an individual has been verified to be under eighteen and the individual is involved in the sex industry

- The age of the individual has been verified to be under eighteen and the individual has a record of prior arrest(s) for prostitution
- Discrepancies in behavior and reported age—i.e., clues in behavior or appearance that suggest that the individual is underage, but he/she lies about his/her age
- Evidence of sexual trauma
- Multiple or frequent sexually transmitted infections (STIs), especially evidence of a lack of treatment for STIs
- Multiple or frequent pregnancies
- Individual reports an excessively large number of sexual partners, especially when it is not age-appropriate (i.e., fifteen-year-old girl reporting dozens of sexual partners)
- Individuals who are under the age of eighteen who express interest in, or may already be in, relationships with adults or older men
- Use of lingo or slang relating to the individual's involvement in prostitution—i.e., referring to a boyfriend as "Daddy" or talking about "the life"
- Evidence of controlling or dominating relationships—i.e., repeated phone calls from a "boyfriend" and/or excessive concern about displeasing a partner
- Individual is dressed in inappropriate clothing (i.e., lingerie or other attire associated with the sex industry)
- Presence of unexplained or unusual scar tissue—potentially from forced abortions
- Tattoos on the neck and/or lower back that the individual is reluctant to explain—i.e., a man's name or initials (most often encountered with U.S. citizen victims of sex trafficking)
- Other types of branding—i.e., cutting or burning
- Evidence that the victim has had to have sexual intercourse while on her monthly cycle—i.e., use of cotton balls or other products which leave residual fibers
- Family dysfunction—i.e., abuse in the home (emotional, sexual, physical), neglect, absence of a caregiver, or substance abuse—these are major risk factors for sex trafficking and can be important warning signs that the individual might be a victim
- Individual may either be in crisis, or may downplay existing health problems or risks
- Individual may resist your help or demonstrate fear that the information he/she gives you will lead to arrest, placement in social services, return to family, or retribution from trafficker[6]

When creating your training program, reach out to survivors in your area for additional insight into vulnerabilities within your community (see chapter 3). Whenever possible, try to work with survivors of commercial sexual exploitation as they can offer unique insight into this crime and victimization. For example, Christine Stark, author of *Nickels,* is a Native American survivor of commercial sexual exploitation.[7] Stark has a wealth of knowledge concerning the prostitution and trafficking of Native women and youth, including sex trafficking on ships that dock in Duluth, Minnesota. Stark exemplifies how a survivor can bring his or her own insider knowledge to the table as well as others if there is a local network of survivors.

If your department is unable to coordinate these trainings, then reach out to local nonprofit organizations for collaboration. There are many organizations across the country working to raise awareness about child sex trafficking and other forms of commercial sexual exploitation and human trafficking. With proper training, a local organization may be able to train others in the community to better assist your department in identifying victims.

Collaboration between law enforcement and nonprofits and/or nongovernmental organizations (NGOs) may also assist in preventing CSEC within the community. With input from law enforcement, nonprofits and NGOs may be able to target those populations most in need of awareness, training, and prevention resources. For example, I recommend awareness campaigns or training workshops for those who may witness traffickers or their allies attempting to engage with youth. This would include security guards for teen hotspots like malls, movie theaters, skating rinks, concert venues, schools, and youth-friendly stadiums or parks. The most obvious signs of such activity would be an adult attempting to engage with youth, via compliments, gifts, and attempts to exchange phone numbers. Be clear about what steps should be taken if a trafficker is suspected to be in the area and engaging with children. If your department has no formal policy in place, refer trainees to call the NHTRC at 1-888-373-7888.

ADDITIONAL RESOURCES FOR LAW ENFORCEMENT AND OTHER FIRST RESPONDERS

I highly recommend the following resources to law enforcement and other first responders while creating local resources and protocols to respond to CSEC.

The National Human Trafficking Resource Center (NHTRC)

The NHTRC is a program of Polaris Project, a nonprofit, nongovernmental organization working exclusively on the issue of human trafficking. The NHTRC offers a national hotline that law enforcement, and other victim advocates, can call 24 hours a day, 7 days a week for referrals when working with child victims of commercial sexual exploitation. Polaris Project's National Contacts Referral Database currently contains more than 3,000 unique contacts for anti-trafficking practitioners and organizations in the field. The NHTRC database contains referrals from all 50 states, the District of Columbia, many of the U.S. territories, and more than 60 foreign countries, including Canada and Mexico.

Law enforcement and other victim advocates can call 1-888-373-7888 in order to speak with an NHTRC hotline specialist about available resources. Ideally, law enforcement and victim advocates should call the NHTRC *before* encountering a victim in order to familiarize themselves with the process and to gain an understanding for what resources are and are not available in the area. Be sure to ask about residential treatment, transitional housing, and/or outreach services. It is also important to seek services from related organizations like those working with sexual assault victims or homeless, runaway, or troubled youth. Law enforcement and other victim advocates must have knowledge of and access to all resources available in one's area, not just those resources dedicated solely to victims of human trafficking.

Reach out to the NHTRC to learn more about other anti-trafficking efforts in your area. They have a confidential online directory of service providers, law enforcement, government officials, task forces, coalitions, individuals, and collaborative initiatives working to combat human trafficking across the country. The database also contains organizations that focus on several issues related to human trafficking, such as domestic violence, sexual assault, runaway and homeless youth, immigration, and refugee resettlement. Polaris Project also offers training and additional resources online at www.PolarisProject.org.[8]

National Center for Missing & Exploited Children (NCMEC)
NCMEC offers a myriad of resources to law enforcement (local, state, and federal) who are investigating cases of missing and exploited children, including analytical and technical assistance services and case management support for children and families. In 2011, NCMEC created the Child Sex Trafficking Team (CSTT), which operates out of their Case Analysis Division. This team is a specialized group of analysts, who handle all requests related to child sex trafficking. This team supports NCMEC's ongoing collaboration with the FBI Innocence Lost National Initiative, as well as handling CyberTipline reports regarding child sex trafficking and missing child cases. Their overall goal is to provide comprehensive analytical services to law enforcement investigations, as well as to link cases of possible child sex trafficking victims to missing child cases known to NCMEC.

Child Sex Trafficking Analysts respond to direct requests from law enforcement for technical assistance and analysis related to potential victims of commercial sexual exploitation and suspected traffickers. Using information from police and other sources, the analysts will conduct detailed and comprehensive searches via multiple public records databases, the National Crime Information Center (NCIC), National Law Enforcement Telecommunications System (Nlets), open-source Internet sites, and NCMEC's own internal systems. These searches have assisted in identifying traffickers, identifying possible child victims, and compiling timelines that corroborate victim statements. For more information, contact NCMEC at 1-800-THE-LOST® (1-800-843-5678).

At the request of law enforcement, NCMEC can also act as a liaison between families of missing children and law enforcement. NCMEC's Family Advocacy Division employs master-level mental health and child welfare professionals who work together to proactively help families, law enforcement, social service agencies, and mental health agencies by providing a support network for child victims and their families. NCMEC can also assist with locating services for commercially sexually exploited victims.[9]

Girls Educational & Mentoring Services (GEMS)
GEMS offers two curricula for training purposes. The first, called the OJJDP CSEC Community Intervention Project (CCIP) Train-the-Trainer curriculum, is "CSEC 101" and sets the groundwork for the agency's innovative Victim, Survivor, Leader training and technical assistance, which is a cornerstone of all GEMS programming. The CCIP Train-the-Trainer curriculum provides a comprehensive overview of CSEC, including the following:

- Understanding trauma bonds/Stockholm Syndrome
- Identification of victims
- Investigating CSEC
- Best practices in programming and prevention
- Counseling techniques for commercially sexually exploited (CSE) youth
- Conducting assessment and intake with CSE victims
- Criminal behaviors and market forces: supply, demand, motivation
- Federal and local laws
- Best practices in investigation and defense
- Appropriate interviewing for victims and perpetrators

- Models for court-based interventions

For more information visit www.gems-girls.org.[10]

Children of the Night (COTN) in Los Angeles

COTN is a privately funded[11] non-profit organization that provides residential services specific for child victims of commercial sexual exploitation, both boys and girls. The program's services include a safe school environment and access to medical and psychological needs, as well as secure and comfortable living quarters with daily activities. COTN offers a hotline to law enforcement and other victims, which is available 24 hours a day, 7 days a week. (Note: The hotline is also available to parents and victims.) COTN's residential services are available to children ages eleven to seventeen, and at no cost. COTN provides nationwide taxi and airline transportation to any commercially sexually exploited child who wishes to enter the program.

COTN is not a locked-down facility; the children can leave at any time. However, it has an extensive security system in place to protect children from traffickers. The COTN program has only two requirements for admission: 1) the child must consent to services over the phone, and 2) the child's appropriate guardian (e.g., parent, social worker, probation officer) must also consent over the phone. Although the intake process requires paperwork (e.g., admission agreement, medical consent), the signing of these papers does not delay the admission of a child into the COTN program. The COTN program accepts children at any time and on any day, including holidays. When possible, the COTN staff will arrange non-stop flights for victims, and they ensure that a child care staff member will be at the airport to escort the child to the COTN program facility. The COTN hotline is 1-800-551-1300.[12] For additional programs that accept child victims from across the country and offer similar housing and services, please call the NHTRC.

APPENDIX C

10 TIPS FOR TEENS FOR PROTECTION AGAINST TRAFFICKERS

1. **Become media literate.** If you don't know what "media literacy" means, research the topic. It is important that you understand how business enterprises are sending you distorted messages via the media in order to make a profit from selling you their products. These messages include: You aren't pretty unless you buy *this;* you aren't cool unless you own *this;* and being pretty or cool is more important than anything else. Popular culture is often rife with negative messages, and traffickers are using these messages to their advantage. Educate yourself in order to be armed against predators. Start with Nicole Clark's documentary, *Cover Girl Culture*; Adriana Barbaro and Jeremy Earp's documentary, *Consuming Kids: The Commercialization of Childhood*; Sut Jhally's *Dreamworlds 3: Desire, Sex, and Power in Music Video*; Jean Kilbourne's *Killing Us Softly 4: Advertising's Image of Women*; or Byron Hurt's *Hip Hop: Beyond Beats & Rhymes.*
2. **Learn different coping skills.** Life in middle and high school is tough. I know this because I was there. It doesn't have to feel so stressful all the time, though. Explore ways to cope with stress. Coping strategies can include meditation, prayer, exercise, yoga, martial arts, writing, reading, music, sports, crafting, and collecting. Please ask for help from teachers or family members if you need assistance with starting one of these activities. A book that helped me with coping strategies was *The Power of Now* by Eckhart Tolle.
3. **Stay involved in extracurricular activities.** It is crucial to do well in school and to stay involved in extracurricular activities. Try out for different sports, clubs, or programs. I promise that good grades and a busy schedule are the most effective ways to overcome middle school troubles and to graduate as quickly and successfully as possible. Trust me on this—I tried running away

from middle school. That route was worse than if I had just stuck things out at school.

4. **Don't be afraid to try new things.** If you have an aunt that offers to take you to the ballet, say yes! If an uncle offers to take you to a sports game, take him up on it! Try new things! Don't be afraid to step out of your comfort zone or away from your friends. I was very afraid to try new things. When my friends inevitably began to try new things without me, I felt very isolated and alone. This is part of the reason a trafficker was able to lure me away from home.
5. **Volunteer.** Volunteering can help you keep things in focus while in middle and high school. There are many different ways to volunteer—from serving food at a soup kitchen to walking dogs at an animal shelter. Check out www.volunteermatch.org or www.idealist.org to find cool places to volunteer. A healthy perspective on your own life will prevent attempted distortion by a stranger.
6. **Learn to say NO.** Our society is saturated with images of sex, and most images of women in the media are sexualized. This teaches young girls that sex appeal equals value. This turns into a domino effect; oversexualized girls are magnets for older, opportunistic boys or men who will push to have their expectations met. Despite seeing and hearing about sex on a daily basis, please know that *you have the right to say NO to anyone at any time, no matter what.* Saying no does not make you less worthy in any way whatsoever. YOU own your body. NOBODY has the right to touch you—no matter what, no matter when, and no matter how far things have gone with a person in that moment or in the past.

   And, guys, despite what you see and hear on a daily basis from music, TV, and from peers—it's OK to wait to have sex. Respect yourself and your partner. Traffickers look for teens who lack assertiveness. Stand up for yourself and others!
7. **Ask questions about sex.** Please know that positive sexual health is not accurately portrayed in movies, music lyrics, music videos, or magazines. These are often very negative and inaccurate depictions of romance and love. Take your time. Rushing to have sex can have disastrous effects. Talk to your partner and seek guidance about issues related to sex.
8. **Seek Counseling!** It is not normal to feel overly sad, angry, hopeless, or empty. Even though so many movie characters and musicians display this exact personality as being *cool* or normal, it is not OK for you to feel this way. You deserve to feel happy and safe. Please confide in a teacher or family member if you are having these feelings. Or, call the Boys Town National Hotline, a crisis hotline for both boys and girls, at 1-800-448-3000.
9. **Understand how child trafficking works.** Traffickers hang out in the same places you do: malls, skating rinks, bus stations, online, etc. Traffickers do not typically look like sketchy characters—they are often young and well-dressed. Traffickers will offer to buy you trendy clothes, shoes, cars, or other expensive items. Traffickers will ask for your phone number; they will ask to see or speak to you alone. Traffickers will tell you how pretty and mature you are, and they may mention knowing celebrities, exotic dancers, models, and porn stars. Traffickers will offer to help you make a lot of money or may offer to help you run away.

   Know this—*no* stranger (man or woman) has good intentions if they offer to help you run away. *No* stranger (man or woman) has anything but personal gain in mind if they offer to help you make money. No matter how cool, how hip, or how fun and friendly they may seem, they mean to harm you. Seek help from a trusted family member or teacher.

10. **Raise awareness!** Start a school club to promote awareness for media literacy and/or human trafficking. You belong to the next generation of advocates who must stand up for your rights and the rights of others. Your voice can make a difference. Believe in yourself and all that you can accomplish!

APPENDIX D

10 TIPS FOR PARENTS TO PROTECT YOUR CHILDREN FROM PREDATORS

1. **Be proactive.** Traffickers try to lure teens away with promises of "a better life." Teens struggling with bullying, peer pressure, or other social issues are particularly vulnerable. The earlier you teach your children effective coping skills, the better.
2. **Extracurricular activities.** Encourage your children's interests. Having a skill helps a child to build self-esteem and self-identity, which is helpful as he or she faces puberty and all the insecurities that puberty brings. A trafficker can easily manipulate a child lacking a strong sense of self. Caution: Don't overload your children's schedules or force participation in activities they are not interested in.
3. **Media literacy.** It is imperative that you discuss with your children what they see and hear in the media. Help them to distinguish between entertainment, advertising, and reality. I promise you that traffickers have a solid understanding of what popular culture is telling your kids. Try watching these documentaries with your teens: Nicole Clark's documentary, *Cover Girl Culture*; Adriana Barbaro and Jeremy Earp's documentary, *Consuming Kids: The Commercialization of Childhood*; Sut Jhally's *Dreamworlds 3: Desire, Sex, and Power in Music Video*; Jean Kilbourne's *Killing Us Softly 4: Advertising's Image of Women*; and Byron Hurt's *Hip Hop: Beyond Beats & Rhymes*.
4. **Do you know who is talking to your child?** Going to the mall was something I did almost every weekend with friends. And this is exactly where I met the man who trafficked me. Today, predators have the ability to look for kids on the Internet. Even though your teenager may look like an adult, he or she is not. Your teens still need your guidance. Note: Predators come in all ages and genders. Women and children, sometimes victims themselves, often help lure unsuspecting teens away with tales of a better life.

5. **It's OK to say NO.** Our society is saturated with images of sex, and most images of women in the media are sexualized. This teaches young girls that sex appeal equals value. Teach your girls that, despite what they see and hear, *it is OK to say no to anyone at any time, no matter what.* Tell your boys, who often feel peer pressure on the subject, that it is OK to wait to have sex. Traffickers look for girls and boys who lack assertiveness and for those who have been exploited in the past.
6. **Teach your child about sex.** If you don't teach your children about positive sexual health, who will?
7. **Spend time, not money.** Advertising is everywhere, from billboards to commercials to magazines. A child is told over and over, "You *have* to have *this!*" A trafficker will often offer to buy trendy clothes or shoes to gain a child's affection or trust. Help your kids understand that money and material things do not equal self-value, self-identity, or trust. Start by spending time with them in lieu of giving gifts.
8. **Exposure.** At fourteen, I felt isolated from the rest of the world. When I met the man who trafficked me, he promised cross-country road trips with visits to exotic lands. I believed him because I *wanted* these things. Expose your kids to other cultures, regions, and interests, even if it's only through media like music, documentaries, maps, and encyclopedias.
9. **Volunteering.** Volunteering can help your child keep things in focus. A healthy perspective on one's own life will prevent attempted distortion by a stranger.
10. **Counseling!** If your child's symptoms of depression or anger are disrupting their school or home life, please seek professional help. Ignoring a child's signals for help will only drive them further away, possibly to seek solace from a stranger.

APPENDIX E

10 TIPS FOR ELEMENTARY SCHOOL TEACHERS AND COUNSELORS

1. **Educate children about media and advertising.** First and foremost, media literacy programs must begin early. Advertisers have hired child psychologists and other professionals to help target children with brand marketing and to distort their perceptions of morality and necessity. Our kids are growing up in a consumer-driven society; therefore, we must teach them about consumerism.
2. **Discuss personal health and etiquette issues like personal hygiene and social manners.** A child who lacks this type of guidance at home is often bullied at school.
3. **Instill programs that cover bullying, self-defense, and coping skills.** Kids must be prepared to recognize peer pressure and bullying, and they must be equipped with ways to deal with it. Coping strategies can include meditation, yoga, reading books, journaling, channeling energy into sports/hobbies/music, and self-defense classes. A child who is confident about defending him- or herself is less likely to buckle under bullying.
4. **Include nutrition education in health classes.** The basic elements for a healthy lifestyle must be instilled early. Make healthy lunch and snack choices available to kids at school. Positive physical health helps to nurture and maintain positive mental health.
5. **Explore different cultures.** Knowledge is power. Expose children to many aspects of the world in order to educate and engage them.
6. **Create a sports tutorship program.** Create space in the weekly schedule to have physical education instructors or tutors work one-on-one, or in small groups, with those kids who struggle with sports. There are tutors for children who struggle with math, why not for those kids who struggle with catching or kicking a ball?

7. **Expose children to a variety of role models.** Today's role models for children consist mainly of movie actors and other television celebrities. This encourages children to aim for one goal: fame. Popularity becomes the definition for success. I strongly encourage educators to promote local young role models involved in music, sports, nutrition, advocacy, volunteering, politics, entrepreneurship, and other areas which promote positivity. Invite these community members into the classroom to speak, or take the kids on a class trip to learn more about the organization or occupation. If that's not possible, raise awareness for these role models and their efforts by hanging posters in school hallways.
8. **Invite local volunteer-based organizations into the schools, especially organizations like Big Brothers Big Sisters; Girls for a Change; and other similar child-focused groups.** School counselors should get to know and have a working relationship with the leaders of these organizations. This way they can recommend connections to troubled kids or to parents of those children who are struggling.
9. **Strengthen a child's self-esteem, self-confidence, and overall self-value with extracurricular activities.** If you see a child struggling, encourage him or her to maintain enrollment in an extracurricular activity. This is most important in the late elementary and/or intermediate school age years. Those children who identify with their strengths in intermediate school will be less likely to lose sight of their self-identity in middle school. If funding is limited for programs like art and music, create incentives for community members to donate their time, money, or equipment; or connect with nonprofits who can help with fundraising.
10. **Connect troubled kids with school counselors.** Identify children whose behavior or personality starts to change, and connect them with school counselors early. Such changes as a drop in grades or a negative change in personality can indicate depression or other mental health or underlying issues. Watch for signs like bruises and cuts, social withdrawal, and running away. If this child is not receiving additional help outside of school, then help them to develop a long-term relationship with school counselors. It takes more than a few counseling sessions for a child to gain trust for an unfamiliar adult. Beth Jacobs, Founder of Willow Way in Tucson, Arizona, also recommends providing a list of resources to children who run away. (See Appendix A)

The building blocks for self-confidence and critical thinking must be laid in elementary school and must continue to build through intermediate school in order to prepare kids for the hormone-driven, self-identity-shaking middle school years. These are the years in which traffickers are looking for troubled teens. This concept applies most to those children missing this type of emotional nourishment and guidance at home.

APPENDIX F

10 TIPS FOR MIDDLE SCHOOL TEACHERS AND COUNSELORS

1. **Media literacy.** Preteens and teenagers must be educated about messages in the media, including advertising. Business enterprises send distorted messages to teens via the media in order to make a profit. These messages include: "You aren't pretty unless you look like *this,*" "You aren't cool unless you buy *this,*" and "Owning *this* product is more important than anything else." Traffickers understand what advertisers and popular culture are telling teens and they are using it to their advantage. Please educate kids about the dynamics behind messages in the media. I recommend the following documentaries, all of which include curricula for the classroom: Nicole Clark's documentary, *Cover Girl Culture*; Adriana Barbaro and Jeremy Earp's documentary, *Consuming Kids: The Commercialization of Childhood*; Sut Jhally's *Dreamworlds 3: Desire, Sex, and Power in Music Video*; Jean Kilbourne's *Killing Us Softly 4: Advertising's Image of Women*; Byron Hurt's *Hip Hop: Beyond Beats & Rhymes*; and Jennifer Siebel's *Miss Representation.*
2. **Coping skills.** Children in intermediate and middle schools are often struggling with a myriad of personal and social issues: bullying, teen pregnancy, peer pressure, poor self-image, etc. Educate students about different ways to cope with stress. A teen that is losing the battle against any one of these pressures can be lured into what a stranger might call "a better way of life." Coping strategies can include meditation, self-defense classes, exercise, writing, reading, music, sports, and crafting. Also, investigate your local child-focused volunteer organizations (e.g., Big Brothers Big Sisters, Girls for a Change, Hardy Girls Healthy Women, among many others) and make this list available to students. Having a relationship with a mentor is an effective coping strategy.
3. **Extracurricular activities.** It is crucial to keep intermediate and middle school kids engaged in activities. Boredom leads to a lack of direction. Traffickers are most interested in teens who lack the guidance and support

to keep them working toward goals. Encourage students, especially troubled students, to maintain enrollment in extracurricular activities.

4. **Exposure.** At fourteen, I felt isolated from the rest of the world. When I met the man who trafficked me, he promised cross-country road trips with visits to exotic lands. I believed him because I *wanted* to see the world outside of my town. Expose your students to other cultures, regions, and interests even if it's only through media like music, documentaries, maps, and encyclopedias. This could include exposure to different interests via field trips as well: the ballet, sports games, the theater, and orchestra concerts. I discovered Bollywood music and dance when I happened upon a program about singer Asha Bhosle in my late teens; it was as if a door to India had been opened.
5. **Volunteering.** Adolescents are hormone-driven creatures. They're angry, they're sad, and they're impulsive. Their lives can fall to pieces at a moment's notice, and it truly feels to them as though life will never get any better, until it does. Volunteering can help a child keep things in focus. Whether it's volunteering at a soup kitchen during the holidays or spending time with a senior citizen at a nursing home. Help your students see the world from someone else's perspective. Help them understand how fortunate they are by helping those less fortunate. A healthy perspective on one's own life will prevent attempted distortion by a stranger. Try to include a volunteer project in your curriculum.
6. **Sexual empowerment.** Our society is saturated with images of sex, and most images of women in the media are sexualized. This teaches young girls that sex appeal equals value. This turns into a domino effect. Over-sexualized girls are magnets for opportunistic boys or men who will push to have their expectations met. Teach preteen and teenage girls that, despite seeing and hearing about sex on a daily basis, *it is ok to say no to anyone at any time, no matter what.* Also, educate teen boys that it is OK to wait; boys often feel pressured to have sex because it would be "uncool" not to. Instill the idea in teenagers that they own their bodies, and nobody has the right to touch them—no matter what, no matter when, and no matter how far things have gone with a person in that moment or in the past. Traffickers look for girls and boys who lack assertiveness and for those who have been exploited in the past.
7. **Sex education.** Knowledge is power. Sex education must go beyond the male and female anatomy. There must be open discussions about the realities of sex and sexuality (including LGBTQ concerns), the characteristics of sexual assault and sexual exploitation, and the potential consequences to sex. Also, there must be open discussions about what *healthy* relationships look like, with or without sex. Our kids are bombarded with messages about sex in popular culture; and, without guidance elsewhere, these messages can be particularly destructive to girls.
8. **Counseling!** If a student's symptoms of depression or anger are disrupting his or her school life, please recommend professional help. Ignoring a child's signals for help will only drive them further away, possibly to seek solace from a stranger. Make available a list of local and national resources to troubled teens (see Appendix A).
9. **Trafficking basics.** Teach children the basics about commercial sexual exploitation, including child sex trafficking and the tactics used by traffickers. There are a few school-based programs available, including The Prevention Project from Richmond Justice Initiative (RJI) and "Tell Your Friends" from FAIR Girls.

10. **Prevention for at-risk girls.** When working with at-risk youth, prevention of commercial sexual exploitation must be a more intensive program. There must be open discussions with at-risk youth about risk factors, the concept of vulnerability and sexual exploitation, influence from the media and other societal factors, etc. My Life My Choice (MLMC), an organization in Boston, offers a ten-week curriculum specific to commercial sexual exploitation for girls who are at a higher risk for exploitation and for girls who have already been commercially sexually exploited. For more information contact Lisa Goldblatt-Grace at LGrace@jri.org.

APPENDIX G

PESS #1—PSYCHIATRIC EMERGENCY SCREENING SERVICES ON JULY 11, 1992*

Physician's Assessment
Emergency Services
Kimball Medical Center

Admission Date: 7/11/1992		**Time:** [unclear]
Patient Name: Smith, Holly	**Sex:** F	**Mar. Status:** S
Date of Birth: 1/19/1978	**Age:** 14Y	**Birthplace:** New Jersey
MV Accident? N	**Comp Case?** N	**Registration Type:** B-Psychiatric Unit
Allergies: NKA	**Remarks:** MEDS; NONE	
Police Notified? Y		**Mode of Arrival:** PD

Nature of Illness:
Patient here for PESS

Physician's History. Assessment & Treatment:
14 y.o. girl with no past medical history. No significant family history. . . . Referred for medical clearance. . . .

*This form has been retyped and includes only the most relevant information.

Diagnostic Impression:
Cigarette burn on left forearm, healing.

Patient referral:
Treated and Discharged

Condition on discharge:
Same

Patient Instructions:
Patient has no active medical problems. . . ; cleared. . . .

Crisis Team Evaluation
Kimball Medical Center
Psychiatric Emergency Screening Services (PESS)
Crisis Team Evaluation

Date: July 11, 1992 **Start Time:** 2:00 p.m. **End Time:** [left blank]
Name: Holly Smith **Date of Birth:** 1/19/1978
Age: 14 **Sex:** Female **Race:** Caucasian
Patient Address: Tuckerton, N.J.
Referral Source: Harbor House **Location of Screening:** Harbor House
Disposition: Hampton Hospital **# Staff Face-to-Face Contact:** 1
 # Collateral Calls Made: 3

Name of Insurance Carrier:
Blue Cross – Medallion

Psychiatric Examination by Psychiatrist?
No

Discharged from Psychiatric Hospital Within Last 30 Days?
No

If Yes, Name of Hospital:
Presenting Problem:
Patient was brought to Harbor House last night for intake and admission by advice of Family Crisis. Patient had runaway for 3 days last week and had engaged in prostitution in Atlantic City. After her return from Atlantic City, she attempted suicide by ingestion of aspirin and ibuprofen totaling 35 pills. No intervention at that time. During intake last night, patient continued suicidal ideation.

Psychosocial Status:
Patient has finished 8th grade at Pinelands Regional and will be attending 9th grade. Patient gets varied grades. An A in computers, B in science and math, and C's in history

and English. She got an F in Study Skills, and a D in gym and industrial arts. She was suspended within the last 2 weeks for fighting . . . parents report fights frequently. She hangs out with a wide variety of friends including "burn-outs" and "sluts."

Her family living at home consists of her mother and father. Father had two previous marriages with three children from those marriages ranging in age from 18 to 27. Mother had 1 marriage resulting in one son, age 21, who is married and lives across the street.

Patient states both her parents are heavy drinkers consuming alcohol daily. Her mother was diagnosed with breast cancer in Oct of 1990 and was in treatment until Sept of 1991. Patient's mother states she still has been given only a 50% survival rate.

When patient ran away, she went with a "pimp" who took her to Atlantic City. She reports to having 7 encounters with "tricks" and making $1000. She had been sexually active once prior to the prostitution. Patient was picked up by A.C. police for soliciting and being underage but did not press charges. They called her parents who picked her up in A.C. She has no feelings about the prostitution and says she just wanted the money so she could buy clothes. Patient admits to wanting to continue prostitution so she can get the money.

Medical Status:
No medical problems or medication taken at this time.

Substance Abuse:
Patient denies any drug use but admits to alcohol consumption. Approximates 2x's a month. No black outs, DT's, tremors.

Psychiatric History:
Patient states she attempted suicide 2 years ago by scratching her arms and saw a psychiatrist through Atlantic City Medical Center. . . .

Mental Status

Appearance:
Patient's grooming and hygiene were good. No make-up. Eye contact fair. Attitude fairly cooperative.

Speech Quality:
Clear, coherent and goal-directed.

Thought Process:
Patient denies auditory or visual hallucinations. No psychotic process evidenced. No delusions. Patient stated "It's not my parents, it's me . . . I kept thinking about bad things that I won't tell you about and wanted to die."

Mood / Affect:
Mood is described as "nothing." Affect flat. No sleep or appetite disturbance noted.

Suicide Assessment:
Patient attempted suicide two times. Two years ago and more recently on Tuesday night of the past week with ingestion of 35 pills—aspirin and ibuprofen. She did not tell her parents and stayed in bed all day feeling sick and experienced ringing in her ears. Patient admits to wanting to die that day. Last night during her intake, she reported wanting to die and having nothing to live for.

Aggressive Behavior:
Patient denies any past or present ideation to hurt others. Patient's parents report frequent fighting at school and socially.

Reasoning:
Reasoning, judgment, and insight appear impaired as evidenced by her impulsivity and poor judgment. She is also presently unable to see reasons to live.

Provisional Diagnosis:
Major Depression, R/O Conduct Disorder

Exploration of Least Restrictive Alternatives:
Patient is currently a danger to self due to recent suicide attempt and impulsive behaviors such as runaway and prostitution.

Disposition:
Psychiatric evaluation is recommended to ascertain dangerousness. Inpatient hospitalization may be required.

APPENDIX H

DISCHARGE SUMMARY #1*

Hampton Hospital
Discharge Summary

Name: Smith, Holly
Admission Date: 07–11–92
Discharge Date: 07–31–92

Demographic Data:
This is a voluntary and first Hampton Hospital admission for this single, 14-year-old white female who lives with her parents in Tuckerton, NJ. She is a nonpracticing Lutheran and is of Irish/Scottish/Native American descent. H is currently in the 9th grade at Pinelands Regional High School.

Chief Complaint:
"I ran away and I became a prostitute and I tried to commit suicide."

History of Present Illness:
The patient presents with a runaway episode two weeks prior to admission. She met with her "pimp" at a local mall and he took her to a motel where he raped her. That night, and over the course of the next day, H had sexual intercourse with three or four men. The next morning she was accosted by the police, however, no charges were brought against her. Approximately one week after this incident, H states that she took an overdose of twenty aspirin and approximately twelve ibuprofen. She told no one at home and "slept all day." The next day H went to Ocean Harbor House where she told staff of her suicide attempt. H was then transferred to Hampton Hospital. H describes the following target symptoms of depression for the two months prior to admission: Sleep disturbance

* This form has been retyped and includes only the most relevant information.

(including insomnia, MNA and EMA), loss of appetite, feelings of hopelessness and helplessness, increased irritability, and dysphoria. She also reports that she drinks when depressed and has consumed up to a half of a fifth of vodka in one sitting.

Two years prior to admission, H got together with a group of peers who practiced cutting themselves. H participated, but in retrospect states that she really wanted to die. H also admits to at least three suspensions from school for truancy and fighting with peers. She has had sexual intercourse with at least five boys from school. She states that things "just happened with these guys" and that she does not have any sexual relations with her regular boyfriends. H has alluded to sexual secrets which she presently refuses to discuss with staff.

H also admits to purging after eating on two occasions, but found herself unable to vomit. She also diets extensively, and has made use of diet pills. She sees herself as "fat."

Past Psychiatric History:
H states that she has seen a psychiatrist in the past, but for only two sessions. She discontinued therapy because she stated that she disliked the therapist. H does not remember the name of the therapist, nor does she remember the dates of treatment. She denies any past inpatient treatment. She has never been placed on psychiatric medication.

Medical History:
Both patient and mother deny any head injuries or seizures. Childhood illnesses included measles and chickenpox. Her immunizations are current.

Family Medical and Psychiatric History:
Family medical and psychiatric histories are unremarkable except for mother's diagnosis in October of 1990 for cancer. Maternal aunt died of cancer in July of 1990.

Psychosocial & Developmental History:
H has three half brothers and a half sister as a result of parents' previous marriages. She is the only child living with her parents presently. According to mother, her pregnancy with H was unremarkable with labor lasting only four hours. H achieved developmental milestones within the normal time frame. In general, H's behavior as a child was marked by daredevil behavior and rocking. Mother states that H was outgoing and had many friends in elementary school and in junior high school H was outgoing, but was more aggressive and had fewer friends. In junior high H has three suspensions, two for truancy and one for a physical altercation with a peer wherein H kicked this peer in the head. H's grades in elementary school were excellent. Her grades in junior high school range from A's to F's. She reports being a student in several honors classes.

H began menarche at age 11 or 12 and is unaware of whether they are irregular. She denies venereal disease. She reports using only condoms for birth control. She also denies pregnancy. Her first sexual experience was at 12 years of age. H smokes approximately one pack of cigarettes per week and she denies military history or legal problems.

Current Family Issues & Dynamics:
Mother is age 42 and employed in a clerical position at a local hospital. Father is 48 years of age and is [a former dry cleaner, currently unemployed]. H describes both of her parents as alcoholics. She states that her parents consume at least one case of beer a day. Although she describes her relationship with her parents as one in which they "get along," she also reports many incidents of physical altercations between herself and each of her parents, which involve them grabbing her by the arm and H pushing them away. The family moved to their [former] residence in 1990. Prior to this move they describe

H as "a caring, sensitive person." After the family moved, H met a girl her age who[se] parents describe as "a tough cookie." Parents attribute this peer's influence as changing H into a disrespectful child without fear of authority.

Mental Status Examination:

Overall, H was neat and groomed for the evaluation interview. Her posture was somewhat tense and facial expression somewhat bland and she was very restless. Physically she is thin and appears her stated age. Her mood was anxious at times, but she was mood reactive. Her affect was constricted and she appeared guarded. Her speech was normal in tone and she verbalized freely. Her thinking was logical and she denied alterations in perception. She denies homicidal ideations but admitted "I want to die." She was oriented to three spheres. H's fund of knowledge was inconsistent, as she was able to name the last three presidents of the United States, but could not name the number of days in a year. She calculated serial 7's slowly but accurately to four digits. Digit span forward was accurate to six digits. Again, she was inconsistent in that she could not name the number of days in the month of February. H's response to similarities indicated adequate abstractive ability. H's three wishes are, "to look good, to have money, and have good things." She sees herself five years from now as "dead." If she could change one thing about herself it would be to "figure out what's going on with me." Intelligence is estimated to be within the average to above average range, however, judgment and insight are extremely limited and impaired.

Assessment:

At this point in treatment it is important to discover H's secrets. Her past suicide attempts and current suicidal ideation make her a candidate for major depression and a trial of antidepressants, although she is resisting this treatment at the moment.

Admission Diagnosis:

AXIS I: Alcohol Abuse
Major Depression with Suicide Attempt
Conduct Disorder
AXIS II: Rule Out Mixed Personality Traits with Borderline Features
AXIS III: None
AXIS IV: SEVERITY OF PYCHOSOCIAL STRESSORS:
Moderate: Break-Up With Boyfriend
History of Physical Altercations With Parents
AXIS V: GLOBAL ASSESSMENT OF FUNCTIONING
Current GAF: 20
Highest GAF in the Past Year: 45

Physical Examination:

Physical examination done at the time of admission revealed no physical problems. It was positive for acne on the face and back and a cigarette burn on the left forearm, which was self inflicted a couple weeks prior to admission.

Laboratory Data:

EKG revealed normal sinus rhythm. Urinalysis was clear. Toxicology screen was negative. Lab scan revealed no elevated levels. CBC was within normal limits. Alcohol screen was negative. RPR was nonreactive. Beta HCG was negative. TSH was within normal limits.

Medical Consultations:
There were no medical consultations.

Psychological Consultations:
Holly was seen by a psychologist in consultation. Dr. [Name Withheld] found her to have symptoms of major depression with suicidal ideation, constricted affect, which when experienced with intensity tended to disorganize her to a psychotic level of thinking, and severe personality problems with defense mechanisms such as projection, denial and other primitive defenses.

Interim Diagnosis:

AXIS I:	Major Depression
	R/O Conduct Disorder
	Ethanol Abuse
AXIS II:	Borderline Personality Traits
AXIS III:	None
AXIS IV:	3
AXIS V:	20

Treatment Plan:
Individual, group and family therapy, creative therapies, psychotropic medication, and psychological testing.

Hospital Course:
Holly was initially very resistant and stubbornly clung to the idea that she would be better off dead. She was very suspicious and had a difficult time forming treatment alliance. She tended to be passively resistant and therefore difficult to engage. However, during the course of her hospital stay she slowly began to form relationships with staff, peers and with me. She talked a lot about her depression and her suicidal ideation and hopelessness. She was able to do some work and accepting the possibility that her life might come to something and that there might be a future for her. She was started on Prozac, 20 mg, and showed a good response with an increased enthusiasm and elevated mood. She had a lot of difficulty in conflict with her parents during the course of her admission. At one point they were stating that they were refusing to bring her home. She felt very rejected and abandoned, although she didn't want to go home to live with them because she felt that rules in the house would be impossible for her to live by. She also stated that she felt her parents were alcoholic, drinking continuously and were making no effort to alleviate that. Finally, at the end of hospitalization, her parents were unable to come up with a residential treatment plan and decided to take her home. She was excited about leaving the hospital, but very apprehensive about how it would be for her living at home.

Condition on Discharge:
The patient's mood was much improved. She had better insight into her situation. However, she had a tenuous grasp on the hopefulness for the future and her intent to make a better life for herself.

Recommendations/Disposition:
She is to immediately start in intensive outpatient psychotherapy multiple times per week and continue on her Prozac. She is to be involved in intensive substance abuse program including AA and NA. Family therapy should continue.

Medications on Discharge:
Prozac, 20 mg p.o. q.a.m.

Prognosis:
Prognosis is guarded as I am not sure that the family is going to be compliant with the above recommendations.

Discharge Diagnosis:

AXIS I:	Major Depression
	Ethanol Abuse
	Conduct Disorder
AXIS II:	Borderline Traits
AXIS III:	None
AXIS IV:	4
AXIS V:	GAF: On Admission – 15
	On Discharge – 45

APPENDIX I

PESS #2—PSYCHIATRIC EMERGENCY SCREENING SERVICES ON AUGUST 7, 1992*

Physician's Assessment
Emergency Services
Atlantic City Medical Center

Admission Date: 8/7/1992
Patient Name: Smith, Holly
Date of Birth: 1/19/1978
MV Accident? N

Sex: F
Age: 14Y
Comp Case? N

Time: 5:46 AM
Mar. Status: S
Birthplace: New Jersey
Registration Type: B-Psychiatric Unit

Allergies: NKA

Remarks: MEDS / Prozac, Ditropan

Police Notified? N

Mode of Arrival: WALK

Nature of Illness:
Patient stays here to see PESS

Physician's History. Assessment & Treatment:
Diagnostic Impression:
Patient Instructions:
Patient referred to Harbor House and Green House. . . .

*This form has been retyped and includes only the most relevant information.

Crisis Team Evaluation
Kimball Medical Center
Psychiatric Emergency Screening Services (PESS)

Date: August 7, 1992 **Start Time:** 7:30 a.m. **End Time:** 12:15 p.m.
Name: Holly Smith **Date of Birth:** 1/19/1978
Age: 14 **Sex:** Female **Race:** Caucasian
Address: Tuckerton, N.J.
Referral Source: Atlantic City Crisis / Family Division
Name of Insurance Carrier: Blue Cross
Location of Screening: PESS Room #2 **Disposition:** [Blank]
 # Staff Face-to-Face Contact: [Unclear] **# Collateral Calls:** 10
Discharged from Psychiatric Hospital Within Last 30 Days? Yes
If Yes, Name of Hospital: Hampton
Psychiatric Examination By Psychiatrist? No

Presenting Problem:
14 y/o single white female brought to PESS after patient was picked up by Atlantic City police for prostitution. Patient was released by Hampton Hospital (7/31) following three week stay after patient was seen by PESS for overdose and was admitted to Hampton 7/11. Parents state patient "seemed fine" since discharge and told parents she was going to Seaside [with friend. Mother confirmed plans with friend's mother]. A.C. police called patient's mother. Patient was picked up for prostitution. [Illegible] reports intent to prostitute but states attempt thwarted when it became known that intended customers were undercover police officers. Patient states she did it solely "for the money" and stated "I'm not afraid of being hurt in A.C. I just don't think about it." Patient has no charge at this time and was released to mother.

Psychosocial Status:
Patient completed grade 8 and will be attending Pinelands High School for grade 9/ Sept. As per 7/11/92 screening grades vary: A – computers, science, math. C – history and English. F – study skills. D – gym, industrial arts. Patient reports she was suspended for fight stating "I kicked some girl I hate." Patient has never worked. Patient reports "many" friends (male and female) from "different crowds." Patient states her and her friends enjoy "driving around, going to parties and stuff."

Patient resides at home with her mother and father. Patient reports good rapport with both but other sources describe patient afraid of father and "family having numerous difficult[ies] relating," patient denies. Father had two previous marriages with three children from those marriages ranging in age from 18 to 28. Mother had 1 previous marriage resulting in one son age 21 who is married and lives across street from patient.

Patient ran away in July and went with a "pimp" who took her to Atlantic City as per 7/11/92 screening. Patient reports while in AC in July she made $800 for "3 tricks" and $200 for 2 tricks in 2 days. Patient and family report patient only received $20 from "pimp" for prostitution. Patient reports she attempted to prostitute while in AC last night but was picked up by undercover AC police.

Patient states long-term relationship at age 11- no intercourse. Patient reports first sexual intercourse age 12 with "some kid [name withheld]." Patient reports it was a "one night stand." Patient states she has had intercourse with approximately 10 people including AC "tricks." Patient reports physical abuse by father one time when father "grabbed patient by shirt and threw her against wall." As per patient's father reacted to a dirty look from patient.

Medical Status:
Mother and patient state patient takes Ditropan 5 mg BID for bladder control problems "wetting pants after giggling" . . .

Substance Abuse:
Patient admits to alcohol use since age 12 ranging from 1 beer to half bottle Jack Daniels. Patient states last alcohol use Saturday . . .Patient admitted to . . . "shakes" within last 4 months after consuming alcohol.

Psychiatric History:
Hampton Hospital 7/11 to 7/31. Discharged 7/31—patient referred to out-patient treatment not followed up due to delay in response. Past psychiatric history—psychiatrist 2 years ago with 6 sessions. No other psychiatric history. Prozac 20mg once daily.

Mental Status
Appearance:
Patient dressed provocatively in black miniskirt, reel top and knee high black boots. Grooming / hygiene adequate. Motor status unremarkable. Attitude evasive. Eye contact poor. Patient defensive.

Speech Quality:
Poverty of content, guarded, coherent.

Thought Process:
Patient denied audio/visual hallucinations. No psychotic symptomatology noted at present. No looseness of association . . . at present. Patient focused on leaving PESS: "I just want to go home and sleep. I'm tired."

Mood /Affect:
Mood irritable and depressed with blunted affect. Patient reports increased sleep—falling asleep in day since Hampton admission.

Suicide Assessment:
Patient denies suicide intent or plan at present stating "I don't want to hurt myself." Patient has two prior attempts. Two years ago—patient slit wrists, no treatment. Last month patient overdosed on 35 aspirin acetaminophen. "I'm not scared of catching a disease or getting killed because it's better to catch a disease and die than to kill myself."

Aggressive Behavior:
. . . Patient admitted to kicking girl in face because she "hated her." Patient was suspended.

Reasoning:
Reasoning at present impaired. Patient does not feel prostitution wrong—adequate way to make money. . . . Current judgment impaired due to patient's trip to AC; without fear of repercussion from prostitution. Insight limited: patient does not see seriousness of behavior or parent response.

Three Wishes:
1. To go to sleep, 2. All the money I want, 3. Perfect life (which patient states would include "good boyfriend, money, people that love me")

Provisional Diagnosis:
Dysthymia; Conduct Disorder by history; Alcohol Abuse

Exploration of Least Restrictive Alternatives:
Patient is currently not a danger to self/others. Patient stating she is not suicidal at present and outpatient is least restrictive alternative at present as patient was just discharged from Hampton on Friday . . .

Disposition:
Patient taken to Harbor House by parents. Greenhouse appointments . . . DYFS recommended.

Notes:
Patient and family deny any components of sexual abuse; however, patient has bladder disorder at present.

APPENDIX J

DISCHARGE SUMMARY #2*

Hampton Hospital
Short Stay Discharge Summary

Name of Patient: Smith, Holly
Admission Date: 08–23–92
Discharge Date: 08–28–92

Identification:
The patient is a 14-year-old white female.

Chief Complaint:
"I was suicidal."

History of Present and Past Illness:
The patient complained that she had been taken to a bar the night of admission by her parents. She said a man tried to pick her up and that reminded her of being raped by her pimp a few months ago. She said her father took her back to the house and then went back to the bar. She called the hospital, saying she was suicidal. The hospital called the police and she was taken to the hospital. The patient had been hospitalized from mid-July to early August in Hampton Hospital and treated for depression and conduct problems, which included running away from home and prostitution. The patient had prostituted herself between these two hospitalizations and the patient also resumed her drug and alcohol use.

Medical History:
The patient has a history of stress incontinence.

*This form has been retyped and includes only the most relevant information.

Mental Status Examination:
The patient is alert and oriented. Speech is spontaneous and goal directed. Eye contact is good. Her mood is depressed. Affect is mood appropriate. She is very manipulative and gamey in her interactions. She endorses suicidal ideation with no current plans and denied homicidal ideation, audio or visual hallucinations, delusions or paranoia. She states that she might want to die sometime soon and that she often wants to die, but has no current plans. Her judgment is very poor and insight is fair.

Physical Examination:
The physical examination done at the time of admission was unremarkable.

Laboratory Data:
The lab scan was within normal limits. She had a mildly elevated white blood count, negative beta HCG and nonreactive RPR. Hepatitis panel was negative. Urinalysis showed 2+ occult blood and trace epithelial and bacteria. The toxic screen was negative. Urine was sent for culture and sensitivity secondary to the patient's complaining of symptoms of urinary tract infection and it showed greater than 100,000 E. coli. The patient also had a negative HIV test.

Medical Consultations:
The patient had a gynecology consult during her hospitalization. Pap smear was done. She has had cultures for GC, herpes, Chlamydia and viral. These are all pending.

Psychological Testing:
There was no psychological testing done.

Hospital Course:
The patient initially came to the hospital stating she wanted to get help and was saying she could no longer live with her parents and needed placement. However, she was unwilling to work with us in establishing placement and was very ambivalent, changing her mind back and forth, stating "O-kay, I'll go home" and then stating, "No, if I go home I'll die." She created a lot of miscommunication between her parents and staff, making everyone aggravated, at which point she would sit back innocently and wonder what the fuss was about. There was a lot of manipulation of staff in an attempt to make them punitive towards her parents. She was unwilling to take much responsibility for her future and was very passive. Towards the end of her hospitalization, when staff and parents were better able to unite, she was forced to make some decisions for herself and take some responsibility. She seemed to be more settled by this closer containment. There were a lot of recommendations made for structure at the time of discharge.

Condition on Discharge:
Condition on discharge was stabilized. She was no longer acutely suicidal or horribly depressed. However, she hadn't made much headway into her manipulative and gamey behavior.

Reccomendation/Disposition:
Intensive individual therapy several times a week. Family therapy and group therapy. Medication management.

Medications on Discharge:
Prozac, 20 mg p.o. q.a.m.

Norfloxacin, 300 mg b.i.d. for urinary tract infection times ten days.
Ditropan, 5 mg p.o. b.i.d.

Final Diagnosis:

AXIS I:	Major Depression
	Polypharmacy Abuse
	Conduct Disorder
AXIS II:	Borderline Personality Traits
AXIS III:	Urinary Tract Infection and Stress Incontinence
AXIS IV:	On Admission – 30
	On Discharge – 60

NOTES

INTRODUCTION

1. A "buyer" is a person (male or female) who purchases—or is attempting to purchase—another person for a sex act. A buyer is often called a "john" or a "trick" when discussed in the context of commercial sex.
2. PL 106–386: *Victims of Trafficking and Violence Protection Act of 2000* was broken down into three divisions: the Trafficking Victims Protection Act (TVPA), the Violence Against Women Act (VAWA), and Miscellaneous Provisions, http://www.state.gov/documents/organization/10492.pdf (accessed August 7, 2013).
3. U.S. Department of Homeland Security, "Trafficking vs. Smuggling," Blue Campaign, http://www.ice.gov/doclib/news/library/factsheets/pdf/ht_tipcard_blue-campaign-june_2013.pdf (accessed September 29, 2013).
4. As noted earlier, the TVPA mandates that force, fraud, and coercion are not necessary to determine sex trafficking cases that involve children (foreign nationals or U.S. citizens) under age eighteen.
5. The term "child sex trafficking" covers all victims under age eighteen; this includes young children, older children, adolescents, and older teenagers. Throughout this book, when I use the term "child" to describe a victim, I am referring to a victim within any one of these age groups.
6. Minh Dang, interview by Katie Couric, *Katie,* January 14, 2013.
7. Theresa L. Flores and Peggy Sue Wells, *The Slave Across the Street* (Boise, ID: Ampelon Publishing, 2010).
8. Shandra Woworuntu, interview by Kristen Saloomey, *Al Jazeera,* May 14, 2013; and Rachel Chinapen, "Human trafficking a United States problem, even a Connecticut problem," *New Haven Register,* May 4, 2013.
9. Shandra Woworuntu, e-mail to author, August 6, 2013.
10. The OJJDP awarded a grant in 2006 to the Salvation Army and its partners (i.e., Girls Educational & Mentoring Services [GEMS], Polaris Project, and the Bilateral Safety Corridor Coalition [BSCC]) to create a training and technical assistance program to assist communities in combating CSEC. GEMS developed the curriculum and the final product was titled the OJJDP CSEC Community Intervention Project (CCIP). http://www.ojp.gov/newsroom/pressreleases/2006/OJJDP06075.htm (accessed July 29, 2013).
11. Rachel Lloyd, interview by John Walsh, *America's Most Wanted: Sex Trafficking Two Hour Special,* February 24, 2012.
12. Polaris Project, *Sex Trafficking of Minors and "Safe Harbor,"* http://www.polarisproject.org/what-we-do/policy-advocacy/assisting-victims/safe-harbor (accessed August 1, 2013).

13. Mira Sorvino, interview by John Walsh, *America's Most Wanted: Sex Trafficking Two Hour Special,* February 24, 2012.
14. James Dold, e-mail to author, August 5, 2013.
15. United States Department of State, *Trafficking in Persons Report June 2013,* letter from Ambassador Luis CdeBaca, http://www.state.gov/documents/organization/210737.pdf (accessed August 7, 2013).
16. *Trafficking Victims Protection Reauthorization Act of 2005,* HR 972, 109th Congress, January 10, 2006, http://www.state.gov/j/tip/laws/61106.htm (accessed August 7, 2013).
17. Tracey Kyckelhahn, Allen J. Beck, and Thomas H. Cohen, "Suspected Human Trafficking Incidents, 2007-2008," United States Department of Justice, January 2009, 2, http://www.bjs.gov/content/pub/pdf/cshti08.pdf (accessed August 7, 2013).
18. Duren Banks and Tracey Kyckelhahn, "Suspected Human Trafficking Incidents, 2008-2010," United States Department of Justice, April 2011, 6, http://www.bjs.gov/content/pub/pdf/cshti0810.pdf (accessed August 7, 2013).
19. Kyckelhahn, Beck, and Cohen, "Suspected Human Trafficking Incidents, 2007-2008," 1.
20. Banks and Kyckelhahn, "Suspected Human Trafficking Incidents, 2008-2010," 5.
21. Ibid.
22. Richard J. Estes and Neil Alan Weiner, "Commercial Sexual Exploitation of Children in the U.S., Canada and Mexico," University of Pennsylvania, September 19, 2001 [revised February 20, 2002], 11-13, http://www.sp2.upenn.edu/restes/CSEC_Files/Exec_Sum_020220.pdf (accessed August 7, 2013).
23. "Testimony of Ernie Allen to the Institute of Medicine Committee on Commercial Sexual Exploitation and Sex Trafficking of Minors in the United States of The National Academies," National Center for Missing and Exploited Children (NCMEC) website, January 4, 2012, http://www.missingkids.com/Testimony/01-04-12 (accessed August 7, 2013).
24. See Michelle Stransky and David Finkelhor, "How Many Juveniles are Involved in Prostitution in the U.S.?," University of New Hampshire, College of Liberal Arts, Crimes Against Children Research Center, 2008, http://www.unh.edu/ccrc/prostitution/Juvenile_Prostitution_factsheet.pdf (accessed August 7, 2013).
25. Daniel Beekman, "Bronx judge sentences 'despicable human being' to max for pimping out 13-year-old girl on craigslist," *New York Daily News,* May 14, 2012, http://www.nydailynews.com/new-york/bronx/bronx-judge-sentences-despicable-human-max-pimping-13-year-old-girl-craigslist-article-1.1078146 (accessed July 27, 2013).
26. Visit www.WalkingPrey.com for a list of recent CSEC cases in the United States.

CHAPTER 1: ARE YOUR CHILDREN AT RISK?

1. Sandra Morgan and Dave Stachowiak, "Physiology of Children in Human Trafficking," Global Center for Women & Children, Vanguard University, Podcast 4, 9:00, http://gcwj.vanguard.edu/eht-podcast/eht4/ (accessed July 29, 2013).
2. Daniel Romer, "Adolescent Risk Taking, Impulsivity, and Brain Development: Implications for Prevention," *Developmental Psychobiology* 52, Issue 3, February 19, 2010: 264. http://onlinelibrary.wiley.com/doi/10.1002/dev.20442/pdf (accessed September 21, 2013).
3. Celia Williamson et al., "Domestic Sex Trafficking in Ohio," research and analysis subcommittee, Ohio Human Trafficking Commission, August 8, 2012: 4, http://

www.ohioattorneygeneral.gov/OhioAttorneyGeneral/files/2f/2ff15706-77ad-4567-b1aa-d8330b5c4005.pdf (accessed July 29, 2013).

4. Investopedia defines "statistically significant" as follows: "The likelihood that a result or relationship is caused by something other than mere random chance. Statistical hypothesis testing is traditionally employed to determine if a result is statistically significant or not. This provides a 'p-value' representing the probability that random chance could explain the result. In general, a 5% or lower p-value is considered to be statistically significant." http://www.investopedia.com/terms/s/statistically_significant.asp (accessed October 5, 2013).
5. Mimi H. Silbert and Ayala M. Pines. "Early Sexual Exploitation as an Influence in Prostitution," *Social Work* 28, no. 4. 1983: 285-289.
6. Celia Williamson et al., "Domestic Sex Trafficking in Ohio," 7.
7. Patricia Murphy, *Making the Connections: Women, Work, and Abuse* (Orlando, FL: Paul M. Deutsche Press, 1993), 18.
8. Ibid.
9. National Center for Children in Poverty, "Child Poverty," http://www.nccp.org/topics/childpoverty.html (accessed September 15, 2013).
10. Rachel Lloyd, *Girls Like Us: Fighting for a World Where Girls Are Not For Sale* (New York: HarperCollins, 2011), 40.
11. Holly Smith, "Neet's Sweets: Human trafficking survivor and entrepreneur bakes to make a difference," *Washington Times Communities,* May 23, 2012, http://communities.washingtontimes.com/neighborhood/speaking-out/2012/may/23/neets-sweets-human-trafficking-survivor-and-entrep/ (accessed July 29, 2013).
12. Ravelle Worthington, "How Sweet It Is: From Sex Trafficking Victim to Success Story," *Ebony,* March 2013, http://www.ebony.com/life/from-sex-trafficking-victim-to-success-story-000#axzz2aPHSur2q (accessed July 29, 2013).
13. Ibid.
14. Tina Frundt, interview by Free the Slaves, "2010 Frederick Douglass Award Winner," https://www.freetheslaves.net/SSLPage.aspx?pid=558 (accessed July 29, 2013).
15. Tina Frundt, Fox Valley Technical College's AMBER Alert Program, *Human Trafficking Why Are We Here,* 2012.
16. Tina Frundt, interview by Lisa Fletcher, "The Stream: Trafficking of Innocence," Al Jazeera, March 20, 2013, http://stream.aljazeera.com/story/201303192347-0022624 (accessed July 29, 2013).
17. Tina Frundt, interview by Free the Slaves, "2010 Frederick Douglass Award Winner."
18. Ibid.
19. Withelma "T" Ortiz Walker Pettigrew, interview by Lisa Fletcher, "The Stream: Trafficking of Innocence," Al Jazeera, March 20, 2013, http://stream.aljazeera.com/story/201303192347-0022624 (accessed July 29, 2013).
20. Abby Sewell, "Most L.A. County Youths Held for Prostitution Come from Foster Care," *Los Angeles Times,* November 27, 2012, http://articles.latimes.com/2012/nov/27/local/la-me-1128-sex-trafficking-20121128 (accessed July 28, 2013).
21. Melissa Snow, e-mail to author, August 5, 2013.
22. Carol Marbin Miller, "Four charged with running foster child prostitution ring," *Miami Herald,* June 25, 2012, http://www.miamiherald.com/2012/06/25/2867962/4-charged-with-running-foster.html (accessed July 29, 2013).
23. Devin Dwyer, "Sex Trafficking of Mentally Disabled Girl Puts Focus on Illegal Immigrants and Crime," *ABC News,* July 28, 2010, http://abcnews.go.com/Politics/immigration-sex-trafficking-mentally-disabled-girl-puts-focus/story?id=11120190 (accessed July 29, 2013); Kelly Smith, "Hopkins High senior

charged with sex trafficking cheerleading teammate," *Star Tribune,* June 4, 2013, http://m.startribune.com/news/?id=210141211&c=y (accessed July 29, 2013); Julie Johnson, "El Dorado Hills man sentenced for sex trafficking disabled girl," *The Sacramento Bee,* July 11, 2013, http://blogs.sacbee.com/crime/archives/2009/09/el-dorado-hills-4.html (accessed July 29, 2013); Chao Xiong, "2 found guilty in Ramsey County sex-trafficking case," *Star Tribune,* July 25, 2013, http://www.startribune.com/local/south/216980531.html (accessed July 29, 2013).

24. Williamson et al., "Domestic Sex Trafficking in Ohio," 6.
25. Jody Raphael and Deborah L. Shapiro, "Sisters Speak Out: The Lives and Needs of Prostituted Women in Chicago," research study, Center for Impact Research, August 2002.
26. Ibid., 4.
27. Ian Urbina, "For Runaways, Sex Buys Survival," *New York Times,* October 26, 2009, http://www.nytimes.com/2009/10/27/us/27runaways.html?pagewanted=all&_r=0 (accessed July 29, 2013).
28. Carissa Phelps, *Runaway Girl: Escaping Life on the Streets One Helping Hand at a Time* (New York: Penguin Group, 2012), 40.
29. Staca Shehan, e-mail to author, March 22, 2013. Emphasis mine.
30. U.S. Attorney's Office, Eastern District of Virginia, "Alexandria MS-13 Member Receives 10 Years for Sex Trafficking of Juveniles," press release, July 1, 2011, http://www.fbi.gov/washingtondc/press-releases/2011/alexandria-ms-13-member-receives-10-years-for-sex-trafficking-of-juveniles (accessed July 29, 2013).
31. U.S. Attorney's Office, Eastern District of Virginia, "MS-13 Associate Sentenced to 292 Months for Sex Trafficking Teenage Runaway Girls," press release, November 4, 2011, http://www.justice.gov/usao/vae/news/2011/11/20111104ormenonr.html (accessed July 29, 2013).
32. Ibid.
33. Williamson et al., "Domestic Sex Trafficking in Ohio," 4.
34. Holly Smith, "Human Trafficking & PTSD: Is there a connection?" *Washington Times Communities,* May 1, 2013, http://communities.washingtontimes.com/neighborhood/speaking-out/2013/may/1/human-trafficking-ptsd-there-connection/ (accessed July 29, 2013).
35. Frances Gragg et al., "New York Prevalence Study of Commercially Sexually Exploited Children," final report, New York State Office of Children and Family Services, April 18, 2007, 53, http://ocfs.ny.gov/main/reports/csec-2007.pdf (accessed July 29, 2013).
36. See chapters 11 and 12 for further discussion on mental health treatment in prevention and aftercare programs.
37. Associated Press, "Two Adults Accused of Forcing Child Into Prostitution," NBC DFW Nonstop, January 31, 2012, http://www.nbcdfw.com/news/local/Two-Adults-Accused-of-Forcing-Child-Into-Prostitution-138407734.html (accessed July 28, 2013).
38. Dale Lezon and Cindy George, "Police: 'Monster' mom admits pimping daughter," *Houston Chronicle,* January 31, 2012, http://www.chron.com/news/houston-texas/article/Police-Monster-mom-admits-pimping-daughter-2855268.php (accessed July 28, 2013).
39. Raphael and Shapiro, "Sisters Speak Out," 4.
40. Williamson et al., "Domestic Sex Trafficking in Ohio," 4.
41. Lesbian, gay, bisexual, transgender, and/or questioning youth.
42. Matt Hennie, "Pasha Nicole gets 14 years in sex slave case," March 7, 2012, *Project Q Atlanta,* http://www.projectqatlanta.com/news_articles/view/pasha_nicole_gets_14_years_in_sex_slave_case?gid=10453 (accessed July 28, 2013).

43. David Ibata, "Go-go dancer sentenced for prostituting teens," *Atlanta-Journal Constitution,* September 5, 2012, http://www.ajc.com/news/news/crime-law/go-go-dancer-gets-80-years-for-human-trafficking/nR4Hc/ (accessed July 28, 2013).
44. Anonymous survivor of CSEC, e-mail to author, October 1, 2013.
45. Williamson et al., "Domestic Sex Trafficking in Ohio," 4.
46. Katrina Owens, *What I Have Been Through Is Not Who I Am* (documentary, co-produced by ECPAT-USA and WITNESS, 2011).
47. Ibid.
48. Gragg et al., "New York Prevalence Study of Commercially Sexually Exploited Children," 53.
49. Geraldine Sealey, "Girls 4 Sale," *Marie Claire,* September 2012, 228-233.
50. Michael Sheridan, "Florida mom sold 6-year-old daughter's body for sex to score drugs: police," *New York Daily News,* March 6, 2012, http://www.nydailynews.com/news/national/florida-mom-sold-6-year-old-daughter-body-sex-score-drugs-police-article-1.1033849 (accessed August 7, 2013).
51. Larry Hannan, "Jacksonville Beach mom pleads guilty to selling sex with 6-year-old daughter," *The Florida Times-Union,* January 30, 2013, http://jacksonville.com/news/crime/2013-01-30/story/jacksonville-beach-mom-pleads-guilty-selling-sex-6-year-old-daughter (accessed August 7, 2013).
52. Anonymous survivor of CSEC, e-mail to author, September 21, 2013.
53. Jody Raphael and Brenda Myers-Powell, "From Victims to Victimizers: Interviews with 25 Ex-Pimps in Chicago," report, Schiller DuCanto & Fleck Family Law Center of DePaul University College of Law, September 2010: 5, http://newsroom.depaul.edu/pdf/family_law_center_report-final.pdf (accessed July 29, 2013).
54. Ibid.

CHAPTER 2: THE "WILLING VICTIM"

1. Kate Price, M.A., "Putting Children First—'Innocence' in Childhood & the Risk for Child Commercial Sexual Exploitation in the U.S.," *Wellesley Centers for Women Research & Action Report,* Fall/Winter 2012, http://www.wcwonline.org/Research-Action-Report-Fall/Winter-2012/commentary-putting-children-first-innocence-in-childhood-a-the-risk-for-child-commercial-sexual-exploitation-in-the-us (accessed September 30, 2013).
2. Rachel Lloyd, *Girls Like Us: Fighting for a World Where Girls Are Not For Sale* (New York: HarperCollins, 2011), 33.
3. Keisha Head has shared her testimony with several media outlets, including a 2012 award-winning Public Broadcasting Atlanta (PBA), documentary titled "How to Stop the Candy Shop," January 30, 2011, http://video.pba.org/video/1771774072/ (accessed October 6, 2013).
4. Keisha Head, interview by Kiss the Limit, *Hands Off This Girl One on One,* November 14, 2012, http://www.youtube.com/watch?v=HEa8CyIbf8E (accessed October 5, 2013).
5. Holly Craw, "Rape at six grooms girl for path into becoming sex trafficking victim," *Examiner,* December 23, 2011, http://www.examiner.com/article/rape-at-six-grooms-girl-for-path-into-becoming-sex-trafficking-victim (accessed July 27, 2013).
6. Savannah Sanders, interview by Pat McMahon, AZTV7/CABLE13, "Savannah Sanders – TRUST Program Assistant," October 4, 2013.
7. Holly Craw, "Rape at six grooms girl for path into becoming sex trafficking victim."

8. Barbara Amaya, interview by Audrey Barnes, *Fox 5 News,* May 15, 2012, http://www.youtube.com/watch?v=2aeMwCqE59k (accessed October 6, 2013).
9. Darkness to Light is a national organization that provides child sexual abuse prevention and response training to parents, communities, and youth-service organizations.
10. Jessica Richardson, e-mail to author, August 8, 2013.
11. Greg Bucceroni, e-mail to author, August 7, 2013.
12. Savannah Sanders, e-mail to author, April 12, 2013.
13. Mimi H. Silbert and Ayala M. Pines, "Early Sexual Exploitation as an Influence in Prostitution," *Social Work* 28, no. 4, 1983: 285-289.
14. Keisha Head, interview by Kiss the Limit, *Hands Off This Girl One on One,* November 14, 2012, http://www.youtube.com/watch?v=HEa8CyIbf8E (accessed October 5, 2013).
15. Margaret Howard, e-mail to author, April 11, 2013.
16. Celia Williamson et al., "Domestic Sex Trafficking in Ohio" (research and analysis subcommittee, Ohio Human Trafficking Commission, August 8, 2012), 4, http://www.ohioattorneygeneral.gov/OhioAttorneyGeneral/files/2f/2ff15706-77ad-4567-b1aa-d8330b5c4005.pdf (accessed July 29, 2013).
17. Keith Burt, "The Sexual Exploitation of Girls in Gangs," webinar, Missing and Exploited Children's Program (MECP), June 2012, http://vimeo.com/44459741 (accessed July 30, 2013).
18. Iceberg Slim, *Pimp* (United States: Cash Money Content, 1987), 167-168.
19. Stacy Lundgren, "Human Trafficking Awareness with Stacy Lundgren, Survivor," [speech, presented by Soroptimist International (SI) of Chico and SI of Bidwell Rancho, Chico, CA, February 24, 2013]; The Stacy Project website, My Story, http://thestacyproject.weebly.com/my-story.html (accessed October 6, 2013).

CHAPTER 3: COMMUNITY RISK FACTORS

1. Refer to OJJDP CSEC Community Intervention Project (CCIP) for more information. "Handout 2.1 Risk Factors for CSEC," http://www.ojjdp.gov/programs/commercial sexual exploitationc_program.html (accessed July 29, 2013).
2. Theresa L. Flores and Peggy Sue Wells, *The Slave Across the Street* (Boise, ID: Ampelon Publishing, 2010).
3. Jody Raphael and Brenda Myers-Powell, "From Victims to Victimizers: Interviews with 25 Ex-Pimps in Chicago," report, Schiller DuCanto & Fleck Family Law Center of DePaul University College of Law (September 2010): 5, http://newsroom.depaul.edu/pdf/family_law_center_report-final.pdf (accessed July 29, 2013).
4. Rachel Lloyd, *Girls Like Us: Fighting for a World Where Girls Are Not For Sale* (New York: HarperCollins, 2011), 40-41.
5. "The Poorest Counties in America," MSN Money, January 12, 2012, http://money.msn.com/family-money/the-poorest-counties-in-america (accessed September 22, 2013).
6. Dawn Turner Trice, "Life After 25 Years of Prostitution," *Chicago Tribune,* March 14, 2011 http://articles.chicagotribune.com/2011-03-14/news/ct-met-trice-prostitutes-0314-20110314_1_prostitution-brenda-myers-powell-rent (accessed July 29, 2013).
7. Tom Ragan, "Theater helps make human trafficking crisis very real in Las Vegas," October 30, 2013, http://www.reviewjournal.com/news/theater-helps-make-human-trafficking-crisis-very-real-las-vegas (accessed November 15, 2013).
8. Tina Frundt, e-mail to author, October 8, 2013.

9. Shared Hope International, "Domestic Minor Sex Trafficking, Las Vegas, Nevada," assessment prepared by M. Alexis Kennedy and Nicole Joey Pucci, Springfield, IL: PIP Printing, March 2008, 2, http://www.northeastern.edu/humantrafficking/wp-content/uploads/Las_Vegas.pdf (accessed July 29, 2013).
10. Audrey Morrissey, interview by WGBH, http://www.wgbh.org/articles/Full-Interview-Audrey-Porter-286 (accessed August 7, 2013).
11. Anonymous former dancer, e-mail to author, September 30, 2013.
12. Anonymous survivor of adult sex trafficking, e-mail to author, September 29, 2013.
13. Edmund H. Mahony, "Man Charged With Sex Slavery," *The Courant,* March 17, 2007, http://articles.courant.com/2007-03-17/news/0703170008_1_indictment-prostitution-related-accused (accessed September 30, 2013).
14. IAHTI means International Association of Human Trafficking Investigators.
15. Emily Tocci, e-mail to author, October 7, 2013.
16. Jeanie Turner, e-mail to author, October 8, 2013.
17. Cvent, "Cvent's Top 50 Meeting Destinations in the United States," http://www.cvent.com/en/sem/top-50-meeting-destinations-us-2012.shtml (accessed July 29, 2013).
18. Shared Hope International, "DEMAND.: A Comparative Examination of Sex Tourism and Trafficking in Jamaica, Japan, the Netherlands, and the United States," (2007), 100, http://sharedhope.org/wp-content/uploads/2012/09/DEMAND.pdf (accessed July 29, 2013).
19. Greg Bucceroni, interview by Dr. Phil, *A Dr. Phil Exclusive: Child Prostitute Links Sandusky to Pedophile Ring,* September 28, 2012.
20. Greg Bucceroni, e-mail to author, June 4, 2013.
21. New Jersey Office of the Attorney General, Division of Criminal Justice, New Jersey Human Trafficking Task Force, http://www.nj.gov/oag/dcj/humantrafficking/downloads/NJ-Human-Trafficking-Brochure.pdf (accessed July 29, 2013).
22. See OJJDP commercial sexual exploitation Community Intervention Project (CCIP) *Routes of Domestic Sex Trafficking in the U.S.,* Handout 1.4.
23. Raphael and Myers-Powell, "From Victims to Victimizers," 6.
24. United States Department of Homeland Security, "DHS, DOT, and Amtrak Announce New Partnership to Combat Human Trafficking," October 4, 2012, http://www.dhs.gov/news/2012/10/04/dhs-dot-and-amtrak-announce-new-partnership-combat-human-trafficking (accessed July 29, 2013).
25. Kendis Paris, e-mail to author, June 5, 2013.
26. Shared Hope International, "DEMAND," (2007), 91-92.
27. Anonymous survivor of CSEC, e-mail to author, January 29, 2013.
28. Daniel Borunda, "Two alleged sex traffickers arrested in El Paso in national FBI effort," *Las Cruces Sun-News,* June 27, 2012, http://www.lcsun-news.com/ci_20940452/pimp-arrested-el-paso-national-fbi-effort?source=rss_ (accessed July 29, 2013).
29. Stephanie Valle, "Pimping suspect waives arraignment," ABC 7 KVIA, July 3, 2012, http://www.kvia.com/news/Pimping-suspect-waives-arraignment/-/391068/15387706/-/s5c9q1z/-/index.html (accessed November 15, 2013).
30. Ibid.
31. United States Department of State, "2013 Trafficking in Persons Report," June 2013, 381.
32. Jim Walters and Patricia H. Davis, "Human Trafficking, Sex Tourism, and Child Exploitation on the Southern Border," *Journal of Applied Research on Children: Informing Policy for Children at Risk* 2, no. 1, March 15, 2011: 3-4.

33. Antonio Castelan, "Riverside Girl Trapped in Tijuana Child Sex Trade," NBC4 Southern California, November 3, 2011, http://www.nbclosangeles.com/news/local/Riverside-Girl-Trapped-in-Tijuana-Child-Sex-Trade—133094943.html (accessed July 29, 2013).
34. Ibid.
35. United States Attorney's Office, Eastern District of Virginia, "MS-13 Gang Member Sentenced to Life in Prison for Sex Trafficking a Child," press release, October 28, 2011 http://www.justice.gov/usao/vae/news/2011/10/20111028santamarianr.html (accessed July 30, 2013).
36. Ibid.
37. United States Attorney's Office, Eastern District of Virginia, "Leader of MS-13 Gang Sentenced to 50 Years in Prison for Sex Trafficking Multiple Teens," press release, June 1, 2012, http://www.fbi.gov/washingtondc/press-releases/2012/leader-of-ms-13-gang-sentenced-to-50-years-in-prison-for-sex-trafficking-multiple-teens (accessed July 30, 2013).
38. Federal Bureau of Investigation, "2011 National Gang Threat Assessment—Emerging Trends," http://www.fbi.gov/stats-services/publications/2011-national-gang-threat-assessment (accessed July 30, 2013).
39. Keith Burt, "The Sexual Exploitation of Girls in Gangs," webinar, Missing and Exploited Children's Program (MECP), June 2012, http://vimeo.com/44459741 (accessed July 30, 2013).
40. National Alliance to End Homelessness, "Youth," http://www.endhomelessness.org/pages/youth_policy (accessed July 29, 2013).
41. Richard J. Estes and Neil Alan Weiner, "Commercial Sexual Exploitation of Children in the U.S., Canada and Mexico" (University of Pennsylvania, September 19, 2001 [revised February 20, 2002]), 30, http://www.sp2.upenn.edu/restes/CSEC_Files/Exec_Sum_020220.pdf (accessed August 7, 2013).
42. Estes and Weiner, "Commercial Sexual Exploitation of Children in the U.S., Canada and Mexico," 11–13.
43. Greg Bucceroni, e-mail to author, April 21, 2013.
44. Estes and Weiner, "Commercial Sexual Exploitation of Children in the U.S., Canada and Mexico," 17.
45. Greg Bucceroni, e-mail to author, April 21, 2013.
46. Estes and Weiner, "Commercial Sexual Exploitation of Children in the U.S., Canada and Mexico," 7-8.
47. Greg Bucceroni, e-mail to author, April 12, 2013.
48. U.S. Attorney's Office, Eastern District of Virginia, press release, "Leader of Crips Gang Indicted for Prostituting High School Girls, April 26, 2012. http://www.justice.gov/usao/vae/news/2012/04/20120426stromnr.html (accessed September 15, 2013).
49. Erica Fink and Laurie Segall, "Pimps hit social networks to recruit underage sex workers," *CNN Money,* February 27, 2013. http://money.cnn.com/2013/02/27/technology/social/pimps-social-networks/index.html (accessed October 6, 2013).
50. Justin Jouvenal, "Underage prostitution ring's leader sentenced to 40 years in prison," *The Washington Post,* September 14, 2012, http://articles.washingtonpost.com/2012-09-14/local/35496088_1_underground-gangster-crips-justin-strom-underage-girl (accessed October 6, 2013).
51. Pierre Thomas and Marisa Taylor, "Gang Members Arrested on Charges of Sex Trafficking Suburban Teens," *ABC News,* March 31, 2012, http://abcnews.go.com/US/gang-members-arrested-alleged-suburban-teen-prostitution-ring/story?id=16046155 (accessed October 6, 2013).

52. Audrey Morrissey, interview by WGBH, http://www.wgbh.org/articles/Full-Interview-Audrey-Porter-286 (accessed August 7, 2013).

CHAPTER 4: ADVERTISING TO CHILDREN AND TEENS

1. Federal Trade Commission, with assistance from Carol J. Jennings and Mary Koelbel Engle, "Advertising to Kids and the FTC: A Regulatory Retrospective That Advises the Present," based on 2004 speech delivered by J. Howard Beales III, 6, http://www.ftc.gov/speeches/beales/040802adstokids.pdf (accessed July 30, 2013).
2. *Consuming Kids: The Commercialization of Childhood,* DVD, directed by Adriana Barbaro and Jeremy Earp, Northampton, MA, Media Education Foundation, 2008.
3. Federal Trade Commission, "Advertising to Kids and the FTC."
4. *Consuming Kids,* directed by Barbaro and Earp, 2008.
5. Ibid.
6. Ibid.
7. American Academy of Pediatrics, "Children, Adolescents, and Advertising," *Pediatrics* vol. 118, no. 6, December 1, 2006: 2563-2569, http://pediatrics.aappublications.org/content/118/6/2563.full (accessed August 7, 2013).
8. MediaSmarts (formerly Media Awareness Network), *How Marketers Target Kids,* 2010.
9. *Consuming Kids,* directed by Barbaro and Earp, 2008.
10. Susan Linn, *Consuming Kids: Protecting Our Children from the Onslaught of Marketing & Advertising* (New York: Anchor Books, 2005), 5.
11. Nick Bolton, "Disruptions: Celebrities' Product Plugs on Social Media Draw Scrutiny," *New York Times,* June 9, 2013, http://bits.blogs.nytimes.com/2013/06/09/disruptions-celebrities-product-plugs-on-social-media-draw-scrutiny/?_r=0 (accessed August 7, 2013).
12. Caitlin A. Johnson, "Cutting Through Advertising Clutter," CBS.com, February 11, 2009, http://www.cbsnews.com/8301-3445_162-2015684.html (accessed July 30, 2013).
13. Trevor Hughes, "Advertising in schools becoming more common," *USA Today,* June 3, 2012.
14. *Consuming Kids,* directed by Barbaro and Earp, 2008.
15. *Cover Girl Culture,* DVD, directed by Nicole Clark, Los Angeles, CA: Zen Pen Films, 2008.
16. Sara Jean Green, "Pimp tells of 'selling' girls with dream," *The Seattle Times,* October 22, 2009, http://seattletimes.com/html/localnews/2010113369_prostitutiontrial22m.html (accessed October 6, 2013).
17. Levi Pulkkinen, "Teen pleads to pimping; 14 other alleged West Seattle Gangsters face sex crime charges," *Seattle Post-Intelligencer,* July 21, 2009, http://www.seattlepi.com/local/article/Teen-pleads-to-pimping-14-other-alleged-West-1305229.php (accessed August 7, 2013).
18. Ken Lee, "Paris Hilton Charged with DUI," *People,* September 27, 2006, http://www.people.com/people/article/0,1539384,00.html (accessed August 7, 2013); Josh Grossberg, "Lindsay Lohan: A Timeline of All Her Arrests (and Boy, There Are a Lot of 'em)," EOnline.com, November 29, 2012, http://www.eonline.com/news/367020/lindsay-lohan-a-timeline-of-all-her-arrests-and-boy-there-are-a-lot-of-em (accessed August 7, 2013); David Caplan, "What Sent Kelly

Osborne Back to Rehab," *People,* January 29, 2009, http://www.people.com/people/article/0,20255295,00.html (accessed August 7, 2013); Justin Ravitz, "Exclusive: Lil Wayne Is 'Not Close to Death,' But 'Drank Too Much Sizzurp,'" *US Weekly,* March 16, 2013, http://www.usmagazine.com/celebrity-news/news/lil-wayne-is-not-close-to-death-but-drank-too-much-sizzurp-2013163 (accessed by August 7, 2013); TMZ Staff, "Myla Sinanaj: I watched Kim K's Sex Tape . . . While Making My Own," *TMZ,* July 27, 2013 (accessed August 7, 2013).

19. *Cover Girl Culture,* DVD, directed by Nicole Clark, 2008.
20. *What a Girl Wants,* DVD, created by Matthew Buzzell, Elizabeth Massie, and Jacob Bricca, Northampton, MA, Media Education Foundation, 2003.
21. Jody Raphael and Brenda Myers-Powell, "From Victims to Victimizers: Interviews with 25 Ex-Pimps in Chicago," report, Schiller DuCanto & Fleck Family Law Center of DePaul University College of Law (September 2010): 5, http://newsroom.depaul.edu/pdf/family_law_center_report-final.pdf (accessed July 29, 2013).
22. David Awasthi, "Cars Used in Filming Transformers 3: Dark of the Moon," *Zimbio,* July 4, 2011. http://www.zimbio.com/Car+news/articles/aH8EfcA7_SJ/Cars+Used+Filming+Transformers+3+Dark+Moon (accessed October 6, 2013).
23. Vanessa O'Connell, "Fashion Bullies Attack—In Middle School," *Wall Street Journal,* October 25, 2007, http://online.wsj.com/article/SB119326834963770540.html (accessed August 7, 2013).
24. Ibid.
25. Linn, *Consuming Kids,* 8-9.

CHAPTER 5: NEGATIVE MESSAGES IN POPULAR CULTURE

1. Victoria J. Rideout, Ulla G. Foehr, and Donald F. Roberts, PhD, "Generation M^2: Media in the Lives of 8- to 18-Year-Olds," A Kaiser Family Foundation Study, January 2010, http://kaiserfamilyfoundation.files.wordpress.com/2013/01/8010.pdf (accessed August 8, 2013).
2. Target, website http://www.target.com/p/women-s-someday-by-justin-biebereau-de-parfum-1-oz/-/A-14091408 (accessed August 1, 2013).
3. Rachel Lloyd, *Girls Like Us: Fighting for a World Where Girls Are Not For Sale* (New York: HarperCollins, 2011), 38.
4. APA Task Force on the Sexualization of Girls, "Report of the APA Task Force on the Sexualization of Girls," American Psychological Association, 2010, 2, http://www.apa.org/pi/women/programs/girls/report-full.pdf (accessed August 7, 2013).
5. *Dreamworlds 3: Desire, Sex, & Power in Music Video,* DVD, directed by Sut Jhally, Northampton, MA, Media Education Foundation, 2007.
6. APA Task Force on the Sexualization of Girls, "Report of the APA Task Force on the Sexualization of Girls," 6.
7. Gretchen Dahlinger Means, Interview with *America's Most Wanted,* "Gang Pimps Take Sex Trafficking to New Lows," June 1, 2012, http://www.amw.com/features/feature_story_detail.cfm?id=4302 (accessed August 8, 2013).
8. Keith Burt, "Sexual Exploitation of Girls in Gangs," Missing and Exploited Children's Program (MECP), webinar, June 20, 2012.
9. Ibid.
10. IMDb, Box office/business for Pretty Woman (1990). http://www.imdb.com/title/tt0100405/business?ref_=tt_dt_bus (accessed October 6, 2013).
11. Burt, "Sexual Exploitation of Girls in Gangs."

12. Suzanne Smalley, "This Could Be Your Kid," *The Daily Beast,* August 17, 2003 (originally in *Newsweek*), http://www.thedailybeast.com/newsweek/2003/08/17/this-could-be-your-kid.html (accessed August 8, 2013).
13. Ibid.
14. Ibid.

CHAPTER 6: VIOLENCE AGAINST WOMEN

1. Celia Williamson et al., "Domestic Sex Trafficking in Ohio," research and analysis subcommittee, Ohio Human Trafficking Commission, August 8, 2012, 6, http://www.ohioattorneygeneral.gov/OhioAttorneyGeneral/files/2f/2ff15706-77ad-4567-b1aa-d8330b5c4005.pdf (accessed July 29, 2013).
2. As a teenager, my friends and I referred to older boys and young men as "guys." At this age, I had no interest in "men," a term I associated with business suits, striped ties, 9-to-5 jobs, and other adult connotations and responsibilities.
3. Gretchen Dahlinger Means, Fox Valley Technical College's AMBER Alert program, *Human Trafficking: Why We Are Here,* 2012.
4. Polaris Project, *Domestic Sex Trafficking: The Criminal Operations of the American Pimp,* http://www.dcjs.virginia.gov/victims/humantrafficking/vs/documents/Domestic_Sex_Trafficking_Guide.pdf (accessed August 8, 2013).
5. A commonly quoted statistic from the Centers for Disease Control and Prevention (CDC) study is that 1 in 4 girls, and 1 in 6 boys, have experienced early childhood sexual abuse. Data and Statistics, Prevalence of Individual Adverse Childhood Experiences, http://www.cdc.gov/ace/prevalence.htm (accessed August 7, 2013).
6. Parents Television Council. "Teen Sexual Exploitation: The Prevalence and Trivialization of Teen Sexual Exploitation on Primetime TV" (Washington, D.C.: July 2013), 14.
7. *Killing Us Softly 4: Advertising's Image of Women,* DVD, directed by Sut Jhally, Northampton, MA, Media Education Foundation, 2010.
8. U.S. Census Bureau, Population Division. Annual Estimates of the Resident Population: April 1, 2010 to July 1, 2012, Released May 2013, American FactFinder, http://factfinder2.census.gov/faces/tableservices/jsf/pages/productview.xhtml?pid=PEP_2012_PEPANNRES (accessed September 15, 2013).
9. U.S. Census Bureau, 2007-2011 American Community Survey. American Fact Finder. http://factfinder2.census.gov/faces/tableservices/jsf/pages/productview.xhtml?pid=PEP_2012_PEPANNRES (accessed September 15, 2013).

CHAPTER 7: THE BUYERS

1. Somaly Mam, *The Road to Lost Innocence: The True Story of a Cambodian Heroine* (New York: Spiegel & Grau, 2009), 43.
2. Lois Lee, e-mail to author, March 1, 2013.
3. Shared Hope International, *Demand. A Comparative Examination of Sex Tourism and Trafficking in Jamaica, Japan, the Netherlands, and the United States* (Washington, D.C.: 2007), 3, http://sharedhope.org/wp-content/uploads/2012/09/DEMAND.pdf (accessed August 8, 2013).

CHAPTER 8: CONTROL AND VIOLENCE

1. Jessica Richardson, e-mail to author, October 8, 2013.

2. Barbara Amaya, interview by Audrey Barnes, Fox 5 News, May 15, 2012.
3. Brittany Green-Miner, "Survivors of sex trafficking hoping for awareness, change," Fox 13 News, April 15, 2012. http://fox13now.com/2012/04/15/survivors-of-sex-trafficking-hoping-for-awareness-change/ (accessed September 30, 2013).

CHAPTER 9: TRAFFICKERS AND THE RULES OF TRAFFICKING

1. Geraldine Sealey, "Girls 4 Sale," *Marie Claire,* September 2012, 228-233.
2. Ibid.
3. Lois Lee, e-mail to author, March 1, 2013.
4. Los Angeles Police Department, "Human Trafficking Arrest NR12319cj," July 11, 2012, http://www.lapdonline.org/july_2012/news_view/51422 (accessed August 8, 2013).
5. Amita Sharma, "Pimps Recruiting Underage Girls In San Diego Through Force And Coercion," KPBS.org, October 31, 2011, http://www.kpbs.org/news/2011/oct/31/pimps-recruiting-underage-girls-san-diego-county-t/ (accessed September 30, 2013).
6. "Police: Pimp Forced Girl To Tattoo Eyelids With His Name," CBS Miami, March 29, 2013, http://miami.cbslocal.com/2013/03/29/police-pimp-forced-girl-to-tattoo-eyelids-with-his-name/ (accessed August 8, 2013).
7. Polaris Project, "Domestic Sex Trafficking: The Criminal Operations of the American Pimp," http://www.dcjs.virginia.gov/victims/humantrafficking/vs/documents/Domestic_Sex_Trafficking_Guide.pdf (accessed August 8, 2013).
8. Ibid.
9. Pimpin' Ken and Karen Hunter, *Pimpology: The 48 Laws of the Game* (New York: Simon Spotlight Entertainment, 2007), 99.
10. Jody Raphael and Brenda Myers-Powell, "From Victims to Victimizers: Interviews with 25 Ex-Pimps in Chicago," report, Schiller DuCanto & Fleck Family Law Center of DePaul University College of Law (September 2010): 2-4, http://newsroom.depaul.edu/pdf/family_law_center_report-final.pdf (accessed July 29, 2013).
11. Minh Dang, e-mail to author, June 26, 2012.
12. Ibid.
13. "Shaniya Davis Update: Mario Andrette McNeill, N.C. man, found guilty of killing 5-year-old; jury weighs death penalty," CBS News, March 29, 2013, http://www.cbsnews.com/8301-504083_162-57586643-504083/shaniya-davis-update-mario-andrette-mcneill-n.c-man-found-guilty-of-killing-5-year-old-jury-weighs-death-penalty/ (accessed August 8, 2013).
14. Russell Goldman, "Utah Mother Tried to Sell Daughter's Virginity for $10,000, Say Cops," ABC News, May 24, 2011, http://abcnews.go.com/US/utah-mother-sell-daughters-virginity-10000-cops/story?id=13676831#.Uc-PcPm3-So (August 8, 2013).
15. M. Alex Johnson, "Indiana woman charged with selling 1½-year-old daughter for child porn," *NBC News* March 8, 2013, http://usnews.nbcnews.com/_news/2013/03/08/17241430-indiana-woman-charged-with-selling-1-year-old-daughter-for-child-porn (accessed August 8, 2013).
16. "Gary Woman Accused of Selling 2nd Child For Sex," CBS Chicago, June 7, 2013, http://chicago.cbslocal.com/2013/06/07/gary-woman-accused-of-selling-2nd-child-for-sex/ (accessed August 8, 2013).
17. Andy Hoag, "Jury convicts grandmother, 68-year-old man in sex-for-cocaine swap of granddaughter," MLive.com, May 19, 2011, http://www.mlive.com/news/sagi

naw/index.ssf/2011/05/jury_convicts_grandmother_68-y.html (accessed July 28, 2013); Tony Perry, "Oceanside Couple Sentenced to prison in sex-slave case," *Los Angeles Times,* May 20, 2013, http://articles.latimes.com/2013/may/20/local/la-me-ln-sex-slave20130520, (accessed July 28, 2013); Vanessa Miller, "Woman accused of human trafficking in Coralville sentenced to supervised probation," *The Gazette,* September 10, 2012, http://thegazette.com/2012/09/10/woman-accused-of-human-trafficking-in-coralville-sentenced-to-supervised-probation/ (accessed July 28, 2013); Ashley (a survivor of child sex trafficking), interview by Lisa Ling, *Our America, 3AM Girls: One Year Later, Oprah Winfrey* Network (OWN), air date February 12, 2013; Federal Bureau of Investigation, Washington Field Office, "Pimp Sentenced to 20-Year Prison Term for Trafficking Four Juveniles Into the District of Columbia for Prostitution," press release, U.S. Attorney's Office, Washington, D.C., November 1, 2010, http://www.fbi.gov/washingtondc/press-releases/2010/wfo110110a.htm (accessed July 28, 2013).

18. National Gang Intelligence Center (NGIC) & FBI's Crimes Against Children Unit (CACU), "Gang Criminal Activity Expanding into Juvenile Prostitution," Intelligence Report, January 31, 2012, 2, http://info.publicintelligence.net/NGIC-JuvenileProstitution.pdf (accessed July 29, 2013).
19. America's Most Wanted, "'Gang Pimps Take Sex Trafficking to New Lows," June 1, 2012, http://www.amw.com/features/feature_story_detail.cfm?id=4302 (accessed August 8, 2013).
20. National Gang Intelligence Center (NGIC) & FBI's Crimes Against Children Unit (CACU), "Gang Criminal Activity Expanding into Juvenile Prostitution," 2.
21. Ibid.
22. Ibid., 6.
23. Ibid., 4.
24. Tina Frundt, email to author, October 7, 2013.
25. Raphael and Myers-Powell, "From Victims to Victimizers: Interviews with 25 Ex-Pimps in Chicago," 5.
26. Gretchen Dahlinger Means, Interview with *America's Most Wanted,* "'Gang Pimps Take Sex Trafficking to New Lows," June 1, 2012, http://www.amw.com/features/feature_story_detail.cfm?id=4302 (accessed August 8, 2013).
27. Ibid.
28. Victoria Kim, "Eight members of alleged sex-trafficking ring indicted," *Los Angeles Times,* August 10, 2012, http://articles.latimes.com/2012/aug/10/local/la-me-sex-trafficking-arrests-20120810 (accessed August 8, 2013).
29. Ibid.
30. National Gang Intelligence Center (NGIC) & FBI's Crimes Against Children Unit (CACU), "Gang Criminal Activity Expanding into Juvenile Prostitution," 5.
31. Keith Burt, "The Sexual Exploitation of Girls in Gangs," webinar, Missing and Exploited Children's Program (MECP), June 2012, http://vimeo.com/44459741 (accessed July 30, 2013).
32. U.S. Attorney's Office, Eastern District of Virginia, "Leader of MS-13 Gang Convicted Of Sex Trafficking Multiple Children," press release, February 23, 2012, http://www.justice.gov/usao/vae/news/2012/02/20120223amayanr.html (accessed August 8, 2013).
33. Polaris Project, "Working with Foreign National Child Victims of Trafficking," webinar https://polarisproject.adobeconnect.com/_a983384736/foreign_national_minors/ (accessed August 8, 2013).
34. Ibid.

CHAPTER 10: THE "RESCUE"

1. The National Human Trafficking Resource Center (NHTRC) hotline is available 24 hours a day, 7 days a week, and can help law enforcement and other victim advocates with placement for child victims of commercial sexual exploitation: 1-888-373-7888.
2. Sergeant Byron Fasset gave a presentation in Dallas, Texas, to participants of the Vital Voices and Hilton Worldwide Global Freedom Exchange, an international program for female leaders working to combat child sex trafficking, Summer 2013.
3. Ibid.
4. Ibid.
5. Ibid.
6. Paula McMahon, "Woman sentenced in child prostitution case had 'horrible' life," *Sun Sentinel,* July 11, 2012, http://articles.sun-sentinel.com/2012-07-11/news/fl-sex-trafficking-sentence-20120711_1_child-prostitution-case-mandi-lynn-bowman-rashad-emon-clark (accessed October 2, 2013).
7. R. Keith Armwood, Letot Center Superintendent, e-mail to author, November 21, 2013.
8. For more information about the HRVT Program, please contact Sergeant Byron Fassett or Detective Cathy De La Paz with the Dallas, Texas, Police Department. To request training from Sergeant Byron Fassett or Detective Cathy De La Paz, please refer to Appendix B: Tips for Law Enforcement and Other Responders.

CHAPTER 11: IMMEDIATE AFTERCARE FOR CHILD VICTIMS OF COMMERCIAL SEXUAL EXPLOITATION

1. By "expert training," I mean training that includes input from survivors. Without survivor input, any training on commercial sexual exploitation is missing a vital component of expertise.
2. LGBTQ means Lesbian, Gay, Bisexual, Transgender, and Questioning. If you are working with LGBTQ youth victimized via commercial sexual exploitation, I recommend reaching out to other service providers who have worked with kids from this population. Try Girls Educational & Mentoring Services (GEMS) in New York City and Courtney's House in Washington, D.C.
3. Carissa Phelps, *Runaway Girl: Escaping Life on the Streets One Helping Hand at a Time* (New York: Penguin Group, 2012).
4. Robert O. Friedel, *Borderline Personality Disorder Demystified: An Essential Guide for Understanding and Living with BPD,* (New York, NY: Marlowe & Company, 2004), 19.
5. To learn more refer to: Holly Smith, "Human Trafficking & PTSD: Is there a Connection?" *Washington Times Communities,* May 1, 2013, http://communities.washingtontimes.com/neighborhood/speaking-out/2013/may/1/human-trafficking-ptsd-there-connection/ (accessed October 2, 2013).

CHAPTER 12: INTERMEDIATE AND LONG-TERM AFTERCARE

1. Examples include Courtney's House in Washington, D.C.; MISSSEY (Motivating, Inspiring, Supporting, and Serving Sexually Exploited Youth) in Oakland,

California; My Life My Choice (MLMC) in Boston, Massachusetts; Girls Educational & Mentoring Services (GEMS) in New York City; Market Your Mind Not Your Body in Charlotte, North Carolina; among others.

2. Joshua Bailey, Co-Founder of The Gray Haven, e-mail to author, November 20, 2013.
3. LMFT means Licensed Marriage and Family Therapist.
4. For more information, please contact Dr. Gaddis at NarrativeTherapyInitiative @gmail.com.
5. MISSSEY stands for Motivating, Inspiring, Supporting, and Serving Sexually Exploited Youth.
6. DIGNITY stands for Developing Individual Growth and New Independence Through Yourself.
7. Rachel Lloyd, *Girls Like Us: Fighting for a World Where Girls Are Not For Sale* (New York: HarperCollins, 2011), 24.

CHAPTER 13: PREVENTION AND ADVOCACY

1. HEAAT stands for Helping to Educate and Advocate Against Trafficking.
2. "Theresa Flores provides tips on trafficking prevention," *Mission Network News,* November 2, 2010, http://www.mnnonline.org/article/14920 (accessed August 12, 2013).
3. ECPAT-USA stands for End Child Prostitution and Trafficking USA.
4. Kevin Poulson, "Pimps Go Online to Lure Kids Into Prostitution," *Wired,* February 29, 2009, http://www.wired.com/threatlevel/2009/02/pimping/ (accessed October 3, 2013).
5. Heather Caillier, Director of Marketing and Development for Breaking Free, e-mail to author, July 8, 2013.
6. Beth Jacobs, e-mail to author, June 10, 2013.
7. American Institute of Philanthropy (now known as CharityWatch), "Tips for Giving Wisely," http://www.charitywatch.org/tips.html (accessed October 3, 2013).
8. Any organization that offers mentoring services to at-risk youth must be trained to spot potential sexual abuse and exploitation. Darkness to Light is a national nonprofit organization dedicated to increasing awareness and prevention of child sexual abuse. Their award-winning *Stewards of Children* training teaches adults in communities and youth serving organizations how to prevent, recognize, and react responsibly to child sexual abuse. For more information, visit www.D2L .org.
9. State of New Jersey, Department of Children and Families, School Based Youth Services, http://www.state.nj.us/dcf/families/school/ (accessed July 31, 2013).
10. The national hotline for Childhelp is available 24/7 and can be reached at 1-800-4-A-Child (1-800-422-4453).
11. Staca Shehan, Director of the Case Analysis Division for NCMEC, e-mail to author, June 17, 2013.
12. Minh Dang, e-mail to author, June 7, 2013.
13. Lawrence Crook III, "Reebok drops Rick Ross over lyric apology fallout," CNN, April 12, 2013, http://edtion.cnn.com.2013/04/11/showbiz/reebok-drops-rick-ross/ (accessed October 3, 2013).
14. 4 Every Girl, http://www.4everygirl.com/learn.aspx.

EPILOGUE

1. AMBER Alert, "Human Trafficking: Why We are Here," training video, 2012.
2. Children of the Night, http://www.childrenofthenight.org/.

APPENDIX B: RESOURCES FOR LAW ENFORCEMENT AND OTHER FIRST RESPONDERS

1. See Toolsi Gowin Meisner, "Shifting the Paradigm from Prosecution To Protection of Child Victims of Prostitution," *National Center for Prosecution of Child Abuse Update* 21, no. 8 (2009); and Rami S. Badawy, "Shifting the Paradigm from Prosecution To Protection of Child Victims of Prostitution," *National Center for Prosecution of Child Abuse Update* 22, no. 8 (2010).
2. Andrea Powell, e-mail to author, November 25, 2013.
3. James Melia, FBI Agent, e-mail to author, October 28, 2013.
4. www.thecode.org
5. Jennifer Silberman, Vice President of Corporate Responsibility at Hilton, e-mail to author, August 14, 2013.
6. Rachel Lloyd, Founder and Executive Director, GEMS, e-mail to author, November 19, 2013.
7. Christine Stark, *Nickels: A Tale of Dissociation* (Ann Arbor: Modern History Press, 2011).
8. Bradley Myles, Executive Director and CEO, Polaris Project, e-mail to author, October 15, 2013.
9. Staca Shehan, Director of the Case Analysis Division, NCMEC, e-mail to author, June 20, 2013.
10. Rachel Lloyd, e-mail to author.
11. COTN has been criticized for accepting funds from and associating with Hugh Hefner, founder of Playboy Enterprises. While I recognize this is a legitimate concern, I have personally toured COTN in Los Angeles and feel confident in recommending their services to child victim of commercial sexual exploitation. As stated earlier, however, I advocate for every community in the United States to work toward creating its own local resources, including in-house and outreach programs that are educated on CSEC and trained to work with these victims. COTN's services are invaluable for child victims of commercial sexual exploitation in need of free and immediate aftercare and for those who must be removed from the community for their own safety.
12. www.childrenofthenight.org.

INDEX